THE ART
OF WOOD CARVING

A STEP-BY-STEP GUIDE TO SCULPTING IN WOOD

WATSON GUPTILL PUBLICATIONS / NEW YORK

THE ART
OF WOOD CARVING

A STEP-BY-STEP GUIDE TO SCULPTING IN WOOD

Photo on page 1:
Zadkine, *The Sculptor* (1939).
Musée d'Art Moderne,
Saint-Étienne, France.

The Art of Wood Carving

Under the supervision of: Jordi Vigué

Text: Josepmaria Teixidó i **Camí** and Jacinto Chicharro **Santamera**
Editing: Carmen Álvarez
Translation: Mark Lodge

Exercises: Camí
With the collaboration of Josep Pons (olive carving)

Collection Design: Josep Guasch
Layout: Camí, Santamera, Josep Guasch
Dummy Book and Makeup: Josep Guasch, Jordi Martínez

Photographs: Santamera
With the collaboration of Josep Cano (olive and mass production)
and archives of the museums and collections mentioned.
Documentation: M. Carmen Ramos
Illustrations: Montserrat Baqués, Jordi Segú, Antonio Muñoz

First published in 1997 in the United States
by Watson-Guptill Publications,
a division of BPI Communications, Inc.,
1515 Broadway, New York, N.Y. 10036

Copyright © Parramón Ediciones, S.A.

Produced by Parramón Ediciones, S.A.
Gran Vía de les Corts Catalanes, 322-324
08004 Barcelona, Spain

Production: Rafael Marfil Mata

Manufactured in Spain
ISBN 0-8230-0294-2
Library of Congress Catalog Card Number: 97-060905
First paperback printing, 1997
1 2 3 4 5 6 7 8 9 10/06 05 04 03 02 01 00 99 98 97

Contents

THE PURPOSE
OF THIS BOOK

Our main aim is to provide an introductory guide to woodcarving, so we shall concentrate not only on the technical aspects but will supplement them with step-by-step descriptions of the creation of six sculptures.

Yet we would be offering only a partial insight into the subject if we were to ignore the theoretical and practical contributions that have been made through history. This was our reason for including a first chapter that, rather than trying to exhaustively cover the subject, aims to provide an overview of the different facets of woodcarving, to stimulate the sculptor's imagination.

The next two chapters are devoted to wood itself and the studio, while subsequent chapters follow a particular order: project, trimming and rough-hewing, or dressing. Each is supplemented with information on the background of the technique used, more for curiosity's sake than as practical advice.

To acquaint the reader with wood, and to arouse his or her enthusiasm, we have allowed ourselves certain literary asides. Our aim is to strengthen the relationship between the carver and the wood, as we believe that being true to oneself and respectful of the material are the keys to this artform.

We have selected the images, classified them, and given our opinions without pretending to be objective. We offer these opinions in the belief that this will enable readers to form their own criteria, confronting their own vision without preconceptions of the aesthetic.

We are searching for that gray area where opposites can combine in harmony; that subtle divide where artistic expression and technical mastery come together; the point at which theory and practice blend. We believe that sculptural significance springs from the results, not the intention. We feel that quality is not based on the abstract or the figurative; it is a different question entirely. In short, we favor a scale of aesthetic values—discussed in "The Aesthetics of Sculpture"—in which first place would go to the sculpture that creates the greatest resonance in the collective subconscious. Despite the above, naturally, we also welcome those who do not share our ideas, and to whom we offer ample material for starting to carve as the reader decides.

To sum up, we should define the elements of the title of this work: *The Art of Wood Carving*. The concept of *carving*—creating a form by removing material—is used here solely in relation to wood, although other materials such as marble, ivory, diamonds, etc., can also be carved, of course. Furthermore, carpenters and cabinetmakers practice *woodcarving*, although here we consider only sculptural carving.

The idea of *sculpture* would not seem to be well defined nowadays. If we consult a dictionary we can see that the classical definition usually concludes with a note that extends its connotations endlessly: sculpture is "anything that can be imagined as such."

So we do not want to define *wood sculptures* too narrowly. Wood can also be sculpted by recycling, joining, twisting, and "anything that can be imagined . . ."

Josepmaria Teixidó i Camí
Jacinto Chicharro Santamera

*Dedicated to our friends who
have helped us with their comments.*

◀ **Michelangelo,** *Christ* (detail).
Polychromed wood.
Casa Buonarroti, Florence.

▲ *Kpelie Mask*
Sénufo, Liberia. 14 ½" (37 cm).
Private collection.

7

HISTORY

This chapter is not intended to offer a systematic overview of what wood sculpture has signified throughout history. We are more interested in providing the future sculptor with the widest range of possibilities based on a sound knowledge of the craft's history. In classifying the information, we have assumed that religion, as a factor that groups together different styles and subjects, has played a more important role than geography, politics, or chronology. Indeed, religion has been wood sculpting's most fervent champion yet also its major critic. Religions have given it their blessing when it could be used to attract the people but have also attacked it to preserve their orthodoxy.

We do not delve here into wood sculpting's sociological aspects but have based our text on the hypothesis that woodcarving has been closely linked to rural societies, whereas stone carving has been more highly valued in urban societies.

The woodcarver's craft has traditionally been concealed by the painter who applied the polychromy. We wish to emphasize the role of the woodcarver, so that the wood, hidden by more "noble" materials, might show itself as it really is.

Our aim is not to study craftsmanship, yet we understand that the concept of a sculpture is more far-reaching than that of a statue. In a century that has so highly appreciated abstract art, we cannot ignore woodcarving's manifestations other than sculpture. These forms, although perhaps originally created with a practical purpose in mind, have succeeded in transmitting all the energy of an art form.

We regret the lack of a specific bibliography on the history of woodcarving in order to confirm the information herein, as the only history of wood sculpture we have had access to dates back to 1912. The absence of sources is even greater in the case of the history of woodcarving techniques.

The information that appears here has been gathered from general studies on the history of art, essays more specifically dealing with the history of sculpture or ethnology, and our direct acquaintance with the carvings of different museums. An appealing road lies before us.

► The Village Mayor—*Cheik el beled* in Arabic—was found in a tomb in Sakkarah and carved around 2750 B.C. from a single block of sycamore, with arms and forearms jointed in. Egyptian Museum, Cairo.

The realistic effect of the portrait is heightened by the encrusted eyes made of copper and rock crystal. The passage of time, which has removed its stucco and paint, has increased its expressivity.

Transitory Dwelling Places for the Spirits

The Reason of Nonreason

"**S**uperstition leads an entire people to prostrate themselves and bow down in fear to a tree trunk, dressed as a saint."

The rationalist logic of Goya contained in this remark on his *Whim 52* does not suffice to explain the importance of linear images in numerous societies.

Indeed, in many cultures the wood sculpture has played a threefold role:

▼ Kalioninge, ritual bird of the Senufa, Mali. 23 ¾" (59 cm). Private collection.

This haughty, stylized figure transmits all the force of the superior spirit that dwelt in it, according to myth.

psychologically, for self-assertion; sociologically, for tribal integration; and politically, for the stratification of society. Today, viewing ancient wood sculptures out of context in museums, we appreciate only their aesthetic value. Nevertheless, certain works arouse resonances of our experiences in infancy.

It might be this infantile vision, more than any rational thought, that enables us to comprehend the images, just as a doll comes alive only when the child wants it to. Though still wood, the sculpture takes on a new dimension, becoming an object imbued with each society's or individual's desires or fears.

Fetishes, totems, holy objects were and are made of wood . . . yet they transcend this state. They are capable of arousing conflicting feelings: a mask can be beautiful and terrifying at the same time, repulsive and fascinating, wood and spirit.

With this childlike vision, which reconciles opposites and endows the inanimate with life, we shall understand why certain sculptures are the dwelling places of the spirit.

Sculptures with a Soul

The main contributions to woodcarving have come from societies outside Europe and Asia. Although each is distinctive, we can group them all under the term *animist* because they interpret the unseen forces of nature as signs of the presence of spirits.

They encompass a wide range of African, American, Australian, and Oceanic cultures. Wood has been basic to all, not only because of its abundance but also due to the belief that it preserves its life force, the tree spirit.

In order to fully comprehend the rationale underlying these sculptures, we must remember that in many tribes the sculptor, before starting work, would endure privations, temperance, fasting, and prayer so as not to unleash the anger of the spirits that dwell in the trees or cause them pain during the rough dressing. Once the carving was finished, the new spirit dweller would be enticed using another ritual or occasionally even deceit.

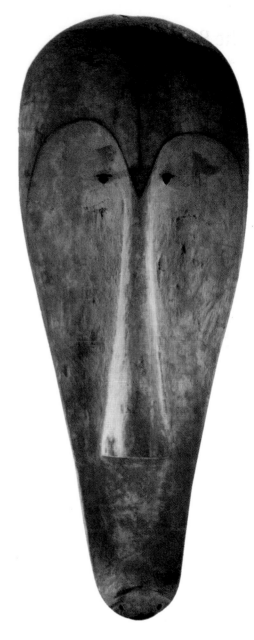

▲ Mask by the Sang of Gabon (19th century). Museum für Völkerkunde, Berlin.

This sober portrait, more of a soul than of a face, is worthy of the spirit of a serious, introspective, profound ancestor.

If the sculpture was beautiful/good (these concepts are usually synonymous), then the spirit, whether a god or an ancestor, would dwell in it for a certain time until it found a more suitable home. It is curious to note that most African tribal spirits prefer novelties, and some have even begun to use plastic, although the spirits of the Fang, Kingang, and Dwane continue to choose the more traditional sculpture.

The Body of the Spirits

There are three forms that are most frequently inhabited by spirits: anthropomorphic images, masks, and totem poles. These all play an important part in holy events: annual feast days, initiation rites, funerals. . . .

The *anthropomorphic images* usually follow strict canons that, even in those places where they are ritually destroyed, live on in the chief's memory, as occurs among the Malanggan in Melanesia.

None opt for realism, since a spirit cannot be similar to a mortal being, although certain guidelines are followed: symmetry, masculinity represented by straight lines, femininity by curved lines. The centers of spiritual energy are stressed—for example, in oversized heads—as are life centers, as in prominent navels and exaggerated genitals. Certain cultures have specific symbolisms: in Oceania the tongue represents strength and wisdom, while in Papua the nose is identified with the phallus.

The arms are usually held at the sides, although in some cultures such as the Tellen in Mali, they are held outstretched. In both cases a single trunk is used.

Some figures appear with additional elements, such as hairstyles or tattoos, to help the ancestors recognize them; geometrical incisions may represent sacrificial marks, a sign of tribal identity, although some are merely for decoration.

Occasionally figures have a cavity in the abdomen to hold magical substances, but when the carving is decked out with such additions as bones, leather, teeth, or herbs, the figure may be a fetish used for black magic.

These figures generally accommodate the spirits of nature or of the dead; one extreme case is that of the Yoruba and Bamileke from Cameroon, for whom multiple births are so important that they honor a dead twin and care for his image as much as the survivor. There are, however, exceptions: among the Fang, the figures represent the rights of inheritance and act as a link with earlier generations; among the Kuba and Bushon of Angola, sculpture is used to glorify their kings; yet Bangswa and Congolese sculptors glorify feminine beauty—art for art's sake.

There is a lesser proportion of sculptures representing animals, as they are considered an inferior life force to humans. They are usually associated with abstract concepts: the bison, lion, or elephant symbolizes strength; the snake or lizard, agility; the tortoise, longevity; the monkey, the recently deceased, while the bird acts as a go-between with the beyond. . . .

The *mask* is an accessory to the dress used in rituals and therefore cannot be fully understood when removed from these ceremonies. Music plunges the wearer into ecstasy while the spirit takes possession of his body.

The sculptor designs the mask, but the wearer perfects it with personal additions.

Masks encourage fecundity, the fertility of the fields; they protect the wearer from the harmful effects of black magic or are merely used for entertainment. In the secret society Poro, for example, the great mask that contains the demon of the forest presides over trials and assemblies, while tiny masks are used in children's education and in the control of women. Among the Bakweles masks help to solve family crises, while the masked Baining of New Britain steal and kill to restore order.

Masks often cover the face, though they can also be worn over the entire head; some are secretly stored away in the ceremonial house.

Totem poles are found especially in Oceania and North America: vertical sculptures as high as the tree trunk allows. In Melanesia they sometimes form part of the local architecture as columns in houses of worship, while in America they stand alone. They usually represent animals and people intertwined and superimposed.

▶ Totem from a Haida village in British Columbia, Canada. Pine wood. Approximately 52 1/2' (16 m). Musée de l'Homme, Paris.

Totems evoke a primitive world that knew no boundaries between spirits, animals, and humans, whose lives were intertwined.

They have come to symbolize several different elements—the spirit of the founder of the tribe, the tribe itself, or the totemic group—while at the same time acting as ceremonial posts or as symbols of prestige or the social hierarchy of the group. Yet they always constitute signs of identification and belonging to a collective that generally operates a system of economic redistribution.

In the New Hebrides there are sculptural groups called graded monuments using up to thirteen elements, one of which is wood. They are intended to signal the social hierarchy of the owner, using abstract forms.

From Nigeria to Alaska, via Hawaii

Africa has a strong sculptural tradition: the terra-cottas from Nok in Nigeria are contemporary with the splendor of Athens. The canons of the *Ife* style remained unchanged from the tenth to the fifteenth century. Bronze found perfection in the *Benin* style (fifteenth through nineteenth centuries), in which it evolved toward naturalism. Wood is also important in this context. Generally small and unpainted, woodcarvings are usually covered with a blackish patina that comes from oils and ritual perfuming.

The hub is Nigeria, from which woodcarving extends through the equatorial region. Among the peoples of Sudan we find a strong tendency toward geometry and abstraction, while in the Gulf of Guinea, forms become less pronounced and more detailed. Wood sculptures show an extraordinary level of develop-

◀ Mask, Aitapé, New Guinea. 18" (46 cm). Musée Napprstek, Prague.

▶ An *imanina*, or large mask worn over the head, that can be as long as 33′ (10 m). Representing a snake with a rectangular head, one is carved by the Dogon of Mali every 60 years.

▼ Medicine holder, Mangbetu, Zaire. Museum für Völkerkunde, Berlin.

ment in the Congo, while in southwest Nigeria, masks possess an intense dramatism.

African masks are highly imaginative and daringly stylized. Particularly noteworthy are the ancient *tellen* figures of the Dogon of Mali, female or hermaphrodite representations with upraised arms. The *tyi wara* masks, to be worn over the head, belonging to the religious sect of the Bambara, are the most stylized and represent elegantly decked-out animals. This same sect has created the *n'done*, whose eight horns represent the myth of creation associated with the germination of millet.

It is curious to see balconies in Gabon full of images of the Fang's ancestors, which protect the bones of the dead and watch over the actions of the living.

In Oceania the bite of the gouge is more obvious than in Africa. Great importance is attached to the female figure, especially the head. Those most dainty come from the Toga in Polynesia. On the Marquesas Islands the images are enhanced with bright red and yellow feathers. The Maori prefer curvy decorations. In Micronesia the spirit Tino de Nukvoro is represented by an

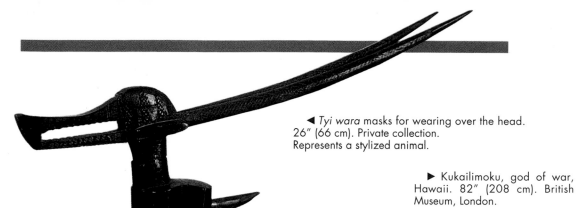

extremely abstract image. The sculptors of the isolated Easter Island are masters of detailed finishing work.

The artist's prestige is usually shared by the entire tribe, although in Melanesia the *asmat* wood sculptors sign their works.

The tribes native to Australia, being nomads, have not developed sculpture as such and paint on the bark of eucalyptus trees, which are easier to carry. The Churinga, however, produce oval pieces with geometrical designs that remind us of their owners' totemic tendencies.

The North American tribes have the most diverse forms of sculpture. These were traditionally colored using rather dull natural pigments, but since the end of the nineteenth century they have incorporated European anilines, which are much brighter.

The most significant sculptures come from the coast that stretches from Oregon to south Alaska. Tribes here carved solid sculptures with few but fine details, and used paints to heighten the contrasts. The masks and doors of the Alaskan Eskimos are truly surprising for their abstract and surrealist designs.

The tall, straight cedars and firs of Canada have been used to make majestic totem poles, which, towering more than 65 feet (20 m) high, announce the noble ancestry of those who build them, turning Haida villages into forests of wood sculptures. Their articulated masks are striking and possess great dramatic power.

The great early civilizations of Central and South America also carved wood images and masks, although these works have been forgotten in favor of their strong, long-lasting works in stone. The ritual use of masks, however, did survive the conquest and drew upon elements of European iconography. The result of this syncretism are masks that combine pre-Columbian gods and the images of Catholic saints.

In order to discover early artworks in wood, we need to visit museums or private collections that specialize in ethnology more than in the fine arts, noteworthy ones being the Musée de l'Homme in Paris and the Rockefeller collection in the Metropolitan Museum in New York.

On the Paths of the East

▶ *Kuan Yin* (7th century), China. Polychromed wood. 42" (107 cm). Rijksmuseum, Amsterdam.

T he Brahmanic religion is a strong champion of sculpture, as it requires objects to contemplate. It makes use of sensuous images to transmit its messages. Because Hindus believe in the eternal return of the soul and the search for permanence, stone is more suitable than wood. Bronze, copper, and tin are also appropriate for expressing the energy of the gods: the dance of Shiva with her many arms is difficult to imagine in wood, for technical reasons. Other materials overshadow wood, which is less appreciated given the abundant amount in India and Southeast Asia. In addition, the damp climate and the disappearance of idols in the face of Islam prevent us from knowing what primitive carvings were like.

Confucianism

C onfucianism, such a determining factor in China's history, considers only intellectual creativity—and therefore poetry, painting, and calligraphy—as worthwhile. Sculptures, on the other hand, are considered mere craftsmanship. Despite this, sculptors decorated the eaves of buildings, which have withstood the ravages of time. Since the eleventh century, woodcarvings have been used for poetry and painting by means of xylography.

Taoism, the path on which opposites converge, stresses the dominance of poetry in China but, together with Zen Buddhism, contributes a new element: the contemplation of nature. Stones, tree trunks, trees, and such are admired as if they were works of art. During the reign of the aristocratic T'ang dynasty, perhaps in the eighth century, people began to manipulate the growth of trees, to enhance their beauty, and from this sprang the original concept of the form of living sculpture we call bonsai.

Japanese Shintoism, the path of the gods, like the refined form of animist religion it is, not only sees art in the landscape but also considers it to be peopled by spirits, whose presence is often related to wood.

The *torii* are the main contribution Shintoism has made to wood sculpture, in this case in the form of abstract structures. They are large lintels that frame the landscape, remnants of the porticos of primitive temples. The large trunks were rough-hewed, straightened, and often painted. Over a hundred torii still remain, spread over the Japanese islands. One of the most noted is the temple of the sun goddess in Isé, which dates back to the third century.

Shinto temples, also made of wood, conserve their ancient structure and resemble organic forms blending into the landscape. The spirit of wood is also a major contributor to the great beauty of the traditional Japanese home.

▶ *Torii* (A.D. 1170), Itsukushima, Japan.
These portals not only adorn the landscape of the Land of the Rising Sun but also represent lintels open to another dimension that peoples the Shinto universe.

Buddha's Path to Mercy

B uddhism is the ideology that has done the most to encourage wooden images. Its subject matter is wide and diverse. The serenity of Buddha himself contrasts with the grotesque vitality of his 17 disciples and the aggressiveness of the Guardians of the Law or the Heavenly Warriors. Some of the sects represent female figures such as the mother goddess or the goddess of beauty and fortune, or characters such as Jizo, the ephebe, or the humorous *bosatsus* angels and even monks who led an exemplary life.

Although originating in India, Buddhism produced its best works in China in the tenth century and in Japan in the thirteenth. We owe the splendor of these Buddhist works to the followers of the Infinite Light (Amitabha in China, Amida in Japan). This popular and individualist doctrine exalts the more touching features of a Buddha who welcomes into his Western paradise all those who have faith in him. Its favorite subject is Buddha-Bodhisattva, the incarnation of compassion and charity and the patron of fishermen and sailors.

Masterpieces were already to be found in the eighth century in the form of two Bodhisattvas, asexual characters who had temporarily renounced Enlightenment to come to humanity's help, known as Kudara and Kule Kannon, each standing almost 6 ½ feet (2 m) tall. They were carved from a single trunk and then decorated and topped with a

bronze flame. Their creator was able to combine in them the mystery of the supernatural and human virtues. Although originally made in Korea, they now stand in a temple in Nara, Japan.

The best Chinese sculptures date from the age of the Sung dynasty (tenth through thirteenth centuries), when an academy was founded that propagated the use of printing. This period represented Bodhisattvas using soft, sublimely spontaneous forms that have a natural grace radiating contented serenity.

Sculptures produced in later times used woods such as sandalwood or camphor. Finishing techniques improved with the use of gold or varnish, and the works became larger, although of inferior quality.

Japan took advantage of Chinese teachings during the military dictatorships of the Kamakura period (twelfth and thirteenth centuries). After earlier works were destroyed, the human style of the Sungs was copied, perhaps for populist motives.

Before this period, carvings in Japan were made from a single block of wood using a technique called *hichiboku*, giving rise to solid sculptures although with deeply wrinkled clothes.

Due to the strong demand for images during the eleventh century, guilds of sculptors were organized and the *yosegi* method was invented. This consisted of joining the wooden parts so that the work could be parceled out. The sculptor Jōchō is said

to have perfected this complicated method, which accurately defined each worker's task in order to achieve uniform results. His most famous work stands in the Phoenix Hall in Byodoin in Uji, near Kyoto. He became so famous that in A.D. 1022 and 1048 he was granted the title of noble by the emperor, something no sculptor had received before.

His descendants inherited the tradition and were known as the School of the Seventh Street. At the end of the twelfth century, one of the greatest artists in Japan was a descendant of this family called Unkei. Unkei led sculpture away from the idea of idealized beauty that was so characteristic of the previous period. He developed realism and was able to reflect the human character in a natural way. He was commissioned to restore the temples of Nara. His best-known work watches over one of these temples, the Todai-ji. It represents two guardians, each over 26 feet (8 m) tall, in a dynamic yet balanced position and with a threatening expression. He carved them in 1203, together with Kaikei, following the yosegi method.

These sculptures gained in vitality thanks to the *Gyookugan* technique, which consisted of inserting glass eyes on which the pupils had been painted first.

This unrivaled period is characterized by quality and quantity: hundreds of Buddhas-Bodhisattva were carved just for the hall of the Thousand Kamons in Kyoto.

Later sculptures were even more detailed in their representation of movement and more violently realistic with the aim of resembling fierce divinities who warded off evil forces; the Buddhist theme, however, began to lose its vigor toward the end of the thirteenth century.

Masks have also enjoyed a long and rich tradition in Japan, where they first appeared in the seventh and eighth centuries and reached their moment of splendor in the thirteenth, when the Noh theater was fully developed. Surprising techniques were used to create the masks, such as hair implants. The results were strangely beautiful, sometimes repulsive, and sometimes moving or frightening.

▲ **Jōchō,** *Amaida Nyorai* (A.D. 1054). Gilded wood. 9'8" (295 cm). Main image in Phoenix Hall in Uji, Japan.
The Enlightened One, with his sensitive features and severe posture, radiates spiritual energy.

▼ **Unkei,** *Muchaku* (late 12th century). Polychromed wood. Placed in the North Octagonal Hall of the Kôfuku-ji. Nara, Japan.
A sober portrait of a monk who led an exemplary life. It exalts not his saintly traits but his real personality.

The Image in the West: I

There is evidence of woodcarvings dating back to the origins of Western civilization, though the sculptures that have survived to this day, such as those preserved in Sumerian tombs, are few and unimportant. Thanks to its dry climate, Egypt, a country where wood is a scarcity, has bequeathed us the finest collection of woodcarvings of the ancient world.

We know that in preclassical Greece wood sculptures called *xoanas* were very popular. They sometimes took the form of dressed, articulated images, and at other times were nude and more associated with the stone *kuroi*. We also know that during the classical era, the Erecteoin, the temple of the caryatids, housed an image of Athena as a girl, cut from olive wood. During Hellenism and up to the Middle Ages, wood was virtually absent from the studios of sculptors, who were more interested in meeting the great demand for marble and bronze. In Byzantium iconoclastic wars destroyed all the religious sculptures, and wood was used only as a base for icons and highly detailed furniture.

Following the considerable contribution by the Vikings during the tenth century, woodcarvings made a strong comeback, especially in the Germanic world. A worthy example of this renaissance is the life-size Gero crucifix, carved in oak for the cathedral in Cologne. During the Romanesque period, wood was preferred over other materials for carving, and during the Gothic and Renaissance periods, polychromy was perfected. Although the Reformation was responsible for removing carved images from the churches of northern Europe, the Council of Trent promoted them so much that workshops had difficulty keeping up with demand, a demand that was to decline with Neo-Classicism.

We will review the role played by wood in these images, as an internal structure, as a support for polychromy, and as sculpting material.

A Core of Wood

Wood is often used as the core to lend greater consistency to a work, as an internal support for sculptures that appear to be precious metal. Worthy examples are the bulls and goats of Mesopotamia. These sculptures make a great display of gold, ivory, or lapis lazuli, yet hide their wooden interiors.

In classical Athens, with its dazzling marbles, the Greeks worshiped an ivory goddess that was dressed in gold but had a wooden interior: Phidias's sculpture of Athena, in the Parthenon, was a wooden structure about 40 feet (12 m) tall that supported over a ton of gold.

In the Christian world also we can find images covered with metal, enamel, and precious stones that conceal an interior wooden support together with relics of the saints they represented. Some were designed to be covered with gilded copper or silver plating. Others, however, were polychromed sculptures that, when donations were sufficient, were covered in metal.

For example, we have Sainte-Foi de Conques from the tenth century, the Virgin of the Vega, Salamanca, from the

▲ *Ram Leaning on the Tree of Life,* from the royal tombs of Ur (2500 B.C.). British Museum, London.
The wood interior of this symbol of life force is covered in gold, lapis lazuli, tortoiseshell, and limestone.

▲ *Virgin of the Vega* (end of 12th century).
This carving, which presides over the Romanesque cathedral of Salamanca, is covered in gold, enamel, and precious stones, lending it a timeless range of colors.

▼ *Mother of God of Castell de Solsona* (13th century). 26″ (67 cm). Museu Episcopal de Vic.
The naive charm of this type of Romanesque carving is heightened by the carefree use of color.

▶ *The Beauty of Florence* (mid-15th century). Polychromed wood. 21 ½″ (55 cm). Musée du Louvre, Paris.
The exquisite nature of the Tuscan Renaissance is captured in this portrait, whose colors reflect its joie de vivre.

◀ **Veit Stross,** *Annunciation* (detail) (16th century). Polychromed wood.
The polychrome technique reaches its perfection with this sculptor.

twelfth century, or Santiago de Compostela from the eighteenth.

Baroque sculptors also used wood for carvings intended for only a day's use, such as funerary catafalques. Bernini's first canopy for the Vatican was intended as ephemeral art, created for celebrating the jubilee year of 1625.

We also find examples of wood being used in the East as a support for sculptures covered in other materials. In China under the T'ang dynasty—eighth century—images of Buddha were fashioned out of clay or lacquer, although their internal structure was made from wood. In Japan, *kanshitsu* was a sculpting technique that consisted of covering a wooden framework with linen, applying varnish containing a special powder, and modeling the resulting black layer.

An Explosion of Color

All cultures have felt the need to dignify, enliven, or sanctify wood by coloring it. Additives such as tar, stucco, or plaster were used to conceal imperfections in the carving and provide a base for polychromy. The latter is generally more symbolic than realist and is achieved by using natural pigments, first tempera and then, since the fifteenth century, oils.

Egypt has bequeathed us many carvings whose color hides the poor quality of the wood itself: palm, acacia, or tamarind, which in their present state appear more expressionistic than hieratic, due to erosion. Small groups representing scenes taken from day-to-day life still display the liveliness of their original colors.

In the Romanesque period there existed many images in wood, a material closely associated with the rural world and light enough to be easily carried in processions. Carvings of a religious nature offer an explosion of color, as they are sanctified by symbolic polychromy, even the relief on doors, lecterns, or altars.

In a Romanesque church, light was directed to highlight carvings that were to be worshiped. A fine collection of these can be found in Barcelona, in the Museu Nacional d'Art de Catalunya.

The three major themes of the woodcarvings are the Virgin, the crucifixion, and Christ's descent from the cross. Mary is presented at the throne of the Savior, in a humble, protective pose characterized by her large eyes and hands. She, or the Child, hold pines, spheres, or books as symbols of life, power, or wisdom. The majesties are the most original medieval contribution to the iconography of the crucifixion. In accordance with their theological position, Jesus Christ is represented in a triumphant pose, dressed as a king and embracing humanity.

There also exist many representations in polychromed wood of the descent from the cross. This theme gave more freedom to the sculptor, both in the distribution of volume and in the expression of feelings.

The taste of the city dwellers, which formed the basis of Gothic art, and the appearance of sponsorship meant that wood had to compete with stone and alabaster; yet these sponsors were also responsible for an increase in demand and the enhancement of polychromed materials. This new form of carving continued with the Romanesque iconography of the Virgin, but over the years the Virgin's image became stylized, more tender, and on occasion even pregnant. This representation of the ideal woman was extended to include saints, reflecting a new form of femininity that culminated in the carvings of the Beautiful Ladies of Bohemia, elegant and finely finished. Sculptors of the Italian Quattrocento also carved charming works in bright colors, representing the Annunciation and portraits of distinguished ladies.

The subject of the Passion became more dramatic, especially following the Hundred Years War. New themes of suffering were included: flagellation, *ecce homo,* piety, the prayer in the garden. . . . The use of such images in liturgical theater was extremely popular in pre-Lutheran Germany. Between 1524 and 1566, thousands of these carvings were burned in the fires of the Reformation's iconoclastic fervor. Contemporary with these images, Germany also developed laical carvings dealing with grotesque themes, the *Danzarines Moriscos* of the Munich Town Hall being a noteworthy example.

▲ *Majesty Battló* (12th century). Polychromed wood. 21 ½" (55 cm). Museu Nacional d'Art de Catalunya, Barcelona.
Life and color come together in this carving from the Catalan Pyrenees.

► *Saint Catherine* (15th century). Polychromed wood. Musée Cluny, Paris.
The ideals of courtly femininity are rendered in carvings in which a naive beauty underlines ugliness.

17

The Image in the West: II, Decked with Jewels

With the re-emergence of cities, there was a considerable increase in the demand for carvings, which was due, perhaps, more to a desire to flaunt them than to worship them. This is confirmed by a requirement that is repeated in numerous contracts: it was compulsory that the images be decked out in jewels and gold leaf, and be adorned by good painters. At the same time, more saints were added, as were new episodes from the Bible, both of which provided more subject matter.

Altarpieces

The Gothic period's major contribution to woodcarving is to be found in its altarpieces, which reached their high point of splendor in the fifteenth century. They depicted Biblical episodes as a form of teaching.

The most sophisticated of the altarpieces were exported, with their stamp of origin, from Brussels to Antwerp. These were oak or walnut triptychs that could be folded over. The polychromy used on them was enriched by the application of new methods. Transparent lacquer was applied over the gold leaf to obtain glazes and an opaque lacquer that was then scratched with a burin, giving rise to the brocade technique. They also added motifs previously made in molds.

Germanic altarpieces were generally made from limewood in the north and pine in the south. The images on them are life-sized. They give an impression of great clarity and lightness, as many have a perforated background. They were produced by the thousands just before the Reformation; the cathedral of Ulm alone had fifty.

In Spain altarpieces covered an entire wall, were divided into squares, and then covered in gold leaf. Although combinations of different woods were used, walnut was reserved for the images. The cathedral in Seville possesses the largest of all.

The most personal of these altarpiece carvers was the temperamental Alonso Berruguete, a determined and independent-minded character who would let himself be carried away by his inspiration and whose contemporary academics would not forgive certain mistakes, the result of his improvisation. When we contemplate the altarpiece of San Benito, now dismantled in three halls of the Museo Nacional de Escultura in Valladolid, we can see how the contortions of his characters and their expressions of contained pain were a forerunner of the works of Juan de Juni, a master of pain and father of the Spanish Baroque.

▲ **Pedro de Mena**, *The Magdalene* (1664). Polychromed wood. Museo Nacional de Escultura, Valladolid.
The soberness of the polychromy highlights the austerity of this penitent saint, whose will is reflected by the gesture of the hand.

◄ **Martínez Montañés**, *Allegory of Strength*, part of the altarpiece at the monastery of the Jeromes of Santiponce, Seville.
The "god of wood," according to his contemporaries, reveals the interior strength via a detail: the fingers.

The distribution and decoration of the altarpiece evolved in accordance with the new Renaissance styles, baroque or rococo, and harmoniously combined the different arts. Although the design is the work of the jointer, it may also be carried out by the sculptor, painter, or architect, such as Berruguete, El Greco, or the Churrigueras.

Wooden Baroque altarpieces were widely developed in Spain. Gold from the Indies was used profusely. Artists, known as *imagineros* (image makers), specialized in carving sculptures that eventually became independent of the altarpiece itself.

Images

Toward the beginning of the seventeenth century, Valladolid, the ancient capital of Spain, and Seville, the door to the Americas, possessed the most renowned workshops of image makers.

Gregorio Fernández is the main representative of the school of Valladolid. His work took Baroque naturalism to its ultimate consequences. Although his clothed figures are stiff, his nudes are masterpieces that, far from being hedonistic, express the last breath of life and the solitude of death. His polychromy makes use of any material that can produce greater realism, and his depictions of pallor, bruises, wounds, and blood clots are minutely detailed.

Thousands of images were carved in Seville for a century and a half, many intended for the Americas. Martínez Montañés represents the height of this school. Although he lived in the Baroque period, his work emanates serenity, balance, order, reflection . . . in a word, classicism. This sober style was well received by his contemporaries, who described him as "marvel of this age and for ages to come." Seville altarpieces of Saint Clare and the Saint Johns or the Christ of Mercy are just some of his masterpieces.

Granada also had an important tradition of image makers. One outstanding example is the versatile Alonso Cano, a disciple of Montañés. His small virgins, with their inward-looking

manner and clothes swirling about the waist, made their mark on Pedro de Mena, although he eventually evolved toward a mystic realism that is reminiscent of the paintings of Zurburán.

. . . and Processions

In Spain, as in southern Italy, baroque carvings invade the streets during Easter Week celebrations. Processions represent a double challenge for the sculptor: they must be designed to be seen from all angles, and because they represent different characters, their poses, gestures, and looks must relate to each other. In addition, as other characters such as the apostles, soldiers, executioners, or thieves were incorporated, the artist could represent them in irreverent postures, such as surprise, incredulity, disdain, or mockery. Being popular characters, they were *dressed,* which saved on carving and polychromy.

Numerous image makers helped to develop the processions. The most noteworthy ones are those mention ed earlier, although we should also include Francisco de Salzillo, the last of the Baroque carvers, who preferred to reject the honors bestowed by the court and execute his detailed work for the brotherhoods of Murcia. *The Prayer in the Garden* is his masterpiece. The last great carvers and polychromers were the Bavarian Ignaz Gunther, with his exquisite rococo style, and the Castilian Luis Salvador Carmona, trained in the baroque style yet influenced by the new Neo-Classic taste, which preferred marble.

▲ **Francisco Salzillo,** *The Prayer in the Garden* (detail of a charming angel). Museo Salzillo, Murcia.

▼ **Gregorio Fernández,** *The Piety.* Museo Nacional de Escultura, Valladolid, Spain.
The master of pain portrays the suppleness of a still-warm yet lifeless body, contrasting two attitudes to suffering.

Noble Woods

◀ *Queen Tiyi* (1370 B.C.). Ebony and gold. 3" (9.5 cm). Egyptian Museum, Berlin.

Time, that great sculptor, has contributed the most to cleaning carvings of what Henry Moore defined as "moss, darnels and other excrescences of the surface that conceal the shape." Thanks to the erosion of surface decoration, we can admire the technical mastery of anonymous carvers who were forced to hide their work for aesthetic reasons or because of the demands of religious decorum.

As is the case with Grecian marble, the sober beauty of antique woodcarvings, free from all polychromy, leads us to doubt whether they could have been conceived otherwise. We can cite examples with widely varying origins: the famous Egyptian *Town Mayor*; a winged tiger from fifth-century Russia, carved with powerful strokes of the gouge; a Toltec serpent; the reliefs on the Romanesque doors of Saint Mary's in Kapitol in Cologne, which retain all their color; or numerous saints recarved by erosion.

In Egypt, however, we also find numerous examples of sculptures that proudly exhibit the material from which they were made, although we should admit that they were carved from the finest woods, imported as taxes from distant countries. We could mention *Ti, the Queen Mother* or the minute ebony portrait of Tiyi, Nerfetiti's mother-in-law, on display at the same museum in Berlin where the majestic limestone bust of her daughter-in-law stands.

Centuries later we find the widest range of reliefs, with finishes that highlight the beauty of the wood, on the doors, lacunars, and furniture of mosques and temples in general.

Even Gothic cathedrals, those representations of Heavenly Jerusalem, took on a more human quality: the introduction of the choir, organ, and pulpit provided three large areas for using noble woods.

Choirs were widely introduced into cathedrals in the fifteenth century. They subtract from the magnificence of the architecture yet also turn the central nave or apse into a more comfortable area, for the chapter's daily use but forbidden to the public. Natural wood provided the desired color and warmth.

The artists revealed their mastery in the canopy, the upper part of the choir, imitating architectural spires.

Prominent artists carved the backrests and would even compete with each other. This is the case of the cathedral at Toledo, carved by the academician Bigarny and Berruguete. Daring use was made of polychromy in 36 reliefs in walnut, barely covered by a fine layer of varnish that appears warm or cool as necessary.

The overflowing imagination of certain carvers found spaces even in the chairs. In the most improbable places and postures they carved fictional characters such as Jehan Turpin in Amiens or busts (Syrlin the Old, in Ulm), designed to be enjoyed for their touch, as should all good sculptures.

Yet the hidden jewels of the choirs are the misericordes, small seats that were used to take a furtive rest while standing. Because they were concealed under the foldable choir stalls, they lacked interest for the clergy and gave even greater freedom to the artist. Here artists would create scenes portraying daily life, fables, or sayings, ironic reflections about the period, revealing their personality in both subject and style. Certain artists such as Mateo Alemán, who worked on the stalls in Palencia, Toledo, and Plasencia, are openly mocking, especially in Plasencia. After the Renaissance the choir stalls were still wood colored.

The backrests, embellished with inlays and gold, reached heights of technical virtuosity. A case in point is the rococo work by Johann Joseph Christian for the abbey in Ottobeuren, with reliefs that produce a great sensation of depth.

Music, that most abstract of arts, resisted all attempts to undramatize Christian worship. The organ became the religious instrument *par excellence* and took its rightful place in churches. The base

◀ **Adrien van Wesel**, *The Meeting of the Magi* (1476). Oak. 30" (76.5 cm). Rijksmuseum, Amsterdam.

▲ **Diego de Siloé,** *The Sacred Family.* Walnut. Museo Nacional de Escultura, Valladolid.

for organ pipes was made of wood, sometimes not even polychromed, and would carry images of atlases, angels, or abstract shapes.

The Counter Reformation gave rise to another area in churches where wood could be used: the pulpit. Flanders saw the most spectacular development of the pulpit: Delvaux (eighteenth century) was one of the specialists in this genre, and in Saint-Davon of Ghent he combined marble and wood. Verhaegen in Malinas showed his exuberance of fantasy and theological complexity by presenting a pulpit situated over a cave and underneath a tree, teeming with all kinds of flora and fauna.

We can also find unpolychromed altarpieces, superior in quality to the organs or pulpits, though fewer in number. It was only during the late Gothic period that the color of limewood or walnut was allowed to emerge, protected only by transparent varnishes that were darkened in certain areas to increase the sense of volume.

Sculptors with a strong temperament, such as Veit Stross, creator of the polychrome altarpiece in Cracow, and Yilman Riemenschneiden, a great sculptor of lined faces, deliberately avoided using color, which disconcerted their patrons, who would occasionally commission the former to paint altarpieces carved by the latter. It is worthwhile remembering that those most in favor of what we have termed the nobility of wood—Stross, Riemenschneiden, and Berruguete—were, paradoxically, those who took polychromy to its ultimate consequences.

There is no evidence that images stopped being polychromed. We should, however, mention certain sculptures.

In Tours during the fifteenth century, there existed a successful school of sculptors in oak and walnut whose works were forceful, though moderate, far removed from the dramatism of their contemporaries. We could mention a Saint John that probably formed part of the Stations of the Cross in Beaugerais abbey. Although it retains traces of color, it is mentioned as an example of dynamic use of the gouge, free from the painter's additions.

The penitent saints were generally represented using a minimum of color. This is the case of the *Magdalene* by Donatello at the end of his life, or the sober *Magdalene* by Pedro de Mena in the Museo Nacional de Escultura, Valladolid.

The underlying strength of the Renaissance is transmitted not so much by the polychrome crucifix of the young Buonarroti as by the *non finitas* maquettes by the aged Michelangelo. Yet it was to be Diego de Siloé, before devoting himself to architecture, who

best expressed the Renaissance ideal of beauty in noble woods in the form of the unpainted *Sacred Family*, a work that combines rhythm and warmth. Siloé, with his *Saint Jerome* for the cathedral in Burgos, introduced Spain to the Baroque style, without the need for polychromy. These attempts were foiled by the demands of the Council of Trent that the saints be represented "with due decorum," which not only meant painting the carving but also priming it, that is, covering it with a base for the color. The sculptor's natural reluctance to this form of manipulation can be seen in a contract with Martínez Montañés: ". . . the carving must be primed so delicately that this work should not even be apparent; it should look like a recently finished work, with nothing to detract from the skill with which the work has been made."

European artists were to wait until the twentieth century before they could free themselves from priming.

► **Alonso Berruguete,** *Moses.* Detail of the choir of Toledo cathedral. The *terribilitá* by Michelangelo here takes the form of a monochrome relief.

Plebeian Sculptures

▲ A corbel from Catalonia (12th century). 26 ¾" (68 cm). Museu Frederic Marès, Barcelona.

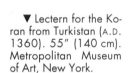

▲ Clog.

▲ Ladle (19th century). 6 ½" (16.5 cm). Canada.

▼ Lectern for the Koran from Turkistan (A.D. 1360). 55" (140 cm). Metropolitan Museum of Art, New York.

We shall now study certain well-carved objects as sculptures in themselves. Beyond their practical purpose they possess a casual elegance, unaware of their own beauty.

There is a vast range of these sculptural objects: the boomerang, with its graceful design, drawn in space; Micronesian canoes, with their asymmetric hulls and sophisticated finish; eating bowls from the Solomon Islands; or the speaker's stools on which the Sepiks of Papua place a branch for each argument they have put forward.

Even objects in daily use can take on surprising forms, from a handle for a flyswatter from Tahiti to a walking stick from Easter Island to the spoons made by the Tlingit Indians of Alaska.

Stools, chairs, pillows, footstools, or armchairs adorned with caryatids by the master Buli from Zaire, although not intended as such, are true sculptures to be found in ethnological museums.

Where architecture makes great use of wood we find a surprising development of relief: the aggressiveness of the Maori forms in New Zealand is moderated by the detailed finishing work. The doors of some houses of the Tlingit surpass European surrealism. Preindustrial Europe also provides examples of numerous farming and handcrafts tools

that are worthy of admiration. We might say the same for other carvings: dolls, toys, spinning tops, and the like. Chess pieces, for example, have attained a high level of stylization and have been adapted to the taste of widely differing cultures.

The same is the case with the fanciful shapes of certain boats. The wavy profile of Viking boats culminates in their magnificent prows; figureheads, be they abstract or figurative, zoomorphic or anthropomorphic, appear in all seagoing cultures. In addition to having intrinsic meaning, whether as an emblem of war or as a mythical or simply ornamental symbol, the figurehead transforms the entire boat into a being with its own personality.

We could also include windmills—in La Mancha or in Holland—Arabic water wheels, and the ingenious artifacts used for extracting water from African wells as forms of sculpture that lend their character to a particular territory.

Even the silhouettes of certain rural churches in Europe become sculptures of the landscape itself. Their fairy-tale forms come alive thanks to the wood that covers them like scales.

The common feature shared by objects that we have characterized as plebeian sculptures is sincerity: they neither disguise their origin nor are ashamed of their practical purpose.

◄ Armchair (1350 B.C.). Decorated wood. Treasure of Tutankhamen. Egyptian Museum, Cairo. A similar one is displayed in the Louvre Museum.

▼ Brossa, Wheel, object-poem (A.D. 1989). Stained and painted wood. 45" (114 cm).

Wood Finds Its Place

In the palaces, temples, and tombs of the great civilizations of the ancient world, wood was originally used for practical purposes; later it was used as an adornment and a symbol.

The throne of the Pharaoh, a sign of divine power—we could mention Tutankhamen's—could not resemble the chairs used by his subjects. It had to be assigned to the best craftsmen to be gilded, polychromed, and encrusted with such noble materials as ivory, precious stones, or exotic woods like ebony.

Perfumed cedarwood, which never rots, was most suited for the sarcophaguses, yet even this wood was concealed by covering it with stucco and paint.

The iconoclastic religions, such as Judaism, Islam, and certain Christian sects, especially the Orthodox groups, opened their temples to abstract relief: the carvings on doors, pulpits, lecterns, although unintrusive, nevertheless contributed to the solemnity of the place of worship.

Islamic craftsmen developed a new technique for the ceilings of palaces, combining skill and creativity. By strapping together small boards of wood, they avoided the effects produced by climatic changes in large single boards and at the same time created a balanced, detailed effect.

In the Europe of great kingdoms and palaces, the golden throne became a sign of power. The solemn hinged seats and walnut furniture of the Austrias gave way to the dazzling and spectacular Bourbon design. The excesses of the baroque style were imitated in all the courts and among the nobility. Even the bourgeoisie, on assuming power, assimilated these aesthetics.

The British crown, in contrast, promoted in the seventeenth century the realist, unpolychromed carvings of Grinling Gibbons, the creator of the choir stalls of Saint Paul's in London, the bishop's chair in Canterbury, and the decoration of Windsor Palace.

In China the emperors of the Ming dynasty ruled from their thrones in the Forbidden City, richly worked thrones that hid neither the color nor the texture of the wood. In Japan, on the other hand, lacquer was used to refine the touch of the wood to the emperor's taste.

Toward the end of the nineteenth century, the Arts and Crafts movement reintroduced the taste for authentic materials. Sculptural furnishings in wood invaded modernist buildings. Even today reproductions of Gaudí's benches are manufactured more as sculptures than as practical objects.

The Bauhaus democratized design and, although stressing functionality, revealed a new concept of aesthetics in which tropical wood stood out among the others.

Nowadays, the use of new materials and the excess of wood veneer have turned solid wooden objects into luxury items.

▼ A Viking boat found in Oseberg. Vikingskepene-Museet, Oslo.

From Panpipes to Stradivarius

▲ *Drum from Baga, Guinea. 52" (132 cm). Musée National des Arts Africains et Océaniens, Paris.*

▼ *Lyre, royal tombs of Ur (500 B.C.). British Museum, London.*

"There are those who decorate their palaces or houses with musical instruments such as organs, harpsichords, monochords, psalteries, harps, pipes. . . . Others with lutes, violas, violins, lyres, flutes, drums. I also recommend this type of decoration, as these instruments, apart from delighting the ear and uplifting the spirit, are also pleasing to the eye if they have been carefully worked by the hand of a master craftsman."

This is how an Italian of the Cinquecento described a custom that goes beyond the mere collection of objects. Instruments competed with Renaissance sculptures because they were also pleasing to contemplate. They were appreciated for themselves as objects. They embodied a form of enjoyment, an metaphysical quality, similar to what was later to be termed abstract art.

This type of sculpture has existed since the origins of humanity, since the god Pan, binding together reeds of different lengths, invented the flute.

Among percussion instruments, the one present in every continent of the world is the drum. In Africa and Oceania it plays a fundamental role in rites, celebrations, and as a daily form of communication. These simple sculptures are made from a single trunk, hollowed out through a lengthwise slit. They are usually set up horizontally, although in the New Hebrides there are vertical sets of drums that often stand over 10 feet (3 m) tall and are topped with carvings of human faces that given them great expressive energy.

In southern Asia, Africa, and Central America we find another percussion instrument—the marimba—whose sound and shape suggest primitive worlds. It comprises a set of graduated wooden bars and primitive resonators, such as pumpkins. The orchestral version, often carved in rosewood, is the xylophone.

Rattles, castanets, sansas, and friction drums are just some of the other percussion instruments with elegant, dignified, sometimes surprising shapes.

Among the most primitive of the wind instruments we find the Alpine horn, a kind of long pipe made from a pine branch split in two and hollowed out, then joined together and bound with roots. Another is the whithorn of Oxfordshire, made from willow bark, studded spirally with sloe thorns, whose form is evocative of an imaginary model of the Tower of Babel. We also find sculptures of wind instruments with a certain surrealist air to them, such as the bagpipe, which uses an animal skin as an airbag, sometimes including an image of the animal.

The Hotteterre family during the seventeenth and eighteenth centuries perfected wind instruments such as the ebony or rosewood oboe.

Among the keyboard instruments, harpsichords, spinets, and virginals are more like pieces of furniture than sculptures, decorated like magical boxes to surprise guests. The grand piano, on the other hand, has a majestic air, and the perfect finish of the wood—or mahogany or walnut veneer—is an invitation to the touch.

String instruments al-

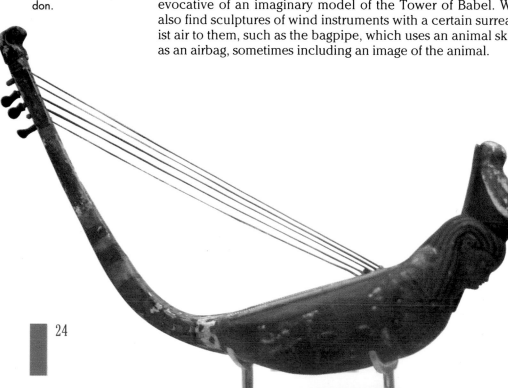

▶ *Eight-stringed harp* of the Fang tribe, Gabon (early 20th century). Musée de l'Homme, Paris.

ing banished by the piano to a dark corner of the drawing room.

Islamic countries possess a wide variety of string instruments which combine different woods and detailed inlays. Their musical function, sculptural form, and expert finish round out their beauty.

The same occurs in the East, especially in India, where certain string instruments are enlarged and decorated with great imagination, having articulated legs, plumage, and other decorations unrelated to their acoustical requirements.

In the West we find many bowed instruments whose shape is an abstraction of the female body: cello, viola, double bass, etc. They also have an upper section, the head, which can be freely carved without affecting their sound. It is common to adorn them with spirals or even realistic looking heads that bring them to life.

After Stradivarius, it is difficult to imagine that the proportions of the violin could be changed, given the absolute harmony of the whole. The woods used were carefully structured: the backpiece of fifty-year-old planewood; the soundboard in black pine or fir; rings in planewood or pine; the violin bridge in maple; fir for the interior; pegs, frame, tailpiece, and chin rest in ebony—seventy parts go into making a violin.

The sculptures of musical instruments are the exact opposite of the romantic concept of creative freedom that has taken over in the twentieth century. They work to order, are subject to strict rules, acoustics are their main concern, and yet they are often able to surprise us with new sculptural forms.

▲ *Drums*, Papua, New Guinea. Polychromed wood. 39″ (100 cm). Private collection.

low for greater creative freedom in the design of the soundbox.

In the British Museum there are Egyptian, and especially Mesopotamian, lyres whose soundboxes, with their strings and tensors, take on the form of the sphinx or are topped with a bull's head. Among the lyres, psalteries, and harps, it was the last that became the most widely used and developed before be-

▶ *Polynesian drum.* Rockefeller Collection, Metropolitan Museum of Art, New York.

◀ Sitar from Timor, Indonesia. Palm and bamboo. 22 ½″ (57 cm). Metropolitan Museum of Art, New York.

A Break with Tradition: The Twentieth Century

▲ Balarch, *The Solitary One* (1911).
This great artist, carving vigorously with the gouge, defined compact volumes that reflect the feelings of the common man.

We have put forward the idea of considering an obsolete tool or musical instrument as a form of sculpture. We believe this criteria, debatable from an academic point of view, is valid when seen from the perspective of the end of the twentieth century. Let us see what has led to this view.

Neither the attempts to free wood from any foreign element (such as paint or stucco) nor the renewal of appreciation for crafts inspired by the Arts and Crafts movement at the end of the nineteenth century managed to bring about this change of opinion.

The break, rather than change, in the Western tradition occurred at the turn of the century: the expressive force of Pacific and African carvers captivated the artists of colonial Europe.

Gauguin was the forerunner. He not only captured the vivacity and spontaneity of the Tahitian painters but realized the sculptural potential of fragments of wood washed up on the tropical shores, bequeathing us several reliefs that symbolized this new approach.

Later, Matisse and Picasso found a new source of inspiration in African art. As early as 1907, Picasso made several wood sculptures in which he stressed the primitivist aspects of that style of art.

What captivated both artists and collectors such as André Derain was not so much the intrinsic value of African sculpture, that power of attracting spirits for which they were originally created, but rather its formal aspects: the distribution of volume and the expressiveness of direct carving. They did not hesitate to define these carvings as true works of art, on a level with the best of European sculpture.

The interest that primitive culture attracted was such that the German Ministry of Colonies, the year the First World War broke out, sent Emil Nolde and Max Pechstein to New Guinea to study it in its original surroundings.

Cubism included wood in its compositions, either literally, by incorporating it in collages, or figuratively, by including it as a subject in paintings.

Expressionism, on the other hand, explored the more communicative aspect of non-European carving; it employed primitivism and painted wood to transmit its aggressiveness with greater force.

Brancusi, who came from a peasant background and was trained as a cabinetmaker, brought new values to modern art: a respect for wood and a search for primordial forms free from all nonessentials. Both aspects come together in his many endless columns. Roughly carved wood contrasts with painstakingly polished bronze and marble.

▼ Boccioni, *Horse + Rider + House* (1914).

Constructivism joined used or industrial woods with other supposedly inferior materials. The maquette by Tatlin for the monument to the Third International is the most well-known work.

We find famous Dadaist and surrealist sculptures in which the main component is wood, although not so much as wood itself but as a recycled object.

New movements appeared ever more rapidly throughout the century that used wood as just another material, even being spurned in favor of novelty materials such as polyester.

The artists in Communist states, especially Poland and Rumania, took their first inspiration from farming tools and later introduced totemic forms, with expressionist tendencies, into urban life.

◄ Gauguin, *Soyez Mystérieuses* (1890). Linden. 28 ¾" (73 cm).
This relief, with its symbolist influence, led to the break with tradition.

► Ibarrola, *Series of Crossties* (1971).
After being subjugated by the industrial era, wood re-encounters its origins.

An interest in trunk sculptures and a certain disdain for what they described as do-it-yourself influenced a new generation of German expressionists in the 1980s who compulsively carved enormous blocks of wood that show the marks of chainsaws.

Under the influence of site art and the surge in ecology, some sculptors have lost interest in the plank and the trunk. They now address the tree and the forest itself.

Major Artists

There are many sculptors this century who have worked with wood on one occasion or another; some have made more frequent use of it, but few have worked exclusively with wood. Although the versatile Ernst Barlach also used other materials, we do not hesitate to qualify him as the main wood artist of this century. He managed to assimilate primitivism and combine it with the Gothic tradition. He appreciated expressionism, yet was not won over by its superficial manners. In his compact forms we find spirit and bluntness, yet also irony and sensitivity. Although his work at first was overshadowed by the flashiness of his fellow artists, over the years it came to become so important as to be a target of the Nazis, who in 1939, a year after his death, destroyed 381 of his sculptures.

▼ **Haussmann**, *Mechanical Head* (1919-1920). Wood, leather, aluminum, and cork. 12 ½" (32 cm).

Ossip Zadkine was one of the first wood artists to capture African influences in large trunks. An enthusiast of direct carving, he would leave the marks of the gouge visible. He evolved from a Cubist preoccupation for pure forms toward a certain symbolic baroque style.

Barbara Hepworth, thanks to Brancusi, discovered another concept of sculpture, different from the Nordic idea, so absorbed with the dignity of monuments to the dead. Contrary to fashion, she vindicated wood as a sculpting material. Her works usually highlight the grain of the wood and the hollowing out. The results are intimate and lyrical.

The origins of Henry Moore ran parallel to those of Hepworth, diverging as he began to draw his inspiration from Maya sculptures. Wood was a suitable vehicle for expressing his interest in organic forms, but due to demand, he came to prefer bronze. Marino Marini admired the Expressionists but took his inspiration from Etruscan art. In his carvings of horses he transmitted the special tension between the force of gravity on the body, the resistance of the legs, and the fragility of the rider. When we consider him outside his historical context, we admire his poetic ingenuity, yet we should remember that, among the Existentialists, Marini also put forward his vision of the Second World War.

Louise Nevelson also merits our attention, as she was one of the few sculptors who assiduously worked with wood. By joining, not carving, she would construct a type of agnostic altarpiece painted in a single color, generally white, black, or gold. Over the past few decades, carving has been revitalized, and today there are many sculptors participating in its future. We cannot list them all, but we must mention the hyper-realists Antonio López and Katsura Funakoshi and the landscape work of Ibarrola and David Nash.

▲ **Louise Nevelson**, *First Personages* (1956). Painted wood.

The absence of literary references and the austerity of color turn this abstract sculpture into a "word" that speaks more to our feelings than to our reason.

▼ **David Nash**, *Ash Dome*. One of the projects of the series carried out between 1977 and 1995. Pastel on paper. 39" (100 cm).

Nature is the protagonist of the flat development of this sculptural work.

WOOD

We will devote this chapter to understanding and appreciating wood, the starting point of our task.

The information presented here will help us to work wood correctly, aware that it is abundant, yet limited.

Thanks to the whisper of the poet and mythology, we will become attuned to the flow of the sap within the tree trunk.

This knowledge and empathy will enable our future sculptures to preserve a breath of life.

The trees on Ox Hill were splendid,
located on the frontier of the great estate,
they were felled with axes and picks.
Can we preserve their beauty?
                                    Mencio

The Columns of the Sky

It is said that several adventurers visited the Land of a Thousand Wonders, or perhaps the Garden of Hesperides or Paradise. The stories don't agree on the name or the location; some say this extraordinary place was in Africa; others, in the Indies or in Indochina. Later mapmakers situated paradise between two lines they called the tropics.

All the travelers claimed that in paradise it was eternally springtime, that millions of species lived there in total harmony. They spoke of two, three, even four layers of vegetation, with trees higher than the spires of our cathedrals.

On one thing all agreed: the sun's rays at midday could not penetrate the dense layers of foliage. They told how when walking in darkness at noon, they trod on the skeletons of roots, concealed under a multicolored carpet. Amazed, they described how the branches of a tree bore fruit and flowers simultaneously, while from others fell a rain of sienna-colored leaves.

But paradise's fame attracted all kinds of hunters. While the Guinean Ucola bathed in clouds and stars, slaves were being traded below. Again in paradise, although distant in time and miles, Vietnamese teak also had to fight off deadly bacteria spread by human war.

Today paradise is fighting for survival.

The Cypress at Silos

Upright provider of shade and sleep
that strikes fear in the sky with your lance.
A jet that almost reaches the stars,
reeling madly around yourself.

A solitary mast, an island wonder,
a seat of faith, a dart of hope.
Today, my ownerless soul chanced upon you
on the banks of Arlanza.

When I saw you—serene, sweet, firm—
I yearned to dissolve and rise up like you,
transformed into crystals,

a black tower of edges,
an example of vertical delirium,
mute cypress in the fervor of Silos.

Gerardo Diego

The Amazon is in flames. Its red scream is visible even from outer space. Its wood is used to liquefy iron, while its rivers are poisoned with mercury; trapped water provides clean energy while strangling life; gold fever has broken out again. People believe that El Dorado lies under the forest's roots. Paradise's forests swallow up freeways while lawyers argue in vain in Stockholm or Rio. Gold fever is still contagious.

Paradise is mortally wounded, according to the neutral computers of the scientists, who add or subtract according to the color of the money they live on. Is it true that half the world's forests have been devastated in the past three decades? That each year 58,000 square miles (150,000 km²) of forest disappear? Or that America has already lost 37 percent of its tropical forest, Asia 42 percent, and Africa 52 percent?

The Food and Agriculture Organization (FAO) is worried about paradise's health: this body, a department of the United Nations, reports that during the 1980s, 600,000 square miles (1,540,000 km²) of tropical forest were lost. Even the World Bank has been forced to recognize that 12 percent of the Amazon has been destroyed.

Whether or not these figures are accurate, some prophets predict that, at this rate, by the year 2015 paradise will be just a memory.

But if paradise disappears, can we still look to the north? Will the woods of cedars of the Haida Indians or Noel's white and green country still exist? No—the Douglas fir and the sequoia no longer compete in height but in fear. Their treetops, at 230 to 330 feet (70 to 100 m) high, fear the industrial winds from the East. Even the maple leaf of the Canadian flag is wounded by acid rain. Far away, in the misty Siberian taiga, the spruce, fir, and larch suffer the consequences of a Cold War in which, although it never turned hot, they are the losers.

Meanwhile, old Europe reforests itself, but on the Flanders pine, on the Black Forest, there falls a strange rain that slowly devours it. The strong oak is sick. Baby elms fight for life, as the great elm, the hundred-year-old elm that gave body to so many saints, the dry elm Machado wrote of, is now only a skeleton on the tired face of the continent.

Today, as before, in the New World, the lungs of the planet, an old Indian, a survivor from paradise, continues to repeat the age-old belief: "Trees are the columns of the sky; the day they disappear, the heavens will fall upon us."

The Tree Test

In our subconscious, in a corner of our being, grows a tree. The structure of our personality has the form of a poplar, an oak, or an orange tree. Perhaps it digs its roots in firmly, its trunk forms knots, or the wind of longing stirs its branches. Perhaps our private tree is serenely rooted in, grows in proportion, and its canopy points to the future.

In the past the nobleman demonstrated his family background using a family tree. Today the psychologist reveals our personality in the form of a tree. Yesterday and today the soul of the poet blends with that of the elm, the pine, or the olive. The sculptor who dares to wound wood is to encounter the corporeality of cedar, teak, or vermilion. If he is sincere, he will sharpen his gouges under the shadow of the tree itself.

All forms of emotions are represented by trees: strength by the sequoia; languidness by the willow; defensive sentimentalism by the acacia, with its lively leaves at dawn and thorns at night; luxuriance by the poplar; the solemnity of the cypress dark in the cemeteries yet welcoming in the Alhambra; aromatic peace by the linden.

Time beats within trees: from winter, the almond tree blooms with perfumed snow and announces spring; the cherry tree celebrates the coming season; the apple tree pours out its fruit in summer, while the beech lends its color to the fall; the fir leads us to Christmas.

All the ages of man are to be found in trees: the terse tenderness of the bud; the greening in April; the surge of spring; the fruit of maturity; the fall of the leaf.

Every possible form is also present in trees: the roundness of the solitary holm oak, the perfect cone of the cedar, the poker shape of the cypress . . . even the imaginary outlines of Bosch.

The tree, like a person, like peoples, can be educated, manipulated, exploited, or defiled. The market gardener does not hesitate to prune the pear tree, which later in spring grows in gratitude, yet when confronted with gratuitous violence, the gardens of Versailles must have cried: "Revolution!" The apple tree generously offered its fruit in Eden, yet today, planted in military fashion, it is forced to produce. The exquisite T'ang dynasty was attuned to the beauty of the maple and gently reduced it to human scale and invited it to live in its halls. Today it is shrunk, priced, and its feelings ignored.

The sculptor, before creating a new form, before carving a new sculpture, must face the triple test of the tree: he must feel its physical presence, empathize with the breeze of its culture's forest, and feel the beat of his own tree.

The Holm Oaks

...

Dark holm oaks:
humility and strength!

...

The oak is war.

...

The pine is the sea and the sky
and the mountain: the planet.

...

The palm tree is the desert,
the sun, and the distance:
thirst: a cool fountain.

...

Beeches are the legend.

...

Poplars are the banks,
the lyres of spring.
What is wrong, black holm oak,
with your colorless branches? . . .
You rise straight or twisted, with
that humility that only surrenders
to the law of life,
which is to live as best as one can.
The countryside itself became
a tree through you, dark holm oak.

Antonio Machado

▲ Hindu woman praying to a tree in the temple of Kanchipuran.

THE EUCALYPTUS
...Illuminated more by its healing vapor than light
The kindest form of compassion.
            ...Celestially good,
the tree is imbued with juice and essence.
Bountiful eucalyptus in the daily flame . . .
Kindness summons me under the eucalyptus.

Evaristo Rivera Chevremont

The forest was and is a place of mystery. Mythology and popular accounts bear witness to this. Perhaps certain forests were the first temples: the Celts use the same word for forest and for sanctuary; in Gaul, until the Roman invasion, temples were unknown. Even today in Japan, a torii indicates the entrance to a forest-temple.

Specific trees have been essential elements in the rites, traditions, and mythology of many civilizations throughout history. Even when the gods adopted human form, they maintained a close relationship with their vegetable archetypes: the olive of Athena presided over the Acropolis, and the laurel, over Olympia. The box tree, firm and persevering, was consecrated to gods as different as Hades, Cybele, and Aphrodite. Atis, in Rome, was identified with the pine. Adonis rose out of a myrrh tree. Again in the East, Brahma turned into a bayon tree. Krishna led his devotees to the shade of a kdamba. Buddha found illumination under a box tree. Jehovah appeared to Abraham in a holm oak. According to certain Pacific myths, human beings themselves originated from a tree. In addition, the tribes of the Philippines, Korea, Central Asia, and Australia have a tree as a common ancestor.

In European mythology the oak—occasionally the holm oak—was the ruling tree, and its golden bough—mistletoe, full of sunlight—the essence. Its worship was associated with both Zeus and Thor, the terrible gods of thunder and rain.

Certain trees, on the other hand, possess negative connotations: the sad willow represents unrequited love; elders are considered a sign of a curse because, according to tradition, Judas hanged himself on one and witches can turn into elders.

The universe itself is symbolized in the form of a cosmic tree that has adapted to each individual place: in Nordic mythology, the branches of the ash tree Yggdrasil hold up the heavens and its roots descend down into hell. The concept of a tree as a world axis is also to be found among the Germans, the linden; in Islam, the olive; in India, the bayan; in China, the kienmu; in Siberia, the birch. The list is endless.

In many cultures—Buddhist, Babylonian, Celtic, and others—the concepts of tree, knowledge, and life are closely related. For example, in the Biblical paradise grew the Tree of Life and the Tree of the Knowledge of Good and Evil. Christianity recovered this image with the Tree of the Cross, as a symbol of the triumph of life over death.

In short, the tree not only symbolizes the connection between the three worlds—subterranean (roots), earth (trunk), and spiritual (leaves)—but also contains the four basic elements: water (sap), earth (roots), air (leaves), and fire (its destiny).

In the Beginning Was Wood

The tree has been universally worshipped, and the essence of this worship lives on in the wood.

Although the trunk with two short branches appears as a symbol of death, it is more usual to find the erect trunk adored or acclaimed as a phallic symbol, as a source of fertility. This is con-

SUMMER/FALL RINGS

SPRING RINGS

◄ A pine whose soft, early rings have been more eroded than those of summer.

► In this cross section of holm oak, we can distinguish the different parts of the trunk. The pith has suffered some disease or harsh weather conditions.

N

S

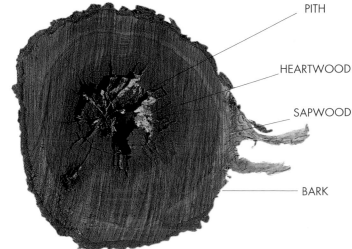

PITH

HEARTWOOD

SAPWOOD

BARK

firmed not only by psychoanalysis but by ancestral rites, related to the May pole, that include spring dancing in Europe and America.

The tree spirit undoubtedly lives in the wood. As we mentioned in the previous chapter, animist sculptors are aware of this and, to become worthy and not suffer reprisals, they purify themselves before wounding it.

In China, wood is considered one of the five elements that make up the universe. It equates with the awakening of the yang, with the east, with the Spring. In India and the classical world, it is synonymous with the raw matter of the universe. The word for wood in Spanish, *madera*, derives from the Latin *materia*, a word of broad significance: nature, wood, material, cast, character.

In the light of tradition, *touching wood* is to touch something sacred, to approach knowledge and connect with life.

Time As Sculptor

When wood was still a tree, it grew with the rhythm of the sun and moon. It will never forget this. With spring rains, the tree grows vigorously. The young growth forms a soft, light-colored ring. This growth subsides in summer and fall. A slower growth forms another darker, more compact ring. Thus, each year leaves its mark on the trunk. When a tree is felled, we can easily calculate its age by simply counting the concentric rings in the cross section of the trunk.

If we look at a section of a trunk, the core may appear a little off-center: the narrower section points north, as the tree grew more toward the area exposed to the midday sun. We can even interpret the climatic changes of the past: an abnormally thick ring indicates a rainy year, while a dry spring will leave a darker, more compact sign. If the tree has survived attacks or fires, these will still be visible in its interior.

The tree's memory is so reliable that it is used by scientists as a first-hand source in interpreting history. As it grows, the vital activity of the tree shifts to the periphery of the trunk, while the interior—the old wood—acts as a support. The area between the bark and the wood, called the cambium, is responsible for growth.

Where lay people see only bark and wood, botanists distinguish between the epidermis, cortex, suber or inner bark, xylem, phloem, cambium, and pith. They refer to normal wood—from the trunk—and to tension and compression—the upper and lower sections of the branches. From the carving point of view, we are interested only in differentiating the sapwood, heartwood, and pith within the trunk.

When we observe a sawed-off trunk, we see that the outermost ring, after the bark, is lighter and more porous. This is the sapwood. In certain conifers, however, such as the pine, a distinct change of color is not visible.

The sapwood is the wood that has just grown and is therefore more moist. The bark and adjacent area, the sapwood, being more "alive," are therefore more exposed to insects and rot, as they contain microorganisms. Generally speaking, bark and sapwood are not recommended for carving.

The heartwood is the old wood, which is usually darker, drier, and harder than the sapwood. It is formed by old rings and accounts for most of the trunk's volume. Over the years, resins and gums take the place of the porous cells that once carried the sap. As the wood hardens, it takes on a new role: that of a support. Its coloring depends on the tannins and others acids that prevent it rotting. The heartwood is highly desirable wood, ideal for carving because it is compact and durable.

There are fast-growing trees such as the poplar that never manage to produce heartwood. Others, such as certain banana trees, olives, and carob trees, do not segregate tannins, so their interior rots and they end their days as living representations of abstract expressionism.

The core of the trunk is the pith. Around this grow the annual rings. Its wood is even darker than heartwood, although it tends to crack radially. For this reason it is not used for planks. Using it in carving entails certain risks.

▲ The moon influences plants' growth. Popular empiricism has no doubts about this. The moment when a tree is felled is decisive for any later cracking of the wood and its resistance to woodworm. One of the common clauses in ancient image makers' contracts was "It will be carved from wood with a good moon."

The winter moon on the wane, when the tree's activity has virtually ceased, is the ideal moment for pruning or felling a tree. The most inappropriate time is when the sun and moon are helping it to grow: first and second quarter moon in springtime.

Nowadays, the lumber industry controls the drying process scientifically. The most suitable woods for carving are those from the tropics. There the climate is more even and therefore the passing of time does not leave such profound marks. For both these reasons, the "good moon" is no longer a concern, except if felling a garden tree.

▼ **Camí,** *Budú* (1987). 17³/₄" (45 cm).
The pith of this ebony was semi-crystallized, and this has been left visible to lend greater expressiveness.

How Wood Develops

Wood's inherent qualities make it ideal for carving: it is plentiful and easy to handle. We might even say that, given its structure, density, temperature, texture, color, and smell, wood is a very "human" substance.

Common wood, however, is perishable, sensitive to insects and to changes in temperature and humidity. Even many years after being cut, it oozes resins, warps, cracks, and breaks open; we could say it continues to develop. Egyptian sarcophagi, for instance, continue to develop.

The Steps in Developing

Wood movements become more pronounced after the trunk has been cut into planks. This is not a random activity, nor uniform, but it does follow a specific order that is not always easy to ascertain. If we understand this order, we can prevent, control, or take advantage of this development.

A tree is impregnated with water/sap drawn up through the roots. It therefore has a far greater proportion of water than air. After cutting, however, the wood either absorbs the surrounding humidity or expels its own if the air is too dry. Water swells wood initially, but when it evaporates, the wood will shrink.

During the drying process, wood can lose a large part of its water until it balances with the environment. A 12 percent degree of humidity is the international standard for considering wood to be dry.

It is surprising just how much liquid wood can contain: one cubic meter (1.3 cubic yards) of freshly cut pinewood, weighing 1,100 pounds (500 kg) and having 80 percent humidity, contains approximately 425 quarts (400 liters) of water.

About 45 percent of the total water contained in a tree is concentrated in the sapwood, as compared to 15 percent in the heartwood. Sapwood, being more porous, is more prone to shrinking than heartwood; wood that has grown in spring develops more than that grown in summer; the wood facing south more than that facing north.

When a plank dries, there is no great change in length. It is the width that can shrink as much as 10 percent from its original measurements. This is because wood is composed of longitudinal fibers. These are long cells that form a network that goes from the roots to the leaves. Because the fibers do not absorb humidity, they do not contract when the trunk dries. Among them, however, there exist other, more porous cells that run across

the trunk and which accumulate or release humidity.

The old wood, the heartwood, has its pores full of resins and other substances. This process has not yet reached the young sapwood. This explains why a plank containing both sapwood and heartwood will warp, because the young wood will shrink more. The plank will twist as if the veins acted as tensors. The closer to the side of the trunk, the more it will distort. These movements are even more marked if the tree was cut when in full growth: "under a bad moon," in popular speech.

Wood tends to continue the development of the tree it was cut from. If the trunk was twisting due to a constant driving wind, the resulting planks will suffer twisting, that is, a double warp. Almond and olive are prone to this effect. The twisting is sometimes so marked that it resembles a wreathed column.

Another factor to be borne in mind is that the outer wood will dry faster than the interior. This contrast can produce cracks, especially if dried suddenly. These cracks spread from the surface to the pith, creating a radial network.

Cracks also develop in a specific way. In the tree the sap seeps into the pith horizontally through more porous areas: the pith rays. When the wood contracts, these spongier areas give way together with the more rapidly growing rings. Sometimes remains of dry sap become

▲ A twisted almond trunk.

▼ The direction in which a plank warps depends on its position in relation to the center of the trunk. Side planks (A) warp more than central planks (B).

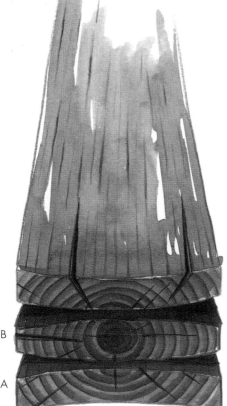

B

A

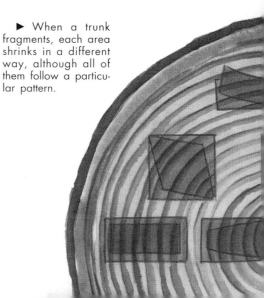

► Fossilized wood.

► When a trunk fragments, each area shrinks in a different way, although all of them follow a particular pattern.

trapped in these rays and appear shiny; this crystallization should not cause us any problems.

We may also encounter other surprises when carving. The trunk may have protuberances, the result of tumors. Urban banana trees are prone to these.

When a tree is still young, it may suffer scars or burns that heal over the years, thanks to the cambium, and are subsequently covered by new rings that alter its concentric pattern. When wood is rough-dressed, these alterations can appear and cause unpredictable changes in the pattern of the interior veins.

Air chambers can also form inside the trunk. These are called colts. They are usually associated with twisting, as the wood can produce empty spots.

The knots are where branches were attached to the trunk. They are the source of most problems, because they are a cause of cracking. In addition, the fibers they contain are extremely hard and resinous. Knots may ooze resin for years, even when they appear to be dry. Since they are more compact than the rest of the wood, they can be removed whole with an accurate stroke of the gouge.

Ancient image makers' contracts usually contained the phrase "using resinless, knot-free wood." Sculptors preferred to extract knots and insert wedges to protect the polychromy. On the other hand, knots usually form beautiful patterns and are highly esteemed in industrial laminates.

The pith generally has similar characteristics to knots. For this reason it is advisable to discard it. Certain trees—olives, for instance—lack pith after freezing during a cold winter. In woods such as ebony, it may be crystallized. It is always a source of problems, although its peculiar characteristics can be taken advantage of for purposes of expression.

The wood of the roots is particularly beautiful, but it requires a specific technique and set of instruments given its hardness and number of knots, twists, and colts.

Wood Development Under Control

Knots were traditionally rubbed with garlic to prevent bleeding; planks were boiled in oil to harden them or were dampened and pressed to straighten out the warping.

Nowadays, wood is sold only after a careful drying process. In addition, world trade enables us to buy tropical woods that have grown at a steadier rate than woods from temperate or cold climates. Their development, therefore, is not as unpredictable and troublesome as before, although we should never forget that wood, even after being cut, is still living matter.

From the beginning of the twentieth century, thanks to Dadaism, the ephemeral has also been valued as art. If we demythologize the idea that sculptures need be eternal, we can transform the limitations of wood into a source of expression, making full use of the idiosyncrasies of each kind of wood.

▲ A dry poplar bleeds because of a nearby fire.

▲ The harder quality of the knots becomes apparent when the wood rots.

▲ The mark left by Dutch elm disease.

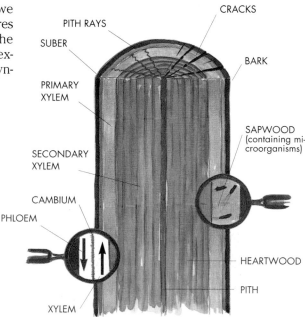

CRACKS

PITH RAYS

SUBER

BARK

PRIMARY XYLEM

SECONDARY XYLEM

SAPWOOD (containing microorganisms)

CAMBIUM

PHLOEM

HEARTWOOD

XYLEM

PITH

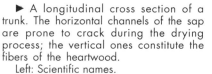

▶ A longitudinal cross section of a trunk. The horizontal channels of the sap are prone to crack during the drying process; the vertical ones constitute the fibers of the heartwood.
Left: Scientific names.
Right: Common names.

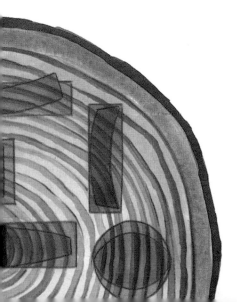

The Wood Industry

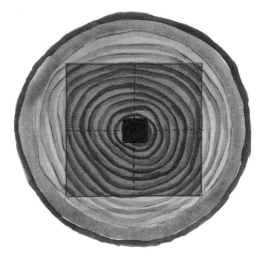

▲ A cross section of a whole beam.

▼ Planks cut parallel.

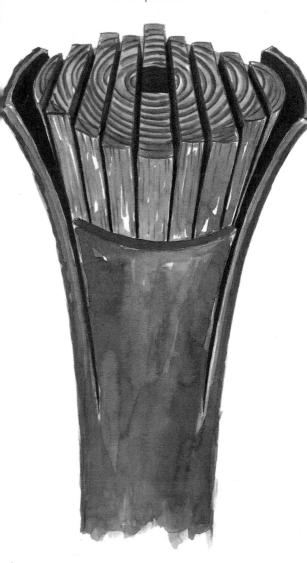

Sculptors and carvers have to deal with an established wood industry. Because our demand is insignificant for this large industry, we are not taken into account when the trees are cut. We have to adapt to the supply available on the market, which, given the demand by carpenters and cabinetmakers, is mostly planks.

Trunks

Ideally, sculptors would have an entire trunk to work with, removing the bark and sapwood themselves. We could then create a sculpture from a single block and avoid the problem of gluing.

There are very few stores where sculptors can buy trunks that have only had the bark removed.

It is easier to find trunks in mountain sawmills, although the variety is limited to locally grown woods. The problem with these small industries is that they are not usually very careful when it comes to felling and drying, as their usual customers—manufacturers of packing boxes, building materials, or paper—are not very demanding in this regard. Using this kind of trunk entails certain risks, as you never know how it will develop.

Beams

On occasion you may find whole beams, rectangular trunks, although quarter beams are also suitable.

On demolition sites and in architectural artifacts stores you may be able to find a beam from an old building. It is worthwhile taking advantage of it, as they are scarce and are ideal for carving. You do need to take precautions in case they contain nails.

Planks

There are many ways of cutting up a trunk: parallel, radial, slanted, rolled, and so on. The most suitable for carving are obviously the widest and thickest. Prices are calculated by volume, and the sapwood and pith are not counted.

Planks were traditionally dried naturally. This system requires a long period of storage, according to the hardness of the type of wood in question: a year for pine, three for beech, and four for oak. Storage must be in a dry place, with ventilation perpendicular to the planks, which should be grouped according to their degree of humidity. Cracks may appear if they are not stacked correctly; the planks should rest on square, level beams. If you look at the partial rings visible on the cut ends of the planks, you can deduce which is the interior face of the plank. Because it will tend

▼▶ Tropical forests are felled at the base for immediate profit.

◄ The trunks are often transported using the old system of rivers. Submerged wood is not attacked by rotting fungi, which require more oxygen in order to develop.

to curve outward, you should place the interior face upward to offset the warping with the force of gravity. The planks should be separated by wooden strips to allow the air to circulate. Cracked ends are inevitable, although they can be improved by using the right paint, applied before starting the drying process.

Today the wood industry uses artificial drying systems and provides the right treatment for each kind of wood.

To avoid any contrast in humidity, vapor has been added to the drying process. This heats up the wood right to the pith, achieving a uniform drying action. Drying rooms usually have automatic devices to inject saturated vapor inside the chamber, depending on the requirements. Success depends on the balance between humidity and temperature.

Using these techniques, the humidity can be reduced to less than 8 percent, although it is unwise to reduce it any further, as the wood's properties may be altered if it becomes too dry. The planks

are also subjected to complex procedures to lengthen their life. They are injected with substances to prevent them from rotting: creosote, copper sulfate, etc. If the wood is subjected to a temperature above 113°F (45°C) and a relative humidity of 60 percent, lyctus and woodworm are eliminated.

Firewood, Paper, and Chemicals

The proportion of wood used in art is insignificant when compared to that employed for other purposes. Baroque altarpieces were not responsible for the deforestation of our woods, nor is sculpture responsible for the destruction of the tropical forests or the boreal taiga. In Africa and Asia, firewood is still the main fuel. Countries such as Mali, Rwanda, Tanzania, Chad, Ethiopia, and the Central African Republic depend on wood for more than 90 percent of their energy. India and China are the two main world

producers of wood, a large proportion of which is used as fuel.

In Brazil, the third-largest world producer of charcoal, well-known multinational companies are keen to eliminate the wood that prevents them from exploiting the riches in the subsoil: iron, aluminum, manganese, copper, gold, tin, oil, tungsten, titanium, zinc, and uranium.

The main use of the northern woods of Canada, Russia, and Scandinavia is for the paper industry: to obtain a ton of newspaper, 3,750 pounds (1,700 kg) of wood are necessary.

Despite this exploitation, it is now possible to take full advantage of every part of the tree, in the form of different products: oils, sugars, varnishes, lacquers, medicine, wax, electrical insulators, explosives, detergents, lubricants, rayon, celluloid, artificial leather, surgical bandages, and a great many others.

▼ These cutting and drying processes are not always carried out in the country of origin. Japan imports entire trunks, while Europe usually imports planks, and the United States, panels for veneers.

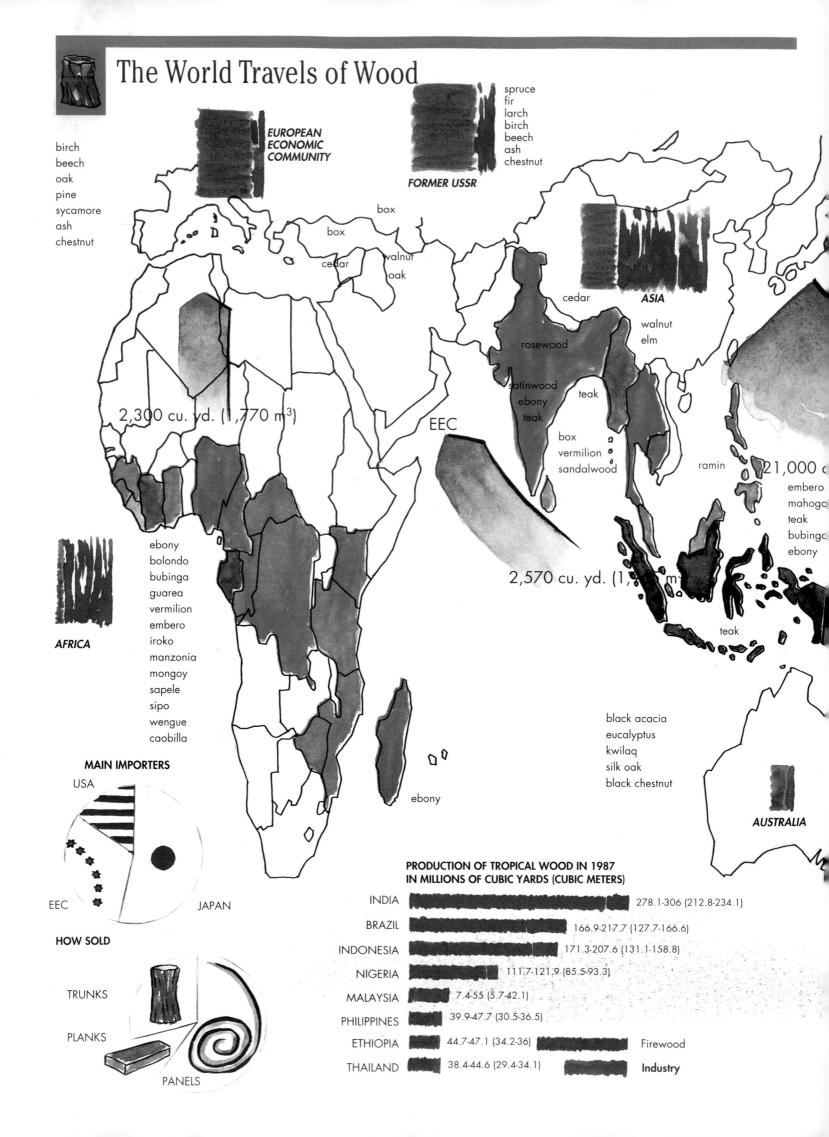

The World Travels of Wood

birch
beech
oak
pine
sycamore
ash
chestnut

EUROPEAN ECONOMIC COMMUNITY

spruce
fir
larch
birch
beech
ash
chestnut

FORMER USSR

box

box

box

cedar

walnut

oak

cedar

ASIA

walnut
elm

rosewood

satinwood
ebony
teak

teak

box
vermilion
sandalwood

ramin

2,300 cu. yd. (1,770 m³)

EEC

21,000 c

embero
mahoga
teak
bubinga
ebony

2,570 cu. yd. (1,   m³)

ebony
bolondo
bubinga
guarea
vermilion
embero
iroko
manzonia
mongoy
sapele
sipo
wengue
caobilla

AFRICA

teak

ebony

black acacia
eucalyptus
kwilaq
silk oak
black chestnut

AUSTRALIA

MAIN IMPORTERS

USA

EEC

JAPAN

HOW SOLD

TRUNKS

PLANKS

PANELS

PRODUCTION OF TROPICAL WOOD IN 1987 IN MILLIONS OF CUBIC YARDS (CUBIC METERS)

INDIA	278.1-306 (212.8-234.1)
BRAZIL	166.9-217.7 (127.7-166.6)
INDONESIA	171.3-207.6 (131.1-158.8)
NIGERIA	111.7-121.9 (85.5-93.3)
MALAYSIA	7.4-55 (5.7-42.1)
PHILIPPINES	39.9-47.7 (30.5-36.5)
ETHIOPIA	44.7-47.1 (34.2-36) — Firewood
THAILAND	38.4-44.6 (29.4-34.1) — **Industry**

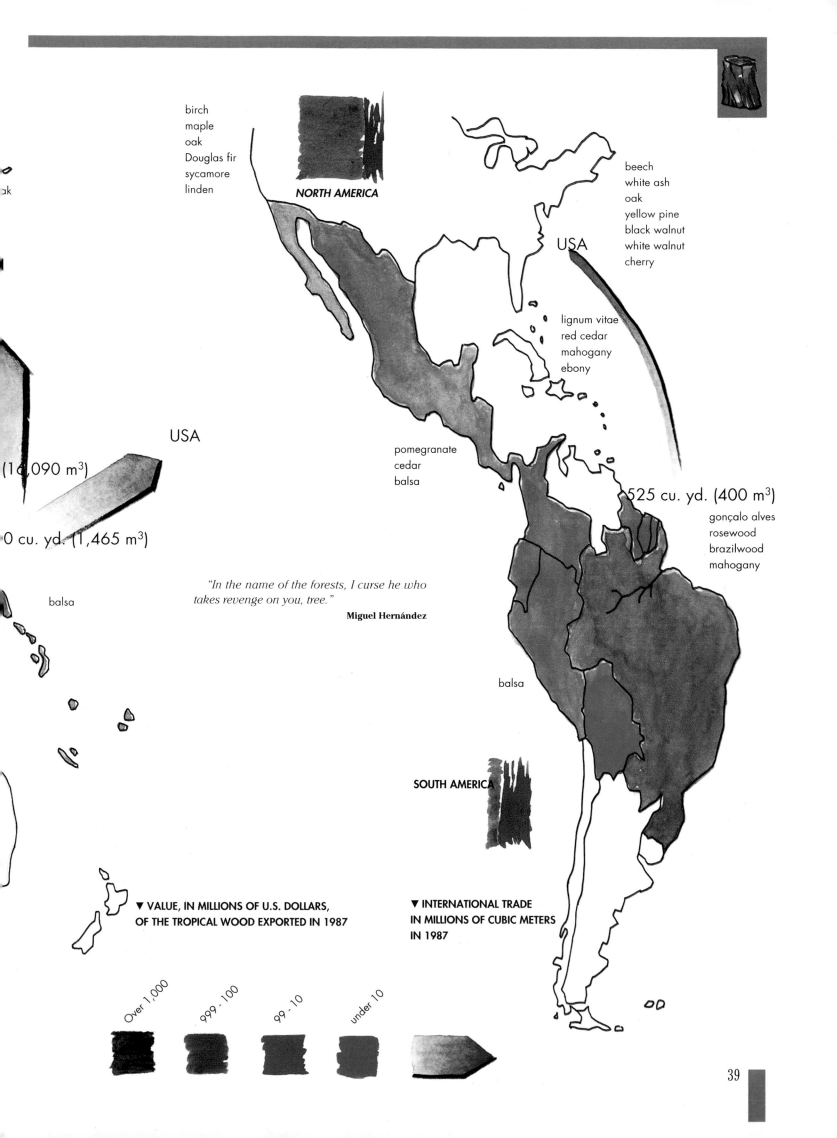

birch
maple
oak
Douglas fir
sycamore
linden

NORTH AMERICA

beech
white ash
oak
yellow pine
black walnut
white walnut
cherry

USA

lignum vitae
red cedar
mahogany
ebony

ak

USA

(16,090 m³)

0 cu. yd. (1,465 m³)

balsa

pomegranate
cedar
balsa

525 cu. yd. (400 m³)

gonçalo alves
rosewood
brazilwood
mahogany

*"In the name of the forests, I curse he who
takes revenge on you, tree."*

Miguel Hernández

balsa

SOUTH AMERICA

▼ VALUE, IN MILLIONS OF U.S. DOLLARS,
OF THE TROPICAL WOOD EXPORTED IN 1987

▼ INTERNATIONAL TRADE
IN MILLIONS OF CUBIC METERS
IN 1987

Over 1,000   999 - 100   99 - 10   under 10

The Personality of Wood

There are many types of wood. Each has its own temperament, as do people. This statement is not senseless, as we even use wood to describe someone when we say, "He's a chip off the old block."

Before trying to "educate" wood, we need to become familiar with its character. If we understand it well, we can bring out its expressive potential. If we are familiar with the different varieties, we can select the one most suitable for our project and predict any technical difficulties we may encounter.

Botanists, in accordance with the shape of the seeds, arrange plants in two main categories: angiosperms and gymnosperms. They also class them into leafy and caducous, depending on the leaves. These categories do not help us, since balsa and ebony, for example, are angiosperms yet do not resemble each other at all. On the other hand, holm oak and oak produce very similar wood, but only the latter is caducous.

For the purposes of this book, the most suitable classifications are as follows: woods that are hard and brittle; woods that can be worked on all four sides. Both of these are ideal for sculpting. The opposite applies to woods that are rather inflexible and weak and the cane-type woods, which are very difficult to control.

This division can be applied to different species of trees and also to the sapwood and heartwood of the same tree. It may be useful when discussing sculpture, but not when we have to buy a particular kind of wood.

Sculptors prefer more functional criteria and differentiate only between soft, semi-hard, and hard woods.

Several factors account for hardness: the degree of humidity, the density, and the internal structure of the vessels through which the sap flows. Here we should point out that hardness is not synonymous with difficulty to work; the opposite is often the case. A very soft wood, such as poplar, is impossible to control because of its long fibers, while boxwood, which is much harder, is easier to sculpt and allows for meticulous detail. Semi-hard woods seldom cause technical problems.

There is such a variety of woods that it is sometimes difficult to distinguish between two similar ones. Even the names are sometimes confused or overlap. It is even more difficult to differentiate between the numerous varieties of the same species of pines, cedars, or rosewoods, for example. On the other hand, the same trunk may yield planks with different qualities, depending on the distance from the roots, as is the case with beechwood. In addition, the same name

may be given to woods that have little in common, such as American oak and French oak.

To confuse matters even more, wood can undergo changes during its processing, be they artificial or natural—which can mislead us even further. Ebony, for example, is scarce and may be replaced by holly, a harder and heavier wood but also dark.

Below we give information that is recommended for beginners in sculpting. We comment on the most common kinds of wood in our markets. The photographs that accompany these examples are life-size.

▶ Note: Abbreviations used in the wood samples on the following pages:
D = density (dry wood and freshly cut).
h = height of tree.
∅ = diameter of trunk.

▼ Chart comparing diameter and height of certain trees.

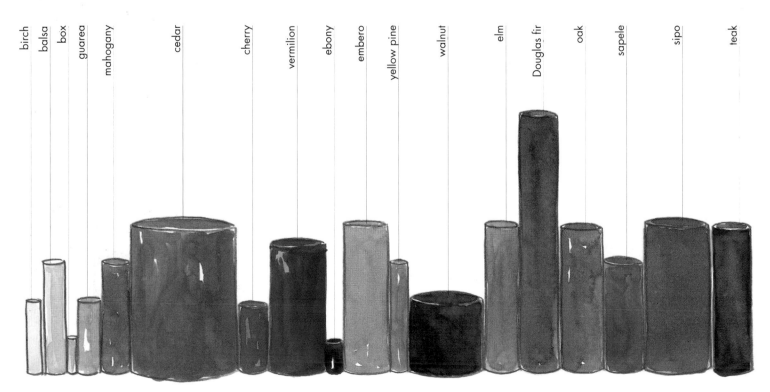

birch · balsa · box · guarea · mahogany · cedar · cherry · vermilion · ebony · embero · yellow pine · walnut · elm · Douglas fir · oak · sapele · sipo · teak

◀ **BOSSE:** *Guarea cedrata*, D 559:650, h 65' (20 m), ø 24" (60 cm). Tropical Africa. Creamy pink color, slightly yellowish, that disappears over time. Fine wood, with fibers twisted against the grain, sometimes forming moiré. Not very fibrous, with resin stains that disappear on sanding. Intense smell. Easy to work, and a sandy shine when polished. Its dust can be unpleasant. Used in quality cabinetmaking, small boats, and pianos.

▶ **BALSA:** *Ochroma piramidale*, D 090:130. h 100' (30 m), ø 20" (50 cm). Costa Rica, Peru. From ivory white to pale pink. Fast-growing tree. Very soft and flexible wood. The lightest and most fragile of commercial woods. Difficult to work and even worse to saw, not recommended for carving. Considered one of the best thermal and acoustic insulators. Used industrially in refrigerated compartments, transport of liquid gases, theater sets, life buoys, models, and above all airplane-modeling kits.

◀ **CEDAR:** *Cedrela adorata*, D 580:80, h 130' (40 m), ø 9' (270 cm). Central and South America, Syria, Asia Minor, Lebanon, the Himalayas, temperate zones in Germany. Color ranges between reddish pink and dark yellow. Straight, soft fibers and close grain. Easy to carve, very uniform and light. Pleasant smell. Repels insects. Stable, resistant to humidity, and durable for exteriors. The tree lives over a thousand years. Due to its size, we can find very large boards on the market. Used for pencils, cigar boxes, musical instruments. The wood most used in ancient times. The Bible treats as a myth the cedars brought from Lebanon to be used for Solomon's temple. Also well-known are the *red Cuban cedar* and *Indian cedar*.

◀ **EMBERO:** *Lovoa klaineana*, D 450:600, h 130' (40 m), ø 4' (120 cm). Philippines and Africa. Color varies from pale gray to golden hazelnut. Not very fibrous; sometimes has countergrain. Easy to carve and resists weather conditions. Easily attacked by termites. Sometimes has dark holes caused by worms. Replaces walnut in some countries. Most suitable for cabinetmaking and molding.

▼ **SAPELE:** *Entandrophagma cylindricum*, D 750:900, h 100' (30 m), ø 40" (100 cm). Uganda, Cameroon, Guinea, Ivory Coast. Brownish red cinnamon color, darkens with the light. Fine wood, with a grooved pattern against the veins and very striking. Very easy to carve. Easily finished. Highly resistant and durable. One of the most widely used in Europe. Occasionally used to replace African mahogany because it is dense, dark, and fine. Seagoing use and furniture in general.

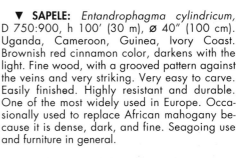

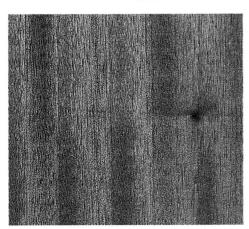

▼ **SIPO:** *Entandrophra utile*, also known as abebay. D 750:850, h 130' (40 m), ø 67" (170 cm). Ivory Coast, Cameroon, Congo, Guinea. Color ranges from pink to red and chestnut. Compact, with fine pores and blackish vein. Is easy to work, finish, and polish. With similar characteristics to mahogany and of superior quality to sapele. Its stability and resistance make it one of the most appreciated African woods. Used for boats and cabinetmaking. An endangered species.

◀ **DOUGLAS FIR:** *Pseudotsuga duoglasii*, D 480:670, h 230' (70 m), ø 40" (100 cm). North America. Does not belong to the genus *Pinus*, despite its resemblance. Toasted reddish brown color, darkens over time. Light, resinous wood with pronounced growth rings. It is carved quite well, is stable and durable. Most useful in cabinetmaking and carpentry.

Semi-Hard Woods

▶ **CHERRY:** *Prunus serotina*, D 680:800, h 65' (20 m), ø 20" (50 cm). North America. Light red color, sometimes with grayish green stripes. Darkens quickly. Very compact wood, with fine texture and straight grain. Can be finished perfectly. Difficult to dry but is then stable and resistant. Other noteworthy varieties are *aliso cherry* in Europe, a little heavier, and *Hottentot cherry* in Africa. The American variety is the tallest and has the greatest diameter. Traditionally used in reliefs and quality cabinetmaking.

▶ **VERMILION:** *Pterocarpus soyauxii*. D 800:950, h 115' (35 m), ø 5' (150 cm). India and Africa. Bright red color that rapidly darkens into violet. Hard yet fine structure; sometimes has countergrain. Easily worked. Highly perfumed. Extremely elastic and resistant. Not attacked by humidity or termites. Used in hydraulic constructions, musical instruments, and knives.

▶ **IROKO:** *Chlorophora excelsa*. D 600:760, h 165' (50 m), ø 5' (150 cm). Africa. Sometimes replaced with teak. Color from greenish yellow to honey brown; darkens over time and the tones become more uniform. Slightly greasy wood, with open pores and intertwining grain: irregular veins, sometimes with moiré. Easily worked and finished. Similar to teak but lighter and less perfumed. Resists water and all kinds of insects. One of the few woods found on the market in large format. Used in shipbuilding and beams.

◀ ▶ **SYCAMORE:** *Acer pseudoplatanus*, D 570:630, h 100' (30 m), ø 24" (60 cm). United States and Canada. Pinkish ivory color. Fine, satiny structure, continuous grain, veined and without any pores. Because the growth rings are not well differentiated, it is hard to distinguish the sapwood from the heartwood. Very slow drying but stable. Resistant to wear, easily worked, and has a perfect finish. Sometimes has the knot called partridge eye. Superior for soundboxes of string instruments, moldings, billiard cues, and marquetry. Highly prized by cabinetmakers since ancient times due to the plasticity of its veins.

▶ **TEAK:** *Tectona grandis*, D 650:800, h 130' (40 m), ø 40" (100 cm). Java, Sri Lanka. There are many varieties but the most prized is from Thailand and Burma. Tobacco color with blackish or greenish yellow veins. Solid wood with compact fiber. Sometimes has moiré. Striking growth rings and a smell similar to leather. Slow drying. Easily worked. Is similar to iroko. Greasy, resistant to water, acids, and insects. Considered the best of all due to its hardness, elasticity, and permanence. Does not shrink nor rust nails. Ideal for shipbuilding, outdoor constructions, ladders, parquet, and scientific instruments. Endangered species.

▶ **BEECH:** *Facus silvatica*, D 650:800, h 100' (30 m), ø 55" (140 cm). Europe. Yellowish white if naturally processed and darkish red if steamed. Dries quickly but is prone to twist and warp. Very easy to work. If green, it is very soft and splits easily. Normally steamed to protect it from woodworm. After steaming, is stable, resistant, and easy to carve. Not very pronounced rings, straight grain, fine and uniform texture. Most suitable for curved pieces and therefore used in toys, turning, and curved furniture such as Thonet chairs. The white *Carpinus betulus* beech is white or grayish and much harder. Used in handles and tool supports, h 80' (25 m), ø 40" (100 cm).

▶ **ELM:** *Ulmus effusa*, D 690:950, h 130' (40 m), ø 32" (80 cm). Central Europe. Generally a light reddish brown. Coarse texture with irregular grain. Strong, porous, and elastic wood, generally with woven fibers. Does not usually split, but tends to bend when drying. Very durable; resists humidity, even when used outdoors. Highly prized wood but rather scarce, despite having six different species. Over the last few decades, Dutch elm disease has practically eliminated native elms from Europe and America. Asian elms have resisted. Used for items that are always in contact with humidity. The black elm, *Ulmus campestris*, from Germany is taller and has a more intense color.

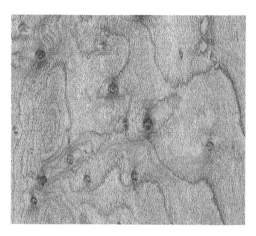

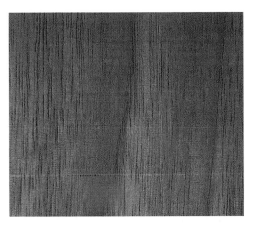

► MANZONIA: *Manzonia altissima,* D 660:700, h 100' (30 m), ø 28" (70 cm). Tropical Africa, mainly Ivory Coast, Ghana, and Nigeria. Gray, brown, or yellowish color with black countergrain. Due to the drying process or light, it can become paler or darker. Dries quickly. Although prone to cracking, is very durable. Fine, regular wood, with dust that can irritate the skin, eyes, nose, and throat. Frequently replaced by walnut, with which it is often confused. Used for rifle butts, quality cabinetmaking and molding.

► WALNUT: *Juglans nigra,* D 670:810, h 65' (20 m), ø 78" (200 cm). Ireland, North America, the Orient. Brownish violet color, darker if from an old tree. Hard, elastic wood with straight, uniform veins. Easily worked. The contrast of its light veins produces a peculiar pattern. Traditionally considered one of the most noble of woods, yet not resistant to woodworm nor insects. Used for cabinetmaking, turning, and molding. Highly appreciated for guns, as it is unaffected by oils and grease. African walnut, *dibetu,* is more similar to mahogany but is twice as tall and more easily worked.

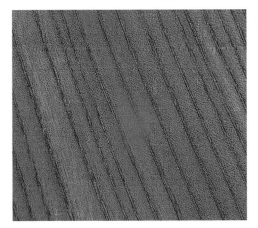

► YELLOW PINE: *Pinus ellitti,* D 850: 1030, h 100' (30 m), ø 16" (40 cm). North America. Strong orangey straw color, darkens in the light and over time. Very broad and pronounced growth rings. Is the pine with least resin and knots. Good for working but cracks easily. Resistant, but often attacked by insects. Used in building: frameworks, beams, staircases. Also known as *melis.*

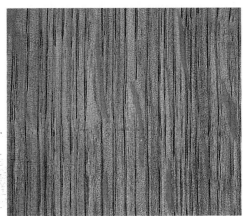

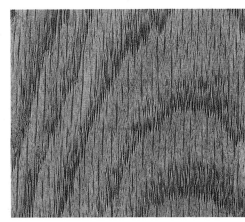

◄ ► OAK: *Quercus alba,* D 630:1085, h 130' (40 m), ø 40" (100 cm). Europe, Iran, Canada. Dark reddish brown color, darkens over time due to the air and light. Grows very slowly and therefore has pronounced growth rings. Coarse texture and straight grain. Easily worked. Slow drying. Highly resistant and durable, although its sapwood is very vulnerable to woodworm. There are 280 different known classes of oak. The French oak is softer and brown colored. *Quercus toza* was used for the roofing of Gothic cathedrals that are still standing. Occurs extensively but is not found in Australia or Africa. With its aroma and resistance to humidity, is ideal for casks used for aging liquors.

Hard Woods

▼ BOXWOOD: *Boxus sempervivens,* D 910:1015, h 26' (8 m), ø 4" (10 cm). Russia, Turkey, Iran, India, North Africa. There exist some 20 different species. Ivory yellow color. Short, slow-growing bush. Compact, homogeneous wood, fine grain and barely visible veins. Heavier and harder than European woods. Easily worked in all directions. Very suitable for small sculptures. Sold by weight. Used for engravings, marquetry, turning, flutes, and cutlery. Its fine grain and hardness make boxwood suitable for making modeling tools.

◄ BUBINGA: *Guibourtia demeusei,* D 950:1100, h 115' (35 m), ø 40" (100 cm). Congo, Guinea. Red or brown with blackish or purple veins. Darkened by light and over time. Very hard, fine wood with pronounced grain. Not easy to work, but can be well finished. When carved, is slightly fetid and can irritate mucous membranes. Highly prized in Japan for its beauty. Used in cabinetmaking, turning, and beams. Endangered species.

▼ BOLONDO: *Erythopheleum ivorense,* D 850:1100. Africa. Greenish yellow or reddish brown color, depending on origin. Very hard and resistant but easily worked. Wears heavily on tools. When polished, can irritate nasal mucous membranes. Used in hydraulic constructions, truck floors, mining beams.

▼ MAHOGANY: *Swietania mahogoni,* D 720:900, h 100' (30 m), ø 28" (70 cm). Mexico, Haiti, Peru, Antilles, Bahamas. Reddish brown or salmon color. Straight fibers, no ribbing, variable grain, generally fine. Does not twist and is easily worked and finished. Very durable, resistant to humidity and termites. Was the first American wood to be industrialized: the ships of the Spanish Armada of the 16th century were made from mahogany from Trinidad. Now used in turning and quality cabinetmaking. Asian mahogany is a dark flesh color. African mahogany is neither of the same botanical species nor of the same quality. The ecological association Greenpeace has organized a boycott on this wood, as ecosystems are destroyed in order to extract it.

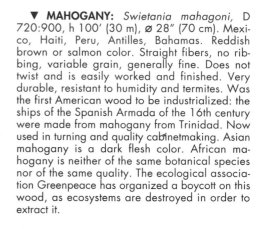

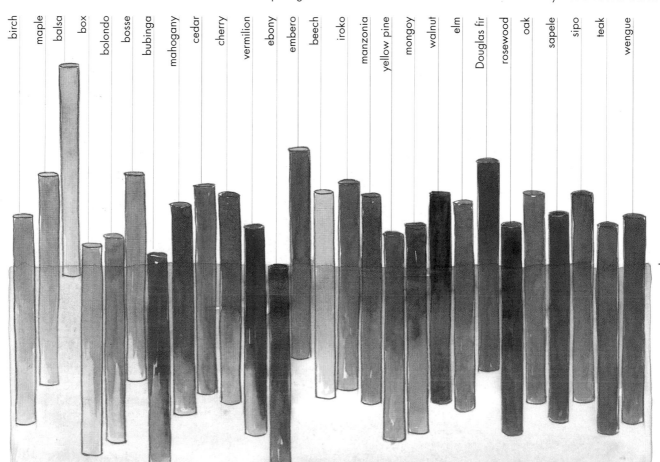

▼ Chart comparing the densities of different woods. This shows how they would float in water.

birch • maple • balsa • box • bolondo • bosse • bubinga • mahogany • cedar • cherry • vermilion • ebony • embero • beech • iroko • manzonia • yellow pine • mongoy • walnut • elm • Douglas fir • rosewood • oak • sapele • sipo • teak • wengue

FLOTATION MARK

At some time most of us have imagined wood as having a particular color, smell, pattern, hardness, and texture. But as we became familiar with the different kinds that exist, we discovered that very few matched our stereotype. Even so, we may still have certain ideas that we think are accurate: for example, wood rots outdoors, wood floats in water, and wood burns in a fire. To correct these ideas, let us examine some examples of different woods.

How can we still refer to "wood color" after seeing the yellowish white of camphor, holly, or spruce; the violet of amaranth; the blue of camwood; the dark red of vermilion, amourette, or ekki; the pink of cherry or ukola; the black of holly or ebony? What is the exact color of pine wood: the cream color of new furniture or the toasted red of old furniture?

The smell of a saw room can make us forget the perfume of sandalwood, the leathery smell of ash and teak, the memories of our infancy evoked by cedar—used for pencils—the aroma of rosewood, or the fetid smell of aloche.

It is difficult to imagine a piece of wood without the pattern of the veins; indeed, the veins of zebrano and gonçalo alves are striking, as is moiré—a pattern in the form of small swirls that we see in teak, bosse, or iroko—or the peculiar, partridge-eye knot of maple. Yet not all woods have veins: pear and cembro, for instance, have none.

Pear wood is one of the most stable and is therefore used for precision instruments such as rulers and T-squares. Others, however, are very flexible and malleable: birch, beech, and poplar can be bent by steaming; linden and balsa by exerting pressure.

Box and dogwood are very soft textured, while balsa is hairy, and teak or iroko, greasy.

We would find it difficult to warm ourselves with box or briar root, as they do not burn, the reason they are used for making pipes.

The density of freshly felled oak, holm oak, beech, ebony, yellow pine, box, and bolondo is greater than that of water, which explains why they do not float. Some, such as pomegranate, guayacan—both used for castanets—and rosewood, still sink even when dry.

There are also nondecaying woods: cedarwood, used for the Egyptian sarcophagi, and camphor are not only free from insects but actually repel them. Neither do termites attack mangle. Iroko resists humidity and insects. Teak neither rots nor rusts nails.

There are also trees that break records. The oldest fossilized forest is in Arizona, with an approximate age of two hundred million years. Also in California, over a thousand sequoias, some over three thousand years old, accompany the sequoia Wawoma, famous because of the tunnel built through its trunk. The drago of the Canary Isles, 3,500 years old, is a survivor of an extinguished species. The baobab trunk of the African savanna is one of the widest: up to 40 feet (12 m) in diameter. Bamboo grows spectacularly quickly: up to 2 feet (60 cm) a day. The Australian eucalyptus is one of the tallest trees. One stands over 500 feet (153 m) tall, which is known as "the tree of fever."

▼ **MONGOY:** *Guibourta ebie*, D 800:900, Africa. Dark brown or grayish color with light and dark stripes. Hard, fine wood. Though not easy to work, has great plasticity. Stable, durable, and resistant to termites. Used in cabinetmaking and decoration.

▼ **WENGUE:** *Milletia lauretti*, D 800:950, Africa. Yellowish brown color; oxidizes quickly on contact with the air and takes on a blackish or grayish tone. Strong, fine wood, open pores, and very elastic; easily worked. Retractile, resistant to blows and high temperatures. Not affected by humidity or insects. Used in cabinetmaking, parquets, knife handles, and tools.

▲ **EBONY:** *Dyospiros melanoxyloin*, D 1000: 1200, h 26' (8 m), ø 12" (30 cm). Madagascar, Cameroon, Mozambique, Nigeria, Gabon, India, the Antilles, Celebes Isles, Mauritius, and Sri Lanka. Blackish brown color or brownish jet, depending on its origin. Highly prized since ancient times for its color and scarcity. A very hard, compact, aromatic wood. Fine pores and difficult to work, although easy to polish and hone down. Very dense, incorruptible. Very difficult to saw when dry. Sold by weight, with or without the bark. Can be replaced by holly. Known in ancient Egypt, nowadays it is used mainly for musical instruments, quality marquetry, and jewelry.

THE WORKSHOP

I n this chapter we will deal with the design of the space for the woodcarving workshop and also with the tools needed for carving. We will concentrate to a certain extent on the gouge, as it is the tool specifically and traditionally used for woodcarving.

In order to serve both the beginner and the person who already has some knowledge of carving, we have provided a range of possibilities so that everyone can adapt them to their own requirements. We end the chapter with a review of the broad sense that the word *workshop* has had throughout the history of art.

Here, in my workshop—urban monastery
I hear the whisper, the wail, the cry of the wood...
Here, in my workshop, two hands and great pleasure.
Inside and out, there grow the fruits of secret accords of
the wind, with the essence of each land, of each wood...
and Kronos, the destroyer, collaborates.

Camí / Santamera

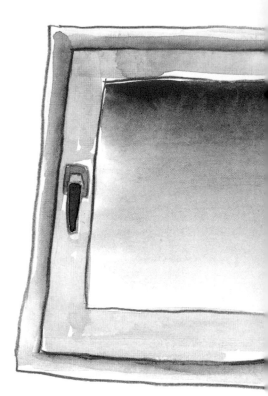

Sculpting requires a suitable work area. Over time, tradition has determined the features of a sculptor's ideal workshop. The most common recourse, and the most advisable, is to use a nearby space such as a storage room, the garage, the attic, the basement, or an old warehouse. It could be said that the perfect workshop does not exist but depends on what you make out of it. Each person has to balance his or her own needs with the available possibilities.

Certain minimum conditions, however, are essential: wood requires a constant humidity and temperature; glues and varnishes need ventilation. To facilitate our work, we need to pay attention to such details as lighting and the arrangement of tools. The most important requisite, though, is layout of the space itself to allow for freedom of movement.

When fitting out the workshop, we need to foresee certain basic requirements: convenient power outlets, acoustical insulation, running water. Safety measures should be observed at all times: keeping electric wires out of the way; avoiding the accumulation of shavings, sawdust, and other flammable materials; and having a recently serviced fire extinguisher handy—plus a first-aid box and posted emergency telephone numbers.

Having ensured the space is safe, we now have to transform it into a work area. If we do not feel comfortable there, our work will suffer; on the other hand, if we overdecorate it, we will lose efficiency.

When organizing the workshop, the sculptor must provide for at least three different, necessary areas: a studio to prepare the project, the workshop itself, and a storage space for wood and finished works.

SPACIOUS BUT COMFORTABLE

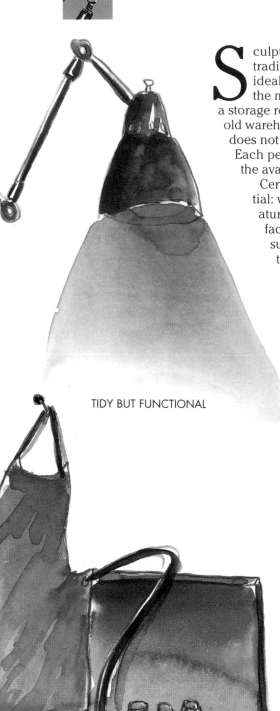

TIDY BUT FUNCTIONAL

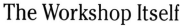

The Workshop Itself

The workbench is the heart of the workshop. For carpenters, it is almost sacred, with its dimensions and material perfectly determined.

Basically, a sculptor needs a large, flat surface for gluing planks and for keeping his tools at hand.

It is also important to have one vertical and one horizontal vise permanently attached to the table to facilitate holding the piece to be carved.

The standard height of workbenches is usually 35 to 36 inches (90 cm), al-

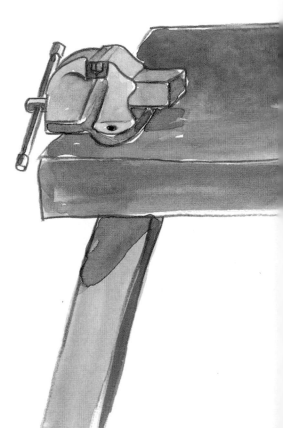

though the ideal height depends on the size of the piece and other factors. If our arms get too tired, we can stand on boards placed on the floor like a platform, adaptable to each circumstance.

If we begin with small pieces, we can make do with a simple workbench. Then we can add such items as a carpenter's table or sculpting easels in different sizes.

We will also need a cupboard to store various materials and large tools.

It is advisable to have a board nailed to the wall to hang and protect the gouges and other tools. It should be made of wood, as it protects them from humidity and keeps them from becoming blunted. To hang each tool, just drive two small nails halfway into the board. Some people even draw the silhouette of each tool to mark its place on the board. Some long strips, separated from the board by small wedges, can be used for hammers, clamps, and rasps.

Experience shows that lack of tidiness in arranging equipment leads to wasting time and getting nervous. The dreamy idea that a bohemian attitude, improvisation, and chaos create art is only a film cliché. To make the best use of your time, you will need to keep everything in order.

It is best to have overall lighting so you can move around without creating shadows. So you also need to plan the layout of power outlets and light sources.

Regarding windows, remember that direct sunlight not only damages wood but also sharpens shadows. This is not the case when windows face north—or south in the Southern Hemisphere.

Traditionally, sculptors' workshops always had a skylight, at a 45-degree angle and facing north, as their main light source. This provided a uniform, diffuse light that enveloped the forms in a kind of *sfumato*.

If we are perfectionists, an adjustable light will be useful when doing finishing work because, if it is used almost as a form of backlighting, it will reveal any faulty strokes with the gouge or unwanted curves or rough spots when sanding.

Last, we should remind you that if you are a beginner in this art and still unaware of your skill or not sure whether wood suits your creative intentions, it is a great risk to set up a complete workshop.

The wisest thing to do is start with the basics: several gouges, a mallet, and clamps. Trimming or silhouetting, the most spectacular part of rough-dressing, can be ordered from a carpenter, as we will see later. This will save time, space, and any unnecessary expenditures on tools.

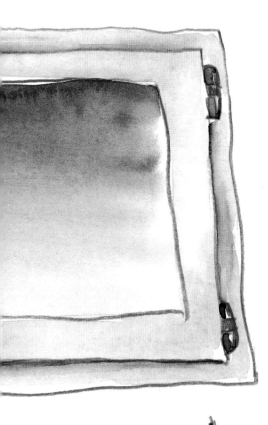

LIGHT BUT NOT SUNNY

N

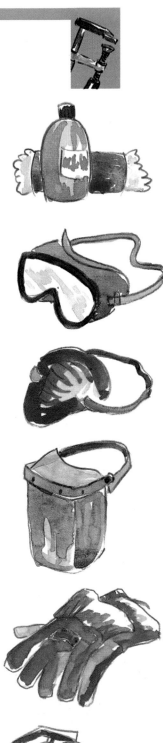

SAFE, VERY SAFE

A Place for Design

B efore starting work, we need to imagine, draw, model. So we need a place in the workshop (free from sawdust) that is clean, comfortable, and well lit. We should be able to relax from the manual work while we visualize and plan new forms.

Any room in the house is suitable, but the studio should preferably be next to the workshop, because an idea often occurs to us while we are working that we can then quickly jot down before it vanishes. Also, if it is close, we can alternate the rhythm of our work and develop parallel projects.

The basic furniture is usually a drawing table with a standard lamp, a board on which to hang projects that require time to mature, and a bookshelf with books for reference or even inspiration.

Studio equipment depends on our skill and method of working on a project. It can be anything from a simple piece of paper, eraser, and pencil to an airbrush or computer, not forgetting Plasticine or modeling clay.

A section of the studio or workshop can be dedicated to projects and maquettes, or models. Here the equipment does depend on our method of working: if we prefer to create maquettes with paper or cardboard, all we need is a compass, ruler, scissors, and glue. Wax requires a small burner to heat it, while clay uses sticks, spatulas, hollowers, and running water. Neutral-colored Plasticine can be used, or polystyrene can be carved, which requires only knives and paper.

To project the maquette onto the trunk, it was traditionally necessary to acquire a machine for pointing or resort to a ruler and scaler. If we intend to carve directly, we can use common materials such as carbon paper or more sophisticated techniques such as enlargers or slide projectors.

Whichever we choose, a detailed list is necessary to buy just the essential tools and materials.

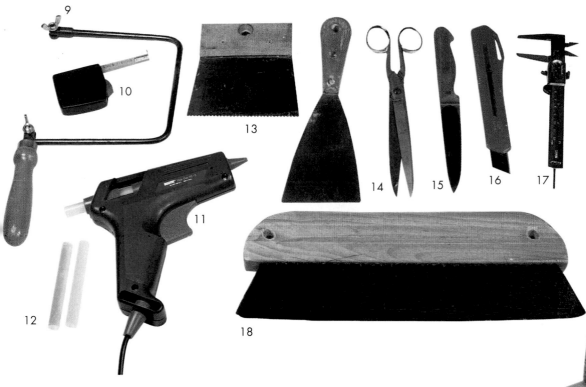

◄► In a well-equipped studio we would expect to find:
compasses (1)
set-square (2)
tri-square (3)
flexible rule (4)
folding wooden rule (5)

level (6)
French curve (7)
ruler (8)
coping saw (9)
tape measure (10)
glue gun (11)
chalk (12)

spatulas (13)
scissors (14)
knife (15)
utility knife (16)
calipers (17)
brush (18)

▼ The material necessary for designing and constructing maquettes will depend on the technique we prefer: pencils and brushes, hollowers, sticks.

► Swiveling stand for modeling with Plasticine or clay.

Storage Space

It is important to set aside part of the workshop for storing wood. A corner with wood waiting to be carved is essential. If we are lucky enough to have more space, why not use it so that we and our friends can enjoy our work?

In the previous chapter, we dealt with wood development, the need to let wood rest for a long time to adapt to the humidity and the temperature. In the following chapter, we will discuss how to develop our projects, how to feel how the trunk breathes. So for both technical and creative reasons, we do not recommend buying a board each time you need one; you must plan ahead.

When storing wood, you should remember what we have said about the causes of warping and splitting. To avoid any unpleasant surprises, the ventilation between the trunks must be carefully arranged. The storage space should be well ventilated but without drafts and, above all, should not be exposed to direct sunlight.

Although in winter or whenever it is cold it is tempting to install a stove in the workshop, fueled by strips of wood and shavings, we must advise against this because it entails two risks: first, abrupt changes in temperature and humidity can damage the wood, and second, the fire risk is obvious.

Even when we strictly follow all the recommendations on how to store wood—horizontally, veins upward—there is only one way to prevent problems entirely: by regular inspection.

When organizing the workshop, it is advisable to set aside a space for storing unfinished works and another for exhibiting your latest ideas and creations. Proper lighting will bring out their best appearance.

It is rumored that several acquaintances of Picasso, after being honored with a visit from the great artist to their workshops and seeing the subsequent sculptures he produced, realized the necessity of having closed cupboards in which to store their most recent works in order to prevent any form of plagiarism.

◀ Wood before being carved: oak (1), vermilion (2), wengue (3), ironwood (4), pine (5), cypress (6), ebony (7), birch (8). Planks stored vertically may warp.

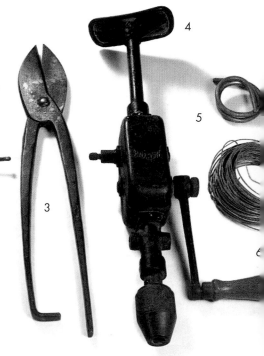

The tools we already have in the house for home repairs (hammer, pliers, saw, glue, nails, etc.) can be the basis for fitting out our workshop.

We can supplement these tools with certain machines. There are numerous models on the market. Most can be used for different purposes depending on the accessories that can be fitted onto them. A drill, for example, can be fitted with bits for drilling, sanding discs, chamois for buffing, or a flexible shaft with a cutter holder for grinding burs.

Different sized clamps are also essential for holding planks when gluing and carving.

There is such a wide variety of sculpting tools that it is necessary to make a selection. Since many are common to both the carpenter and the cabinetmaker, we shall concentrate on the most specific ones, classifying them in accordance with the traditional process of carving.

▲ Electric plane.

▶ Scroll or saber saw.

▶ Drill.

▲ Rubber support and sanding discs.

▶ Drill with table attachment and flexible shaft for different grinding burs.

◀ Though not specifically for sculpting, the following will be useful:

clamps (1)
drill bits (2)
metal shears (3)
hand drill (4)
solder (5)
wire (6)
hammers (7)
crescent wrench (8)
borers (9)
broad chisel (10)
chisel (11)
screwdriver (12)
soldering iron (13)
tongs (14)
pliers (15)
block and curved
  plane (16)
white glue (17)

Tools for Trimming

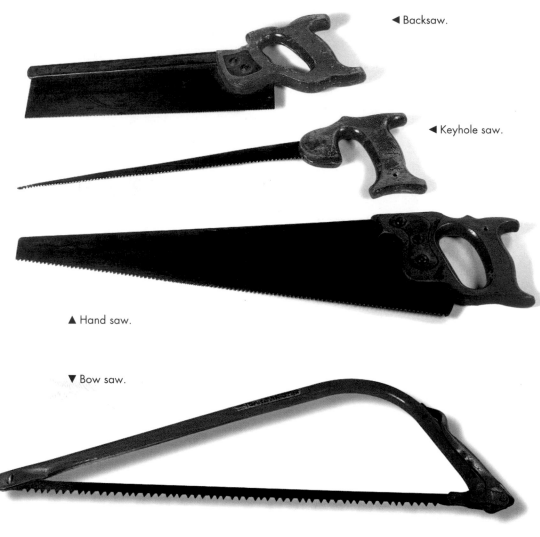

◀ Backsaw.

◀ Keyhole saw.

▲ Hand saw.

▼ Bow saw.

▼ Chainsaw.

The easiest way to begin a carving is to draw the silhouette and hand it to a carpenter who has complex precision machinery that would be considered a luxury in a sculptor's workshop: bandsaw, circular saw, bench drill, and such. But if we wish to do the trimming ourselves, we should obtain an electric die grinder, chainsaw or a simple traditional handsaw.

More sophisticated machinery exists that can cut and rough-dress so easily that it removes any need to trim. If, for instance, we have a die grinder, we can adapt a special saw chain to the disc, smaller than a chainsaw's. This will come in handy for shallow cuts and rough-dressing.

A special cutting disc can also be fitted to the same die grinder. If we use it perpendicular to the wood, it will cut through it. Depending on the angle, it will rough-hew it, more or less deeply. If used parallel to the wood, it will act as a plane.

Great care should be taken with all machinery, especially electrical devices. Attach protectors and, above all, ensure that removable parts are well fixed. Follow the instructions that come with all multi-purpose devices, for better performance and maintenance.

Traditional saws, however, are not obsolete. They are still useful for cutting up planks or small protuberances. Made from hardened steel, their teeth are slightly bent in alternating directions to prevent overheating. This means that the cut is wider than strictly necessary.

Although saws are sold without an instruction manual, and despite the fact it seems obvious, we should remember to use a saw gently, with a steady and constant back-and-forth motion. The pressure applied should be minimal on the forward morement and none on the backward movement.

If you lubricate the sawteeth with bar soap or, even better, fat, the saw will move more smoothly and you will prevent it rusting when not in use. Now and then you should stop and clean away the accumulated resin and sawdust to prevent the blade from becoming blunt.

Sharpening a saw is a slow and painstaking process, done with a triangular file. A saw set is used to restore the slant of the teeth. Specialized workshops can do these jobs for us.

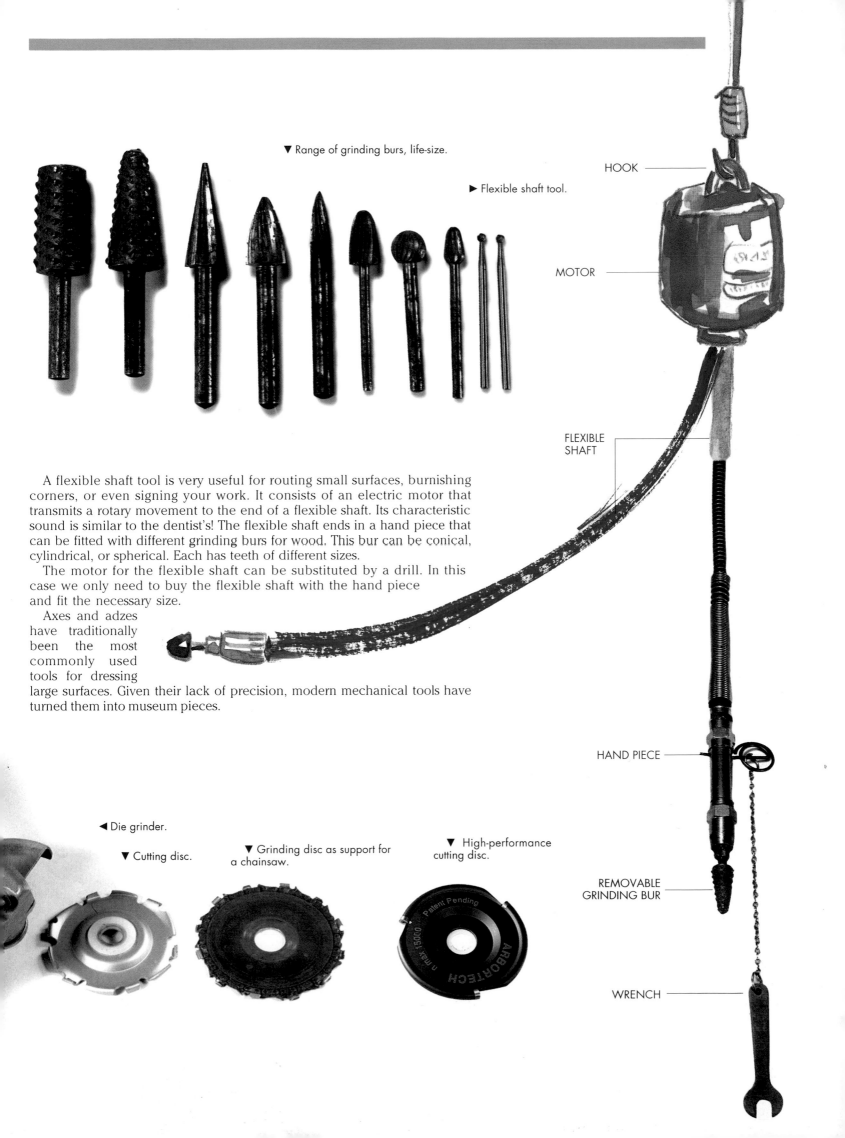

▼ Range of grinding burs, life-size.

► Flexible shaft tool.

HOOK

MOTOR

FLEXIBLE SHAFT

A flexible shaft tool is very useful for routing small surfaces, burnishing corners, or even signing your work. It consists of an electric motor that transmits a rotary movement to the end of a flexible shaft. Its characteristic sound is similar to the dentist's! The flexible shaft ends in a hand piece that can be fitted with different grinding burs for wood. This bur can be conical, cylindrical, or spherical. Each has teeth of different sizes.

The motor for the flexible shaft can be substituted by a drill. In this case we only need to buy the flexible shaft with the hand piece and fit the necessary size.

Axes and adzes have traditionally been the most commonly used tools for dressing large surfaces. Given their lack of precision, modern mechanical tools have turned them into museum pieces.

HAND PIECE

REMOVABLE GRINDING BUR

WRENCH

◄ Die grinder.

▼ Cutting disc.

▼ Grinding disc as support for a chainsaw.

▼ High-performance cutting disc.

Carving Tools

Nowadays, many sculptors who carve large blocks of wood prefer the marks of the machine to remain visible. But if we wish to control our work down to the last detail, we will need the sculptor's tool par excellence: the gouge.

Before dealing with gouges, we should remember its two sister tools, which are commonly used by carpenters but can be of great use to us also: the chisel and wood chisel.

The *chisel* is used for deep, narrow cuts called *mortises*. Made of steel, it is square, narrow, and thick, with a highly beveled cutting surface. It is used parallel to the cut we want. It is very useful when we want to join two pieces.

A *wood chisel* also made of steel, is broader and thinner, with a rectangular cross section and sloping cut. It cuts obliquely to the wood and is used for rough-dressing.

The chisel and wood chisel require handles that are traditionally made from wood, reinforced with two met-

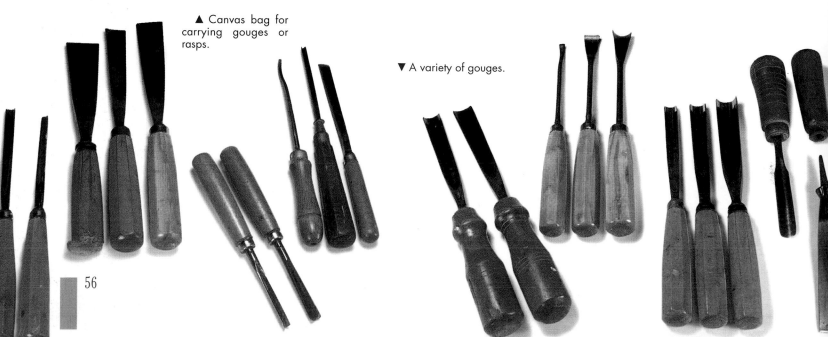

▲ Conical, cylindrical, and bell-shaped mallets.

▲ Canvas bag for carrying gouges or rasps.

al bands to prevent them from splitting as they are struck with a metal hammer.

The *gouge* is still the sculptor's hallmark, as the pen is for the writer. Computers and die grinders make life easier for both professions, but the pen and the gouge transmit the creator's strength more spontaneously. They constitute his signature and leave his mark.

Gouges are made from steel, but unlike the other tools, they are not solid but layered, and are not necessarily flat. They are really wood chisels adapted for working curved surfaces.

The enormous range of gouges on the market is the result of combining two variables: the size and shape of the *blade*, and the type of cutting profile, or *mouth*.

In regard to blades, we find *straight* and *curved* gouges or a combination of both; *elbow* if the cut of the curved end is beveled upward; or *counter-elbow* if the mouth is open under the curve of the blade.

In regard to the mouth, we have flat gouges, half-round, *tubed*, which are more curved than the previous ones, and *V-shaped* if the cutting edge is in the shape of an angle. There are also gouges with intermediate curves. For example, there are half-round gouges that are so open that they can almost be confused with flat gouges.

Professional gouges usually have a blade about 4 inches (12 cm) long when they are new. There are over a dozen types with different sized mouths that range from 2 mm to 30 mm. There are also gouges with specially shaped mouths, used for a limited number of tasks.

Choosing the kind of gouge that best suits us is fundamental. To make this eas-

ier, we show here a chart of the most common ones. Because it is all too easy to get carried away and collect a large number of them, only to find that later we use just a handful, we highlight the main ones. We should also remind the beginner that he or she will have enough with two or three straight, half-round gouges between 5 and 20 mm, which we have indicated in magenta.

The gouge can be struck with the hand for detailed work, although the most common technique is with a mallet.

Mallets are made of wood and used for striking the wooden handle of the gouge. It is obvious that a mallet would crack or warp if used like a hammer for nails or metal. In the same way, the handle of the gouge would split if struck with metal.

The quality of a mallet depends on both the hardness of the wood and the structure of the fibers. The tighter and more entwined the fibers are, the longer the mallet will last. The best mallets are made from rosewood, box, or the pith of elm or holm oak, although the easiest to find are made from beech and ash.

The design of the sculptor's mallet has remained unchanged since the times of ancient Egypt: the impact surface is curved and the handle is short. Both factors ensure accurate blows. The most common shape of the body of the mallet is bell-shaped, although we can also find conical, cylindrical, convex, and even square mallets.

In the following chapter, which deals with the process of carving, we will discuss the correct use of the gouge and mallet.

▼ A variety of gouges.

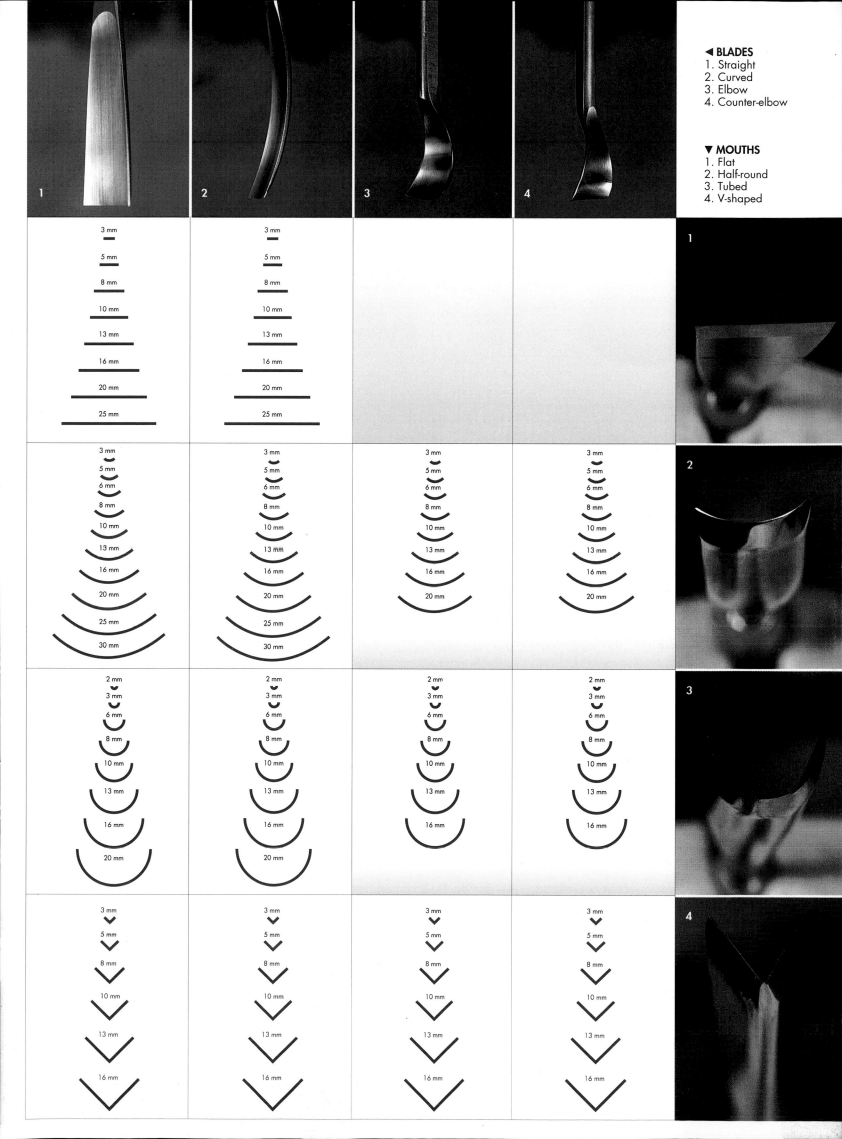

◄ BLADES
1. Straight
2. Curved
3. Elbow
4. Counter-elbow

▼ MOUTHS
1. Flat
2. Half-round
3. Tubed
4. V-shaped

Sharpening and Care of the Gouges

▼ Oil bottles.

▼ Hand stones.

▲ Tabletop sharpening stone.

Some craftsmen are proud to use the same gouge as their parents. They remind us of those pencils that we used to sharpen until there was nothing left. Gouges, like pencils, can become blunt through wear or a blow. The process for sharpening a gouge can be divided into three stages: grinding, sharpening, and finishing.

Grinding cuts back the beveled area and removes any damage, such as nicks, to the cutting edge. *Sharpening* defines the cutting edge. *Honing* perfects the edge.

Gouges are sold in hardware stores or stores specializing in knives and are usually sold ready to use, although some brands offer only ground gouges, that is, with the bevel but no cutting edge. So it is a good idea to have grinding stones in the workshop right from the beginning; these are made of Carborundum and are lubricated with a light oil.

So before beginning to carve, it is necessary to learn to sharpen. Take the gouge in both hands and rub the bevel with a sideways back and forth motion against a flat grinding stone greased with a few drops of oil.

The cutting edge of the gouge dulls with use. So we should sharpen it as soon as we notice any roughness when drawing it across the wood. When it is sharp, we have to correct the bevel and finish the cutting edge. Hold the gouge with your least able hand and with the other rub the two sides of the edge, from inside outward, with a round-edged stone slightly finer than the previous one, which is also greased.

As we carve, and especially with finishing work, it is necessary to sharpen frequently to ensure a clean cut.

The knots in wood, the wood's hardness, dropping the gouge, or simple wear from usage will eventually blunt

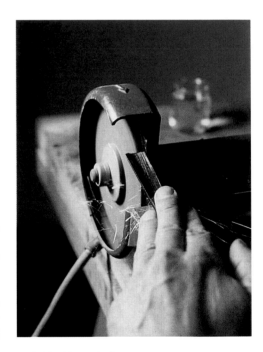

▲ Machine grinding.

▼ Handle and parts of a gouge.

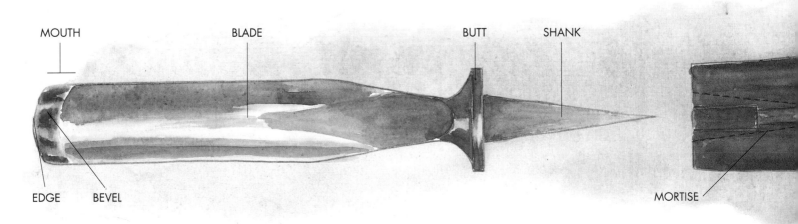

MOUTH   BLADE   BUTT   SHANK

EDGE   BEVEL   MORTISE

the gouge. To correct this we will need a grinder.

Grinding is delicate work that requires expertise and a grindstone. For this reason, we recommend waiting until you have several blunt gouges and then taking them to a specialist. If we grind them ourselves, we have to interrupt the process several times to prevent the gouge from heating up, in which case the steel would lose its temper and become brittle.

Although certain brands of gouge have plastic handles, good handles are still made from wood. We recommend the handle not be cylindrical but rather be ribbed to prevent your hand from

▼ Electric grinder.

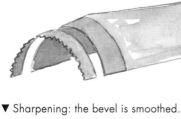

▼ Grinding: the steel is cut back until any damaged areas are removed.

▼ Sharpening: the bevel is smoothed.

▼ Finishing: the cutting edge is refined.

▲ Hand sharpening.

▲ Hand finishing.

HANDLE

slipping. Unlike wood chisels, gouges should not have a metal band, as this would hurt when struck with the palm of the hand, and the wood mallet will not damage it as much as a hammer does chisels.

If we buy gouges and handles separately, we will, obviously, have to attach them. *Fitting the handle* is easy: using a fine drill bit, make an initial hole in the center of the handle, almost as deep as the shank to be fitted. Using a thicker bit, drill a new hole halfway along the first. This way we create a two-sized hole inside the handle that will act as a mortise for the gouge shank.

We then insert the shank in the mortise of the handle, and to secure it, we simply strike the handle down onto a table until it is firmly attached. If there exists any play between the shank and the mortise, we can use our knowledge of wood as a living being: if we dampen the hole in the handle, the wood will swell to grasp the shank. If this is not sufficient, we can always insert small wedges.

Finishing Tools

▼ 1. File card.
2. Wire brush.

▲ Rasps: 3. Small Surform.
4. Flat replaceable blade.
5. Handle for replaceable blades.
6. Handle with half-round
replaceable blade.

► Files.

▼ Traditional rasps.

► File teeth.

► Rasp teeth.

When we have finished with the gouge, we can proceed with the smoothing and polishing. For this we will need rasps, files, and knives. The *rasp* is a most suitable tool for woodworking. It is made of steel and its entire surface is regularly toothed. The teeth are produced by incisions made with a burin that raises the steel. This granular surface is the abrasive part used for reducing, roughing, and polishing.

There is a great variety of rasps. If we classify them according to the size of the teeth, we have coarse, semi-coarse, fine, and extra-fine rasps. When beginning to model, we will use mostly rough rasps, while for the finishing touches we will require extra-fine models.

Depending on the shape, we can classify rasps according to their cross section: rectangular, square, round, half-round, knife, etc. Whether we choose one or the other will depend on the characteristics of the surface to be worked.

Rasps are useful for defining, finishing off detailed work, reducing prominent parts, rounding corners, etc.

The rough surface of *files* has less relief than the surface of rasps and is more densely covered. The steel has been reduced using straight, crossover cuts over the entire surface, producing grooves that file and polish, although more superficially than the rasp.

There are as many kinds of files on the market as rasps, given the different combinations of size, shape, and thickness of the teeth. They are used mainly for finishing off the work carried out with the rasp, as they leave the surface smoother. We can also use them for sharpening other tools, such as saws and knives.

There is a special sort of small files called *riffle files*. Similar to modeling sticks, these tiny tools are held in the middle, as each end has a differently roughed surface. They are useful for working minute detail into the nooks of the wood.

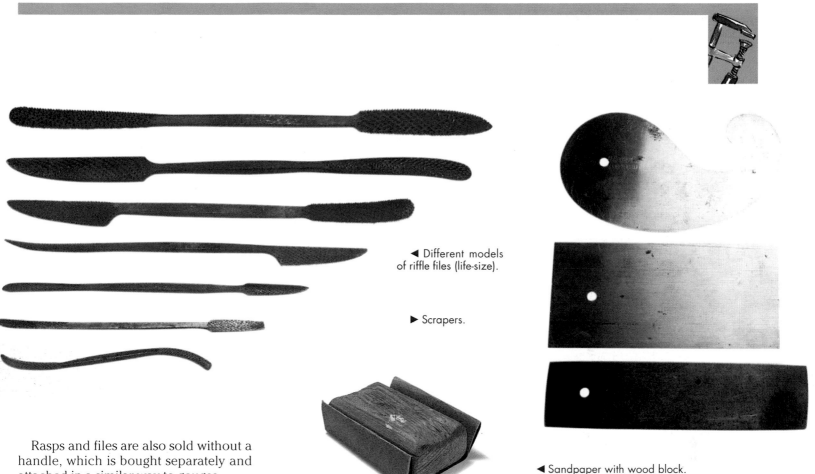

◀ Different models of riffle files (life-size).

▶ Scrapers.

Rasps and files are also sold without a handle, which is bought separately and attached in a similar way to gouges.

Both tools are used with both hands; with one we hold the handle firmly and with the other we guide the point. To prevent uneven surfaces, you must maintain a steady pressure. If the rasp is too coarse, it will scratch the wood; in this case you will need a finer model. If we rasp without following an order, we will raise splinters, so it is best always to apply the tool in the direction of the grain. If we need to cut across the grain, we should choose a finer-toothed rasp or file.

The spaces between the teeth easily get clogged with resin, dust, and sawdust. A metal brush is used to clean them out.

Although a file leaves the surface reasonably well polished, it also lifts up the ends of the fibers. *Scrapers* are used to sever these.

Scrapers are fine strips of steel with straight edges, that is, without a cutting edge. They are used to smooth the rough ends of the wood during rasping. Because they are also used by carpenters, they are easy to find in hardware stores.

Later we will explain how to use them, always in the direction of the fibers. For the moment, their edge must not be sharpened. If this should happen, we should restore the original cutting angle using an extra-fine file.

Last, we need different grits of sandpaper. We can apply it more easily using a small block of wood or buy a specially designed wood or cork accessory.

If we need to finish large surfaces, electricity can help to lighten the work, thanks to an orbital (finishing) sander or, for even larger surfaces, a belt sander. However, these machines belong more to carpentry than to wood sculpting, as they are usable only on flat surfaces.

◀ Sandpaper with wood block.

▲ Orbital sander.

▶ Belt sander.

There Are Studios ... and Studios

What we have described so far we could ironically describe as the workshop of the romantic, a place where an individual can unleash his creativity. This chapter will provide us with a more objective historical perspective of this subject.

The idea of the workshop in the history of art covers three concepts: the place, the equipment of work, and a group of apprentices with their master.

It is no easy task to find information about the characteristics of the workshops and tools used in the past and the most common techniques. There are two main reasons for this: the secret nature of the guilds and the motivation of the researcher, more concerned with the results than with the means used, more with the aesthetics than with the technique.

Like all guilds, the image makers jealously guarded the secrets of their techniques. Tools evolved in accordance with their needs. Some masters would design them depending on how they worked.

Focusing on the workshop itself, we must remember that during the Middle Ages, many workshops were located in European abbeys.

The workshops later moved to the cities. Their customers, mainly the Catholic church, would approach them with precise commissions. Sometimes the finished work would be held for a certain time for use as an advertisement. Transport was always a problem, so packing was done with the utmost care.

If we study the culminating point of Western wood sculpture during the Catholic baroque period, we will see that the team working with a sculptor was very similar to those of other guilds. The master, the assistants, and the apprentices followed a strict hierarchy regarding their work, assignments, and responsibilities. This tradition of guilds was also found in the East. We should remember that in ninth-century China there already was an academy, and the followers of Jōchō in Japan were known as the School of Seventh Street.

The master, known today as the artist, was mostly in charge of contracting and finishing the work. If a direct carving, he would do it himself to ensure the correct movement and proportions. If the carving was to be enlarged by pointing, his task was to create a small-scale maquette. The enlargement, a more routine job, was left to his students. It was the custom for the artist himself to carve the faces and hands, and this was specified in many contracts. The commissioner thus ensured a minimum standard of quality.

There are few exact details about the number of assistants and apprentices. The only reference we can find in certain documents is the formula "he had a large number of assistants," to underline the category of the artist.

An image for a baroque altar would pass not only through the hands of this artist. A carpenter would first prepare the block of wood, and after the altar was carved, it would be sent to a painter's workshop for the polychromy to be added and finally to a joiner, who was responsible for the final positioning and decoration of the surrounding area. Some image makers, such as Alonso Cano, Berruguete, or J. S. Carmona, were also master painters. They thus had their work more under their own control. At different times and in different places, however, it was forbidden for the sculptor to apply the polychromy.

If we read that an anonymous work "is from the workshop of . . . ," it may mean the carving was made on the master's premises and under his direct influence. In a broader sense, it may be a reference to one of his disciples or it may simply indicate that we lack sufficient evidence to attribute the work to the sculptor in question.

► Egyptian relief showing a couple of sculptors.

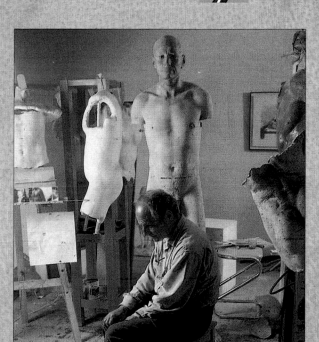

Nature, too, has its own workshop: in the Southern Hemisphere there is a constellation called the Sculptor's Workshop, better known simply as the Sculptor.

Not All Carvings Are Unique

A single idea can give rise to different interpretations: the story of a miracle, for instance, can give rise to different images; different because they depend on the memory of the medieval cleric who saw

◄ The workshop of a modern polychromer who continues to follow the traditional steps of his antique craft.

► Workshop of the hyper-realist Antonio López.

the original and commissioned the work, and different because of the imagination, skill, and material available to the local carpenter.

From the Renaissance onward, engraving popularized works of art. An engraving could be the starting point for the creation of a new sculpture. Artists did not idealize the idea of an original, or one-of-a-kind, work as we do today. At that time, an artist was renowned when he was able to improve on the maquette. So it is quite usual to find several copies of the same carving.

Neither was it strange for a sculptor to copy his own work. We can see almost identical images signed by the same artist. In such cases, to reproduce the prototype, the artist would use the technique of pointing and so needed to equip his workshop with one of the devices used for this task. This system was enhanced with the arrival of the pantograph, which in turn gave rise to the modern systems of industrial reproduction.

Today there are factories in which five, ten, even twenty-five sculptures can be copied at the same time. A prototype is made of a resistant material such as

metal resins, and by means of complex machinery similar to that used for copying house keys, different trunks are simultaneously hewn. Although this type of machinery is usually accurate, the carvings are generally finished with the gouge to give them a more unmanufactured touch.

◄ **J. S. Carmona** *The Christ of Mercy* (18th century). Atienza, Spain.
There exist two virtually identical carvings of this same Christ, in Nava del Rey and La Granja, Castile, signed by the same sculptor.

► Mass production of carvings.

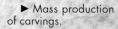

THE PROJECT

I n art, technique and creativity go hand in hand.
Technique can be taught, while creativity is difficult to transmit through the written word, and this is not our intention.
Instead, we will limit our text and allow images to communicate with the subconscious and suggest different sources of inspiration: such sources as nature, the work of other artists, the wood itself . . . even aesthetic and philosophical notions that might seem to inhibit the mind but more often serve to free it.

Later we will deal with how to materialize our ideas in a maquette and from there to the wood itself.

This chapter also comments on certain techniques used in the past.

◄ In the workshop of the sculptor Henry Moore, in Perry Green, England: Santamera observing a sketch during his interview with the artist in 1982.

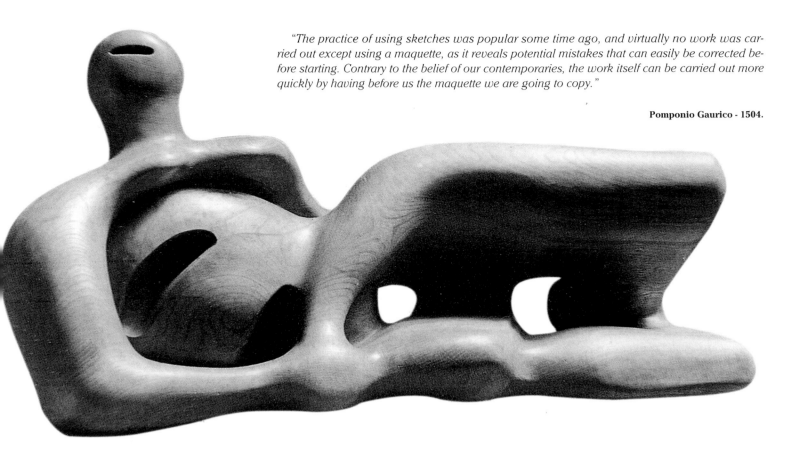

"The practice of using sketches was popular some time ago, and virtually no work was carried out except using a maquette, as it reveals potential mistakes that can easily be corrected before starting. Contrary to the belief of our contemporaries, the work itself can be carried out more quickly by having before us the maquette we are going to copy."

Pomponio Gaurico - 1504.

▲ **Henry Moore,** *Reclining Figure* (1959-64). Elm wood. 89 ³/₄" (228 cm).

◄ Clay maquette and enlargement in plaster before being cast in bronze.

A Thousand and One Forms

The Creative Process

Being creative entails discovering, imagining, shaping something that does not yet exist. Our genetic background and cultural heritage are no doubt important, yet creativity also requires a double form of learning. On the one hand, we need to assimilate, consciously or unconsciously, our experiences to use as a source. And at the same time we need to acquire the technical mastery necessary to materialize our ideas. Having something new to say and knowing how to express it require years of maturing and patient exercise.

Having reached this stage, the artist needs some time to create an original form. In many African tribes this period of time is spent on rites carried out by the artist. In our own culture we find similar references:

"Gregorio Fernández . . . would never sculpt Christ, Our Lord nor the Virgin Mary without having previously prepared himself through prayer, fasting, penitence and communion, so that God would grant him the necessary grace."

After this reflective period, when no solution seems available and the artist is on the verge of giving up, the right half of the brain receives what psychologists call insight, in a sudden, unpredictable way. This insight causes a certain amount of stress, which in turn stimulates the artist. This stress has been termed *estro*, in a comparison with mammals' period of heat. Since this is a passing phase, it is advisable to have the right materials on hand to make maquettes.

▼▶ Nature teems with ideas.
There they are to be copied. If they sow their seed in us, a thousand and one ideas will spring up in the future.

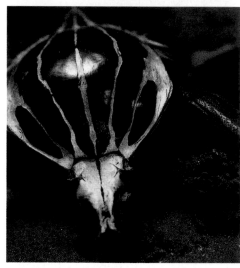

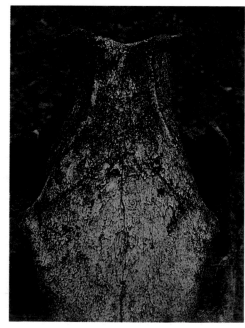

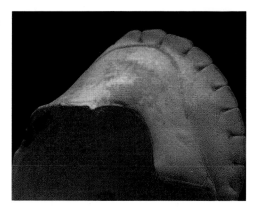

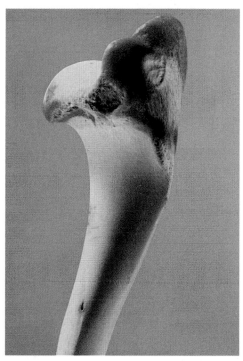

"Before painting bamboo, we need to let it grow inside us."

—Su Dong Po (11th century)

A Thousand and One Ideas

Feelings, fiction, characters, ideas, myths, gods . . . have been captured in wood. History is a whirlwind of projects.

When inspiration is not forthcoming or is sterile, it is best to turn to the masters.

One day, our gouges will overflow with ideas.

◄ **Leiro,** *Carrion* (1987). Chestnut and graphite. 86 ½" (220 cm).

"The more distant the model, the more vigorous the inspiration."

—Lu-Chi (3rd century)

▲ **Basterretxea,** *Bigarrena eguzki-lore* (1975). Wood. 42" (107 cm).

▲ **Barbara Hepworth,** *Oracle* (1960). Painted wood. 52 ½" (133 cm).

▲ **Ángel Ferrant,** *Figure 4* (1957). Painted wood. 19" (48 cm).

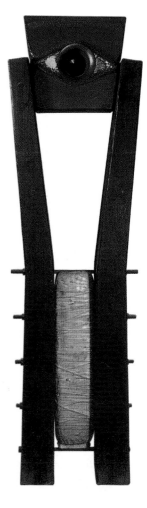

▲ **Subirachs,** *Polyphemus* (1964). Processed wood. 69 ½" (177 cm).

▲ **Riu Serra,** *Frightening Wind* (1990). Sapele. 21 ³/₄" (55 cm).

▲ **Manolo Valdés,** *Infanta 1* (1985). Wood with encrusted iron. 78 ³/₄" (190 cm).

▲ **Subirà-Puig,** *Leather Torso* (1987). Oak. 78 ³/₄" (200 cm).

▼ **Marino Marini,** *The Miracle* (1955). Painted wood. 65" (165.5 cm).

► **Arp,** *Milestone.* 25 ¹/₂" (65 cm).

◄ **J. M. Muñoz,** *The Pagoda of the Abyss* (1987). Holm oak, oak, and lead. 78 ³/₄" (200 cm).

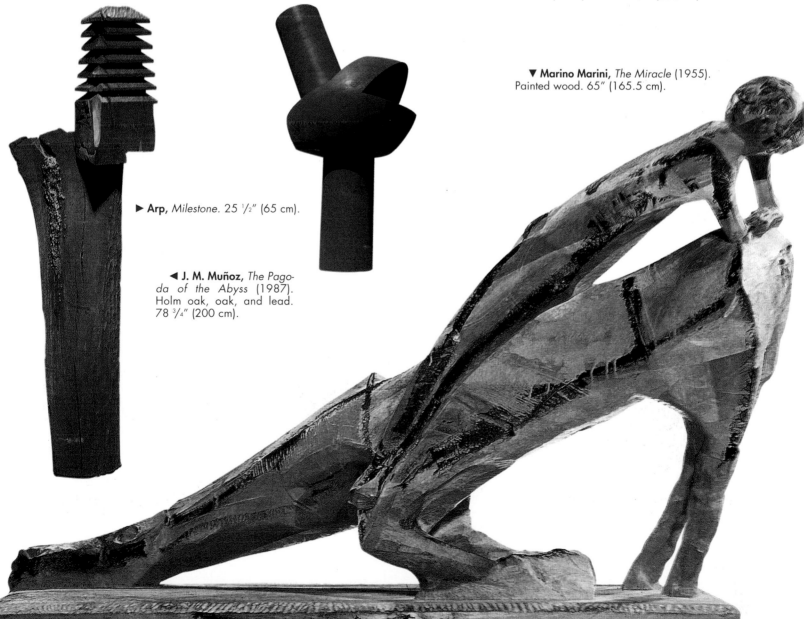

From Wood to Idea

Our project may be inspired by the shapes of nature, history, etc., but it can also spring from the wood itself.

Latent within the wood is a form that the sculptor's eyes can discern. "Carving," Michelangelo said, "consists of eliminating all the excess material so that the sculpture that lies within can awake and emerge."

Each person sees a different sculpture within a trunk or block of wood. Each person projects his or her own idea into the limited volume of the wood, an idea-shape that has slowly evolved.

It is probable that your first attempts to visualize your sculpture will produce mistaken forms, either too small or too large. Only time and contemplation of the wood will enable you to acquire the skill to fully explore all the potential of the wood you have before you.

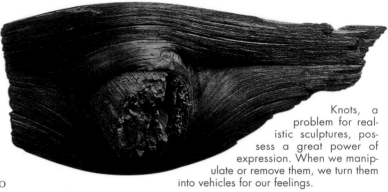

Knots, a problem for realistic sculptures, possess a great power of expression. When we manipulate or remove them, we turn them into vehicles for our feelings.

◄ **Camí**, Numen (1995). Walnut. 30" (76 cm).

Branches suggest many different forms that multiply as the position of the wood is shifted.

▼ 1. *Bust of a Woman* (2500 B.C.). Partially painted wood. 24" (61 cm). Egyptian Museum, Cairo.

2. *Female Ancestor*, Bambara art from Mali. Musée National des Arts Africains et Océaniens, Paris.

3. *Virgin of the Descent* (12th century). Museu Nacional d'Art de Catalonia, Barcelona.

Within a trunk slept African spirits, Egyptian officials, Romanic virgins . . . until a hand awoke them. Forms lie inside the trunk, waiting for their metamorphosis.

1

2

3

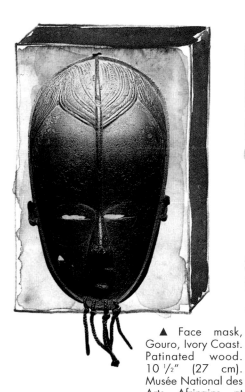

▲ Face mask, Gouro, Ivory Coast. Patinated wood. 10 ¹/₂" (27 cm). Musée National des Arts Africains et Océaniens, Paris.

▲ The goddess Hathor (350 B.C.). Cedar. 18" (46 cm). Metropolitan Museum of Art, New York.

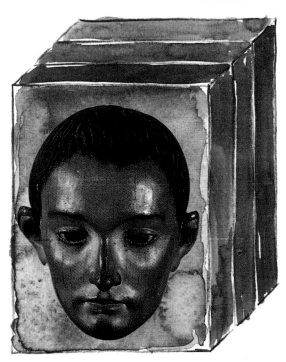

▲ **Alonso Cano,** *San Diego of Alcalá* (detail) (17th century). Polychromed wood. Private collection, Madrid.

▼ **Venancio Blanco,** *Reclining Christ* (1988-91). Valsaín pine. 86 ¹/₂" (220 cm).

▼ **Jasans,** *Near the Sea* (1974), Sapele. 14" (35.5 cm).

A block of wood hides a world of potential sculptures. Some are evident, while others. . . .

We can also construct the block of wood to suit our idea.

When we have formed an idea, either following an abstract inspiration or a simplified version we have already sketched while building the maquette, this is the moment to pause and ask ourselves whether we are on the right track, to consider our aesthetic criteria.

The Aesthetics of Sculpture

After drawing the sketch or sketches (the more the better), it is best to judge them from a distance, figuratively speaking, to let them mature. If no version seems to surpass the others, we will need to make others, synthesizing the previous ones. The final project is always the result of a long, slow process. A stroke of genius, however, can also appear when what we have called an idea-shape emerges above the others.

Only time will tell if a work is art. The reputation of the sculptor, a passing vogue, the price . . . these may all dazzle us, but in the final instance, it is the sculpture itself that shows its worth.

Being a slow process, it is impossible to improvise, even after many years of practice. To make the work appear more spontaneous, it is good to remember the saying "Spontaneity should be well thought out."

Before Art, the Basics

The following points should be taken into account:

Choose the right wood or, alternatively, adapt to the potential of the wood available. If soft, we can make it more expressive. If hard, it permits detailed finishing work.

Sculpture has volume, whereas painting, photography, and cinema only represent it. When improvising, it is easy to spot a sculptor who thinks in two-dimensional terms. Volume requires the space to be conceived in three dimensions. In addition, a sculpture is solid and heavy and it is up to the sculptor whether this quality is heightened or lessened.

All sculptures possess dominant lines of force: vertical planes lend firmness, resistance, a monumental air, while horizontal planes suggest relaxation, passiveness, submission. Diagonal and convex lines suggest tension, movement, action. Wood is more suited to representing softness than hardness, though if we succeed in reversing this . . . ?

Sculpture is three-dimensional: the spectator must move around it. The mannerists achieved this by resorting to a helicoidal composition. The sculptors of the statues carried in religious processions had to consider an endless number of viewpoints, as proposed by Benvenuto Cellini.

The size of a sculpture should be in proportion to the distance and the context: a sculpture that appears enormous in the workshop can seem insignificant in the open air. Where it will be placed, therefore, is a point to bear in mind. If it is to be placed on a raised stand, it will require a certain disproportion to appear proportioned to the spectator. If it is to be framed, it can blend into the background or stand out. In both cases, great care should be taken with the front view of the work. If the public has easy access to it, the detail must be thorough.

The sculpture may be contained, or it may reach into the surrounding space in different ways:

A Romanic virgin, for example, occupies little space in relation to its mass, while a baroque angel, with wings, legs, and arms simulating flight, invades the surrounding space. The difference would become clear if we had to pack the two sculptures.

Wood can also frame a space, creating an internal volume, as is the intention of Barbara Hepworth.

Sculptures appear to create an aura that redefines space, either as a focal point that attracts the attention (the image on an altar, for example, or a totem pole in a landscape).

Academically speaking, sculpture is proportional and has always been based on mathematical structures through history. The concept of the canon and the golden section has a numerical basis. Even Gothic naturalism is based on simple geometric forms.

Breaching these proportions, however, can highlight expressivity. The vision of the sculpture as a whole depends on the balance or counterpoint of its different parts.

Though static, a statue can suggest movement. A sensation of repose is related to the supernatural—Romanic majesty, the serenity of Buddhas radiating reverence, veneration. Movement, on the other hand, transmits strength, energy, dynamism. One or the other can depend on the direction of the grain. A wavy rhythm is the easiest to achieve with wood.

A single work may combine both movement and repose when an ascending figure is placed on a rigid base. Certain figurative works, for example, show legs that remain firm while clothes and body contort.

It is more difficult to represent potential movement, that strength that Michelangelo was able to instill in his marble sculptures. Despite this, certain works by Juan de Juni, for example, combine potential movement with the stillness of the volume.

Movement can also be the result of capturing an instant. In this sense it also represents time. The floating angels, holding lamps, to be seen in baroque churches are still a surprising sight. They are the representation of movement taken to its ultimate consequences. All that can be added are articulations to resemble real movement. Sculpture requires time and expresses time. Marble captures an instant, whereas wood evolves and, being a living being, can age well or badly. Joints, cracks—over the years it can take on an appearance that was not intended by the sculptor; time itself becomes the sculptor.

Expression is one of the aims of art. In a realist work, the face and the hands are fundamental, to the extent that sculptures to be dressed ignore all other details. Exaggeration and disproportion are expressive techniques, while balance is also worthy of being expressed; abstract sculpture, like music, expresses feelings.

The work is given the final touches during the finishing process.

The sculptor's work ends where the spectator's criticisms start. An unfinished appearance, the marks left by the gouge, the polishing, and polychromy are required by the idea. An affected style is the punishment for hesitant work.

Sculptures have their own color, and any change in texture can alter it. Paint can be used to blend together or differentiate the planks that form the sculpture, to highlight details, rhythms, and elements. Glazes and transparencies can be used to create chiaroscuro. The brocade technique, letting the gold show through, is the one that most fully explores the potential of the internal light of a sculpture.

If We Wish to Produce Art . . .

Here we should like to outline a few ideas without intending to create any new rules.

Although it is a truism, it is worth remembering that all sculptures have a dual value: sentimental and objective. We may appreciate a carving because of the effort we have put into it, because it brings back memories, because it symbolizes our nationality, or simply because it is ours. Yet its real, more objective artistic value will only emerge over time, when the work is divested of all living memories, like an Alaskan mask in Europe or the portrait of a stranger; if it is still impressive, it may be art.

The traditional goal of an artist was to surpass all previous models. Since the beginning of the twentieth century, the aim has been to break free of preconceptions. Glorifying one criterion or another leads to judgments unrelated to a work's intrinsic value. The fleeting fashions that resulted from avant-garde movements against the nineteenth century were treated with irony by Dalí: "Don't insist on being modern. It is the only thing which, whatever you do, you will always be" (*Los cornudos del viejo arte moderno*, Barcelona, 1990, p. 46).

The concept of a *work of art* has been a paradox throughout history. Martín González recalls: "Surpassing a theory through creative pressure is no less admirable than satisfying and developing the same theory. Art is as rule based as it is anti-rules" (*The Key to Sculpture*, Barcelona, 1990, p. 39).

We believe the theories of the Chinese Hsieh-Ho are still valid; because he is referring to painting, we shall freely adapt his ideas to sculpture. Hsieh-Ho establishes a hierarchy of accumulative values. Only works that reach the top level would be worthy of being considered art. Hsieh-Ho holds that too many works conform to pre-established models, by art or tradition. He recalls that there are many works that become popular or buy their popularity through advertising techniques. He underlines that many sculptures are reasonably well composed; the volumes, lines, and colors are all adequate, something that can be learned. He places a certain value on those works that make full use of the potential of the material used, as this requires knowledge. He appreciates the few works that transmit the carefulness or energy of the artist (once the technique has been mastered, the gouge is an extension of the hand). Lastly, he mentions the very few sculptures that, connecting with the collective subconscious, give rise to a resonance of the spirit. (Werner Speiser, *El arte de los pueblos, China*, Barcelona, 1961, p. 117).

◄ **Alonso Berruguete,** *Sybil* (1526-32). Polychromed wood. Museo Nacional de Escultura, Valladolid, Spain.

From the Idea to the Maquette

► A simple axis surrounded with Plasticine, ready for modeling.

After these aesthetic considerations, we turn back to our project. Let assume we already have an idea and must now put it down on paper.

First, we will probably find the initial sketch lacking, as a flat drawing neglects problems that only become apparent when volume is involved, and this requires three dimensions. Drawing a sketch or building a maquette will help us to understand, observe, judge, and modify without jeopardizing the form we are creating. We do not recommend confining yourself to a single model. It is better to make several and select the best. Venancio Blanco, for instance, made fourteen models before materializing his representation of the first instant of the Resurrection. They were all rejected by the brotherhood who had commissioned the work.

You can ignore the maquette stage and begin to carve directly, but this method is not recommended. However clear we think our idea is, it is better to model it using material that is easy to alter.

There are several ways of making models. You should choose the one you are most familiar with, provided it suits the project. Though there exist specific manuals on this subject for those who wish to learn more, here we will include the fundamental points. The maquettes will be made by the addition or removal of the chosen material.

Modeling of Maquettes

Malleable materials such as wax or clay have often been used by sculptors for making their maquettes, or models. We recommend using clay or Plasticine. If we use clay, which does not need to be fired, we can ignore the technical problems that affect ceramicists. If we use Plasticine, it should preferably be neutral in color, similar to wood or gray, because color can distort our perception of form.

Before making the model, it is useful to have a central structure, or armature, around which we can distribute the added material.

▼ The filling for a maquette can be pieces of cloth or tied-up newspaper, while the surface should be modeling material.

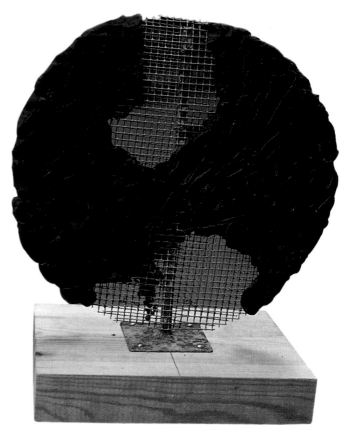

► Wire netting, preferably galvanized, enables us to create a more consistent interior.

If the sculpture is to be mainly vertical, we will need an axis. For a small maquette, simply drive the tip of a long nail into the center of a board and then cover with the modeling material.

Because it is essential that the axis not move, it may be preferable to make a sturdier structure. We can replace the nail with a strip of wood, held upright by small angle irons, or something similar, such as a square-shaped tube. Any of these items can be nailed to a wooden base. If we nail two wooden strips underneath the base to act as feet, it will be easier to move the model around.

For small, horizontal maquettes, we can do away with the axis, though larger works will perhaps require a more complete armature.

If the model is voluminous, we can fill the inside with such materials as paper, cloth, or foam. We can tie them to the axis with wire, attempting to reproduce the form from the outset.

For certain maquettes we will need to build an armature with different axes, covered and attached by wire netting. Remember that galvanized netting, being more rigid, will be handy for geometric forms, while standard netting, being more malleable, can be used for more organic forms. We can use this netting to build up the shape around the axis. Then we cover it with clay or Plasticine, adding or removing material until we have the desired form.

Subsequently, using our hands or with modeling sticks, we can begin to add material to the original shape. This should be done while turning the model, so as not to lose the overall effect, creating the larger surfaces before outlining the details.

Because the finish depends on the ultimate material, wood, we need not spend any time on this.

Once the maquette is finished, the vertical and horizontal axes are marked using squares. These lines will indicate the main reference points when transferring or enlarging this model onto the block of wood.

We can also shape the maquette using the wire netting itself and then cover it with damp plaster gauze. In this case we cannot add or remove material, so greater mastery of the form is required. This technique, called *draping*, is useful for building full-scale models. Again, it is not necessary to include details, but it is still essential to indicate the basic axes that will then be transferred to the block of wood.

▶ Elements for making an axis for modeling.

◀ Armature for more complex structures.

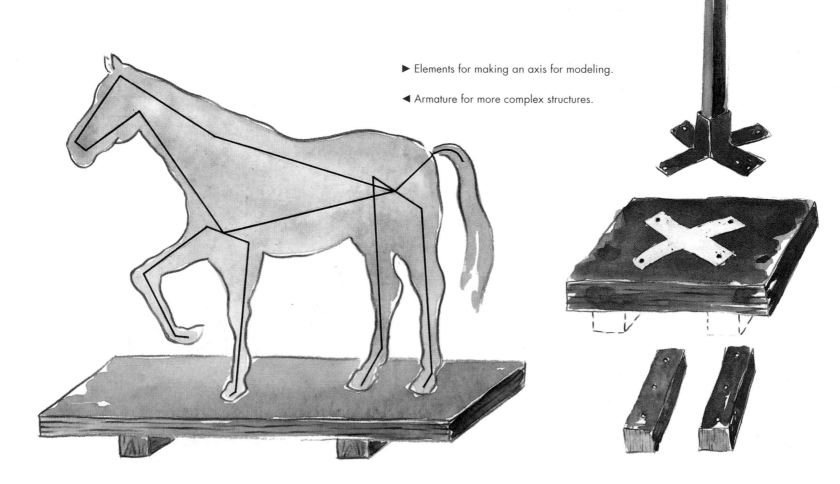

▲ 1. Axes and profiles are marked on the six sides of the block.

▲ 2. Material is removed until we have a cube-shaped silhouette.

▲ 3. We are approaching the definitive form.

▼ 4. We can simplify the task by complementing the form with Plasticine.

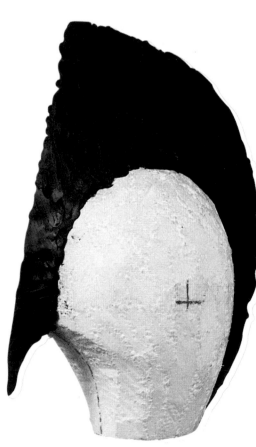

Carving Maquettes

If you have had little or no practice modeling clay, it is better to use polystyrene, as this is good practice for the final process. In this case we obtain the form by reducing the material, that is, by removing polystyrene. We can manipulate any soft material, such as soap, pumice stone, or wax, but we recommend polystyrene, medium or heavy density polyurethane, because there is an ample supply of it and because it produces cleaner, firmer results than other materials.

Using these materials, we begin to carve with a knife, razor, or utility knife, following the basic steps we will deal with later under carving: indicating the axes, projecting the drawing over the surface, trimming, planing, profiling, etc.

Combined Techniques

There is no reason to resort to a single technique. Because maquettes are not to be definitive works, we can start with one material and complement it with any other, malleable material. We could start, for instance, by modeling polystyrene and then add clay so as to economize on materials and work. Or start with certain organic objects—bones, stones—as did Henry Moore and then add Plasticine to transform them.

▼ **Leonardo da Vinci**, *Flora* (detail) (1501-6). Painted wax. 26 ½" (67.5 cm).
During the Renaissance it was fashionable to present sculptures modeled in wax. This vindicated the intrinsic value of models.

The Maquette: Not the Definitive Work

The maquette is a mere stage in the process of carving, so it is not necessary to pay too much attention to detail. It is important not to depend too much on the model, for the final work will use a different material and will probably be a different size. It is more a reinterpretation than a copy. A slight error in the proportions of the maquette, when enlarged, can alter the appearance of the whole. In addition to this, the wood we have chosen also has its own properties, different from those of the material we used to make the model. Given this unpredictable situation, it is advisable to modify the model as the wood is carved to plan the subsequent stages of the work.

Although the maquette is generally considered ephemeral art, if we have the chance it is worth admiring the models of the classics, as they carry the mark of the artist, a mark that is easily lost when the work is enlarged by his assistants. The sensibility of the artist can sometimes be felt more vividly looking at his maquettes rather than the later, definitive work.

The further back in history we go, the more difficult it is to find examples of models, as the master carvers tried not to be limited to a specific project in their contracts. It is said that J. S. Carmona, for example, would only show a vague sketch-maquette that he would then claim back.

▼ This model, of painted terra-cotta, acts as a reference point. The definitive work will have to adapt to the wood used.

▼ During carving, this pine trunk started to twist at the thinnest point. The wood suggested a movement, and it would have been a mistake to blindly follow the maquette.

▼ **Camí,** *Organic* (1986). Commissioned work, in pine. 80 ³/₄" (205 cm).

From the Maquette to the Wood

Once the maquette is finished, we have a decisive step before us, one that requires a sculptor's intuition: to visualize the model inside the block of wood we wish to sculpt. It is best to start with simple forms. Despite what we said earlier concerning the importance of maquettes, we suggest you sculpt a simple, flat form as your first exercise. We will begin by cutting out a stencil. For this we can use the sketches made earlier, enlarged to the actual size of the sculpture. We can begin by cutting around the perimeter of the sketch, placing this silhouette on the wood, and transferring the drawing. Carbon paper can also be used and removed, and the lines then reinforced.

So as not to lose the overall vision of the work, also draw in the main axes on each plane of the wood.

Now we can begin to rough-dress the wood, and as we progress, we must redraw the model, especially the axes.

As a second exercise, we suggest increasing the complexity by projecting a symmetrical three-dimensional shape. Here again, we begin by drawing the front and side silhouettes on two pieces of paper. Then, using any method, we transfer both drawings to the wood. Since this is a symmetrical figure, there is no need to draw the rear side if we are trimming with industrial methods. But if we are going to rough-dress the wood ourselves, we should turn the paper back to front and transfer each drawing to the opposite sides of the block. As in the previous case, we should mark the

▲▶ The simplest way of reproducing a flat form is to cut out a stencil with the silhouette of the sculpture and draw it on the wood. We can then begin to trim.

main axes and go over the lines as often as necessary.

Moving on to a more difficult exercise, we can embark on an asymmetrical volume. The process is the same as before: after observing the maquette in three dimensions and using the axes as a starting point, we draw the multiple silhouettes on six pieces of paper. We then transfer the main lines to the six sides of the block, not forgetting the

base. We should take great care when reinforcing the basic lines that define the form and the movement. Then we can join several lines with others by rough-dressing. As in the previous cases, we must constantly redraw the sketch until the planes meet.

When we have a certain command of this, we can do away with the paper stencils and use a squared platform, which can be the same as that used for holding the model. Using a grid and a square, we project the vertical lines on the maquette itself, beginning with the axis of the four sides. These lines can then be complemented with other horizontal, equidistant lines. The result of this will be a model subdivided into small, imaginary cubes. The block of

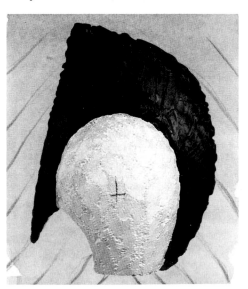

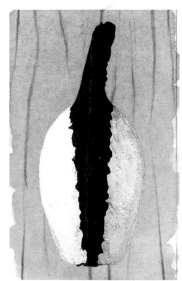

◀ Although this is a symmetrical three-dimensional form, the front and side views are different, so we need to draw the two silhouettes on corresponding sides of the plank.

wood is then also divided into squares and, using the maquette as a guide, we then draw the silhouette on every side. These lines will help us to maintain the correct proportions. To change scale, simply enlarge or reduce the size of the grid squares on the block of wood. The section on pointing offers still other solutions. Of course, these are not the only possible methods. We can resort to others, such as projecting and drawing the shadow of the model on the wood or using slides of the different

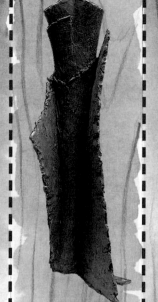

sides projected on the block and situated at the right distance to obtain the desired enlargement. With practice, we can even draw directly on the wood itself.

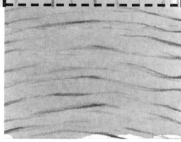

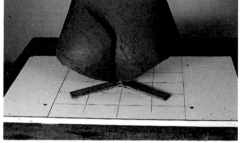

▲ Imaginary "unfolding" of a block of wood from which we will carve an asymmetrical volume. It is advisable to draw the silhouettes on the four main sides and also on the upper and lower sides.

Another way of transferring the maquette to the wood consists of:

▲ 1. Squaring the base that supports the model.

◄ 2. Using this grid, drawing vertical lines on the maquette with the aid of a square.

▲ 3. Drawing horizontal, equidistant lines on the maquette to obtain a grid pattern.

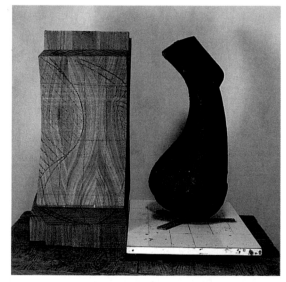

▲ 4. Drawing a grid pattern on the block on every side and, with the maquette next to it, drawing the silhouette using these lines as a guide.

Ancient Techniques

"*All their belongings are as ingeniously fashioned as if they had the most complete of tool-boxes. . . . Their creativity and skill in all manual jobs are equal, at least, to those of any other nation.*"

This is how Captain Cook described the sculptors of the northeast Pacific tribes in his logbook. We should point out that the craftsmen of every nation at the end of the seventeenth century had reached their limit in regard to technical mastery: he is comparing them with the image makers of the baroque period.

Even today African woodcarvers can create art virtually without carving. They do not use a bench vise or clamps. With one hand they hold the wood and carve with the other. Practically their only tool is a small ax with an oblique edge. They use it to rough-dress and, holding it by the blade, to carve. For the finishing touches they use knives and burins. Hollows are formed using a red-hot iron. For polishing, they use chips of stone, flint, or a kind of carpenter's plane.

The technique and tools of the tribes of Oceania and North America are very similar.

All work from a single trunk. They are limited by the size of the trunk, yet, paradoxically, this stimulates their imagination, their wits sharpened by their limitations.

In ancient Egypt the main body of a sculpture was hewn from a single trunk. Then arms and forearms were added, sometimes with joints.

The creators of Romanic Christs used similar techniques: a large trunk for the body, generally hollowed out from behind, and two for the arms. Other Romanic sculptures usually come from a single hollowed-out trunk, although jointed work is not uncommon. On the contrary, the joiner's task was considered one of the most delicate stages of the process.

The hands were almost always carved apart. The joiners used the folds of the sleeves to fit the hands onto the sculpture so that the join would not be visible. During the Renaissance it became customary to hew the hands and head in the trunk and then cut them off and work on them separately. This tradition of carving the hands separately still exists in modern industrial and nonindustrial carving.

During the eleventh century in Japan, the Yosegi method was invented. This consisted of working the different pieces of wood separately and then joining them together. In this way many sculptors could work at the same time under the orders of the master. Jōchō, using this technique in A.D. 1053, directed the carving of a 10-foot (3-m) Buddha. In 1204 Unkei and Kaikeo perfected the system and erected two 26-foot (8-m) sculptures.

In Europe during the Renaissance, especially during the baroque period, the system of constructing blocks of wood became popular. Before this, clay or wax maquettes were made or simple sketches drawn. In direct carving, the maquettes were marked with a grid, and compasses with curved points were used to indicate thicknesses and distances. The most common method, however, was to enlarge the image using the pointing system.

The block would be formed by four planks glued and fastened with bars or hinges. This allowed the sculptors to leave the interior hollow. They were not averse to using bent nails or bolts to reinforce the joints in those areas that were to remain out of sight.

It must not always have been this way, for Pacheco, the father-in-law of Velázquez, deplored the custom of ignoring the "wood inside." He did, however, defend the practice of concealing and reinforcing cracks and joints with wooden wedges and strong glue.

▼ A modern woodcarver in Kenya. Thanks to their creativity and skill, he and his compeers do without technical instruments.

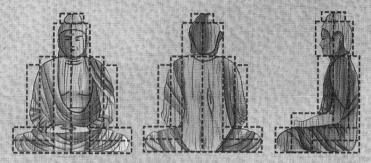

▼ Example of the Yosegi method: layout for the carving of Amida Nyorai.

▼ The join of the forearm of an Egyptian woodcarving.

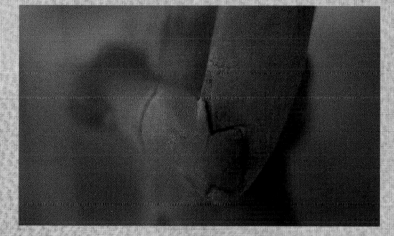

▶ Small Egyptian figure with articulated arms.

▼ A Buddha that has lost an arm, revealing the hollow interior of the trunk.

The most common method was using cloth or sacking soaked in plaster and glue.

Although these statues were then covered with more than fifteen layers of plaster and glue to form the basis for the polychrome, the wood finish was carried out with great care. Once the carving was finished, it was *surfaced*. This consisted of correcting small errors using paste and glue. Knots were either extracted directly or burned out. If this was not possible, the surface of the knot was roughened and rubbed with garlic to stop it from bleeding.

Below we include a couple of formulas for making the glues used in the surfacing process before the polychrome was added. The first belongs to Pacheco: "The piece of mutton is placed in the water before being washed, then it is rinsed four or five times until the water runs clear, because cleanliness is important. . . . It should boil until thick and then be tested on the palms of the hands." If the glue had to withstand a cold climate, he recommended adding parchment and ram's or goat's ears. He recommended removing the fat when it had cooled.

An even more exquisite recipe comes from Pomponio Gaurico (Florence, 1504). He suggested fish glue or "also a mixture made from crushing limestone, mastic and cheese in identical measures."

Tools that are no longer used but were important in rough-dressing and trimming or silhouetting were:

The *iron wedge*, which, when struck with a long-handled metal hammer, separated the fibers and split the trunk in half. Hard wooden wedges, struck with a mallet, were also used.

The *ax* was used for the initial rouging. Unlike the wedge, the ax could cut the fibers and could therefore be used in all directions. The were axes for all purposes. The hatchet was the easiest to handle. The length of the handle is in proportion to the weight of the ax blade.

The *adz* was the basic tool for rough-dressing. It was known as early as the Egyptians. The ones with a large handle were used with the trunk held between the feet. Short-handled adzes made precision cutting easier.

▲ Traditional ax.

▲ Egyptian adz.

▲ Traditional adz.

▲ Egyptian mallet.

PREPARATION AND TRIMMING

I n this chapter we are going to deal with the most important task for the sculptor: establishing the proportions, which in classical terms was called *proportioning*.

We will discuss how to construct blocks and use trimming and roughing tools.

We will also deal with the advantages and risks of working with trunks, beams, or posts.

The chapter ends with a reminder about the techniques invented for copying a sculpture as faithfully as possible.

"Not everyone who knows how to rough-dress wood knows how to proportion, profile and polish it; and not everyone who knows how to polish knows how to paint, how to put the final touches of perfection."

Juan de la Cruz

Constructing a Block

When beginning to carve, it is best to start with the simple forms we can obtain from a single plank. Then we will increase the complexity by building blocks from several planks glued together; we will deal with this further on. Finally, we can take on trunks and beams, which entail more problems.

We should never apply glue in a random fashion; remember what we discussed in chapter 2: you must understand the nature of the wood you are working with, take into account the position of the plank in the original trunk, and foresee how the wood will develop in the future.

After the wood is chosen, the maximum dimensions of the sculpture must be determined. Then we can cut up the plank to obtain fragments we will call *cuts*. We can glue these cuts together until we have the desired width or height. To avoid unpleasant surprises, consider the following:

First we must choose the plank correctly. This means the most suitable for our project in regard to size, hardness, grain, color, etc. When calculating the necessary length, to obtain the correct thickness, we must bear in mind that, when planing to smooth the sides, we will lose some wood. Also, the ends of the plank will be removed, as they are usually cracked and moldy. The sapwood is also discarded, though normally it has already been removed. The most difficult thing to foresee is interior cracks.

The most common sizes of planks on the market range from 6 to 12 feet (2 to 3.5 m) long; about 12 inches (29 to 30 cm) wide; and 2 to 2 ¾ inches (5 to 7 cm) thick.

In the workshop we can discern any warping by looking at the end of the plank. If it is present, we can plane down the most bowed part with an electric plane until the surface is flat. If we did this after splitting the planks, we would

FORMING A BLOCK
OF WOOD WITH TWO
CUTS FROM THE SAME
PLANK

◀ 1. After removing the ends, the two parts most distant from the pith are attached to each other.

complicate the task unnecessarily, as the plane would have to avoid all the new plank ends.

Before gluing, it is necessary to plane the face of the plank, even though it appears flat; this way we will roughen it slightly and the glue will adhere better.

To avoid unnecessary work in the future, we should plane and glue the part opposite the pith, where the growth rings spread out more. It is not necessary to smooth the other side, as this will be roughed and carved.

When planing the plank or removing superficial rough ends with a sander, we can see the true structure and color of the wood, which were hidden by the light and by the marks left by the machine cutting. If we dampen part of the polished wood, the shine will disappear and we will be able see the true tonality. Obviously, we can carry out these tests with any beam or trunk of wood, not just planks. A sound knowledge of the pattern of the grain and the different tonalities of the wood will enable us to choose the ideal part for the most visible section of our project.

7

8

FORMING A WIDE BLOCK

◀▼ 4. A heartwood plank. The pith is removed and the rest glued.

FORESEEABLE SHRINKAGE

◀▼ 5. Side plank. The two cuts are attached by their heartwood.

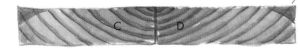

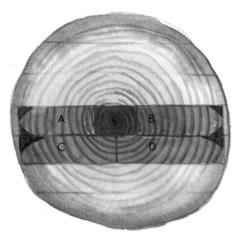

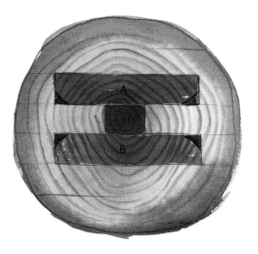

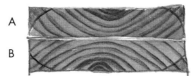

A

B

◄▲ 2. Correct join between two side planks of similar origin.

►▼ 3. Adequate join between two side planks of different origin.

C

D

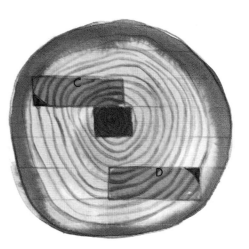

The next stage is to cut up the plank. Not all saws are suitable for this. We recommend using a bow or table saw, as a keyhole saw will not suffice.

We can then proceed to glue the different cuts, not forgetting that the glued areas develop over time and the new distribution of the grain may form patterns that interfere with the final form of the sculpture.

If we truly understand the development of the wood, we will see why we must join the two most distant parts of the pith: on shrinking, one will apply pressure on the other (fig. 2). If we attach them the other way around, the shrinkage will finally separate the ends (fig. 7).

To form a block using two cuts, the plank is smoothed, cut up, and the parts overlapped as if folding on an imaginary hinge attached to the cut edge (fig. 1). We should avoid letting the grain form circles, as this would indicate that we have glued two sides that will tend to shrink in opposite directions (figs. 7, 9).

Planks that are too wide may include the pith, and if this is the case, it is preferable to saw it off, discard it,

10

and glue the two remaining fragments, keeping the same orientation they originally had but without the pith. This will avert any later changes in the wood (fig. 4).

If we need a width that cannot be found in the stores, we can join two cuts, glued along the sides, attaching heartwood to heartwood (fig. 5). This will prevent the heartwood and the sapwood from coming into contact, as each shrinks at a different rate (fig. 8).

If the sculpture is to be of some considerable size, we will need to form a large block using more than two cuts. In this case it will be more difficult to prevent the wood from developing further.

The planks should be selected with utmost care. The safest are those that contain fragments of the same growth rings. The ones closest to the sapwood or pith should be avoided. Planks that, seen from the end, have barely curved grain are ideal for joining without problems (fig. 6).

Usually we will have to content ourselves with joining the most similar woods available, combined in such a way that they prevent each other from developing. In all cases, avoid joining cuts that come from close to the pith to others from the sapwood (fig. 10).

9

◄ 7 to 10. *Incorrect* gluing that may split over time.

◄▼ 6. Ideal origin of cuts for forming a single large block of wood.

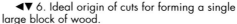

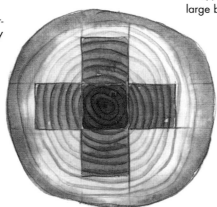

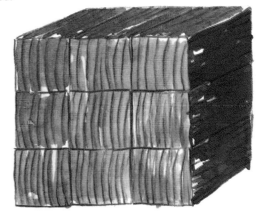

Gluing and Pressing

◄ Forming ridges in the surface so the glue will penetrate more easily.

Before gluing, it is important to bear in mind the final form of the sculpture to save on materials and work. A well-thought-out distribution of the cuts will simplify the trimming process. To create an arched form, for example, we do not need a rectangular block; we can simply add different sized cuts roughly approximate to the final form. When forming a block using different cuts, we must remember which surface is going to be the carved exterior of the sculpture. Gluing lines should be situated in secondary areas and great care taken when selecting and joining the grain patterns so that they do not distort the form of the sculpture.

You may find it tempting to join small planks of different color, although we feel this is more sensationalist than expressive. If we do so, we must select woods of similar hardness; otherwise, the glue will tear the softer wood and later, when it is sanded, it will reduce too much.

To calculate the length of each cut, we can draw a full-scale silhouette of the project on a piece of paper. We then draw parallel lines on it, the distance between them equal to the width of the plank. The drawing will then indicate the length of the cuts we need.

It is a mistake to be too generous with the wood for surfaces that will not be visible, but neither is it wise to be left with so little that we cannot correct an error. The wood should be reduced, however, and all that might retain humidity and cause splitting in the future should be removed.

Once the planks have been cut up and we have checked that the silhouette fits the project, we can start to glue. Use good carpenter's glue. Although it is white or beige, it turns colorless when dry. It is a synthetic resin with a low water content and is easy to apply and strongly adhesive. Drying takes between 10 and 12 hours. We do not recommend contact glues because they are usually not as adhesive. Neither should any stronger glues be used, as they can crack soft woods and some semisoft ones.

This gluing will be stronger the more it penetrates the surfaces to be attached. These should be smoothed so that they match, but not too much; otherwise the glue will run off them. Some-

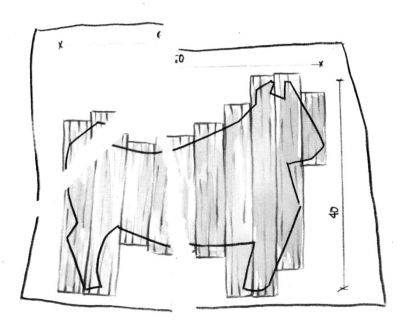

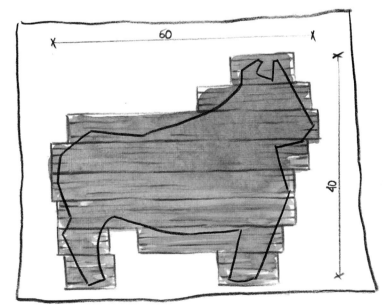

times a rasp is drawn along the fibers to create tiny ridges and make for better adhesion.

The glue should form a thin film between the cuts. Using a paintbrush or roller, we spread the glue lengthwise and then crosswise a couple of times, until both surfaces are impregnated. We then wait a few minutes. After checking the face and direction of the grain, we place one cut on top of the other.

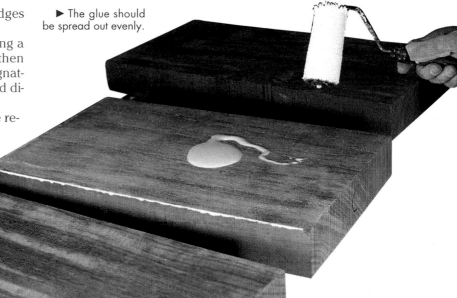

► The glue should be spread out evenly.

Excess glue will seep out around the perimeter. This we remove with a glue spatula and then wipe with a cloth. If we have applied too much glue, we will notice that one cut slides over the other. If there is too little, none will ooze out around the perimeter. In both cases it is best to separate the cuts and start again.

The glued cuts are immediately pressed together to attach them firmly. The ideal press is, of course, an industrial one, as commonly used by carpenters, because it applies a uniform pressure over the entire block. Since we probably do not have one, we can use clamps. Starting from the center of the block, we attach as many clamps as possible evenly over the surface until we reach the edges. In this way any excess glue will seep out. The greater the pressure, the better the join.

After 5 or 6 hours we can remove the clamps, but the block will not be ready for trimming until 12 hours have elapsed. For roughing, it is preferable to wait a whole day.

If the block becomes unglued during carving, we should give the cuts time to separate and then fill the crack with glue, using a spatula, and again apply pressure with the clamps.

Gluing is a simple process to understand, but it entails certain technical difficulties, especially when dealing with large blocks. As on other occasions, a carpenter's help may be necessary.

▲ We should only combine woods of similar hardness.

► Industrial press.

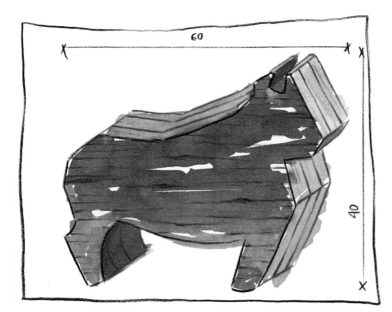

◄ Proper distribution of the cuts not only simplifies the task but can also affect the aesthetic result.

Clamping

To carve properly, you need to attach the wood firmly to the workbench. This should be done in such a way that it does not interfere with your work. It is also important to place the wood at one end of the bench, which, in turn, must be placed so that you can walk around it and observe your work from all angles. The wood must not be able to move at all, especially when you are working with bow saws, rasps, or any tool that requires both hands to be used. When sculpting, the work must be totally immobilized. The better it is secured, the better the work with the gouge, which in turn means a better sculpture.

The essential tools for gripping a plank, a block of wood or a trunk are the table vise and the clamp.

For traditional trimming, the wood for sculpting is firmly gripped by the table vise, if the thickness of the wood permits it. This facilitates sawing by hand. If the vise is large, it can also act as a base for small sculptures during the carving process.

Different sized clamps allow us to adapt to each circumstance. The clamp should always grip the wood firmly to keep it from moving when struck. The fear that this may happen will make us lose time, rhythm, and precision. The only part of the clamp that should be above the wood is the top bracket. If the clamp were fitted the other way round, it would be a constant nuisance.

Right from the beginning of the process, decide which parts of the wood will have the sole purpose of acting as support points. These can then be cut off later without spoiling the sculpture.

By using these clamping points, we can apply the clamps without fear of damaging the sculpture, so it is best to leave them attached until the last moment, after the finishing. However long we wait, though, we will eventually have to remove them. Then we can support the wood on wedges, odd pieces of wood that, if necessary, can be cut to size. Because the clamp is to grip the sculpture until it is completely finished, we can use pieces of cloth to protect the wood from the metal.

We should take the same precautions when we want to preserve the organic form of a trunk and find it difficult to designate clamping points. Wedges can be nailed or glued to a larger board that is then anchored to the table using clamps.

BENCH VISE

HAND CLAMP

ROTATING CLAMP

LARGE CLAMP AND WEDGES

▼ Although heavy pieces of wood are immobilized by their own weight, we should still prevent any movement by using wooden strips attached to the workbench with clamps.

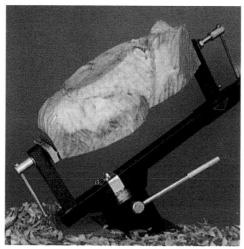

This is called a *bed*. We can place the sculpture on it in such a way that it can be swiveled while we carve. The right fit can be obtained using small strips, pieces of cardboard, polystyrene, or pieces of cloth.

In certain cases, the solutions offered above may be insufficient for large trunks or excessive for miniatures. Let's study some other solutions.

To grip a large trunk, we can form a bed on the bench itself. This is done using clamped wedges to create a "negative" of the sculpture. A combination of bed and large clamps, capable of gripping both the wood and the bench, will provide more stability. We can also use cloth or sponges to prevent the brackets from moving. If we are dealing with a very heavy trunk, clamping is less of a problem because the trunk's own weight immobilizes it.

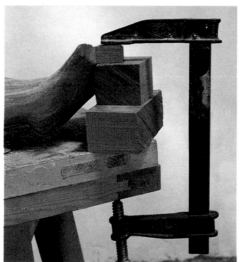

When carving a small sculpture or a flattish relief, we can screw or glue the wood to another, larger piece of wood that will act as a base. When gluing, we should insert a piece of paper to make the pieces of wood easier to separate later. When we have finished, a simple blow or leverage with a chisel will suffice to separate them.

▲ Bed constructed from the wood left after trimming.

If the board we have chosen is too thin to be strong but has the right dimensions for trimming, we can reinforce it by nailing another piece of wood at the ends. Because the nails are positioned outside the perimeter of the drawing, there will be no problem when sawing off the excess wood. If the sculpture is high-relief, with the sides also carved, we can screw the rear side to another, larger board and clamp this one. On separating the wood from the base, only the marks of the screws will be left.

It is not difficult to find other solutions for each problem. The important thing is that the wood should not move or be damaged by contact with the clamp. It becomes increasingly important to take precautions as your work reaches more advanced stages. If we use a chamois cloth or rag to protect the sculpture from any abrasion or scraping, our sculpture will thank us for it.

◄ ► More examples of immobilizing large sculptures by using wooden strips attached to the workbench with clamps.

Traditional Trimming

To facilitate the roughing process, save time, and check that the form we have imagined really fits the wooden block, we use the trimming or silhouetting procedure.

This consists of removing excess wood from the outline we have drawn. When we do so, the form we have imagined for our project will emerge for the first time.

When trimming, it is preferable to cut rather than carve, as this will save time and effort. The process was traditionally carried out using a handsaw. If one is not available, we can use a broad chisel.

If the drawn form is simple—with straight lines or large curves—the bow saw is used to obtain the silhouette because it saws easily through the cut.

If, on the other hand, the form is complex—zigzag, wavy, or a combination of straight and curved lines—it is best to trim in two stages.

First, using the bow saw, we make several cuts perpendicular to the line of the silhouette and, if possible, also perpendicular to the grain of the wood. These should be parallel cuts, close together and deep enough to come nearly into contact with the drawing.

Then, using a broad chisel or flat gouge, these parallel strips of wood are cut away at the base. They will come off cleanly if we cut following the direction of the wood fibers. If, on the other hand, we have to cut across the fibers, we recommend using the saw.

Under no circumstances should we cut down to the outline of the form itself. It is wise to leave just a few millimeters around the perimeter, especially at the beginning, because if there is not enough wood, the entire volume of the sculpture has to be reduced. The sculpture would then be somewhat smaller than planned. Any mistake will force us to redesign our idea, although we recommend discarding the wood and starting fresh.

Don't forget to leave several fragments outside the line uncut to act as clamping points for holding the piece firmly on the workbench throughout the entire roughing process. These clamping points should be preserved as long as possible for easy carving. When the carving is finished or the points become a nuisance, they should be removed.

▲ Before trimming, it is best to draw the largest outline.

▶ Detail of the clamping point that we will leave uncut when trimming.

▼ We begin the process making perpendicular cuts to the grain.

◄ Using a flat gouge and following the direction of the fibers, we can cut off the sawed fragments cleanly.

▲ When trimming, we also remove areas affected by the larvae of xylophagous insects.

◄ Finishing off the traditional trimming process.

Industrial Trimming

I f our aim is to sculpt large works, traditional trimming will be too slow and tedious. In this case we exchange the handsaw for an industrial saw. Although the tool is different, the technique is the same as before.

The best course of action is to take the block of wood to a workshop equipped with a circular saw. This can cut close to the drawing because it can follow the lines with great ease. Even when the surface is highly complex, this type of saw enables us to trim using parallel cuts, just as we explained earlier.

We should never forget to draw the clamping points so that they can also be trimmed. Remember also to collect the sawed-off pieces, as they can be used later as wedges to immobilize the sculpture through the entire carving process.

If we are dealing with a very large block, we should leave four or more clamping points, at least two on each of the larger

◀▼ Trimming bolondo and vermilion with an industrial band saw.

▼ Comparing the maquette and the bolondo after the first side is trimmed.

▼ The bolondo before and after trimming the front and rear insides of the figure.

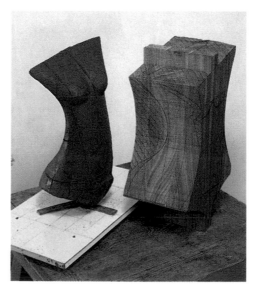

surfaces. If, due to their size, these points should be a hindrance, they can be cut down during the carving process.

This will not only make our job easier but will also allow us a better view of the volume we are forming. Here again, the sawed-off wood can be useful as wedges.

It is preferable to begin with simple forms: the trimming process described so far involves symmetrical forms whose front and rear are parallel. Yet with experience we can start to draw asymmetric profiles and carry out double trimming.

In this case, it is best not only to draw the two main silhouettes accurately but also to join them across the width of the block and, when cutting, to follow the resulting slant. We must be very sure of ourselves when sawing because any mistake means either reducing the size of the sculpture or gluing on the sawed pieces, which, we repeat, always come in handy.

If the form we want can be revolved around a concentric axis (sphere, cylinder, cone, etc.), we can use a wood lathe. A carpenter is unlikely to have the

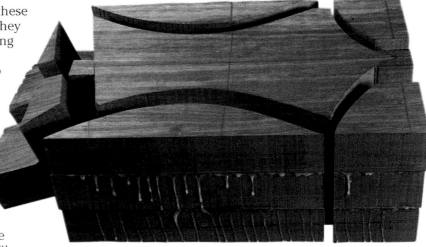

▲ During trimming, the volume of the sculpture emerges from the block.

appropriate equipment, so we need to turn to another specialist, the wood turner.

Not all woods are suitable for turning. Soft and fibrous woods often are troublesome, as are very hard types.

During turning, two clamping points are left at each end, and we should remind the specialist not to remove them because they will be useful for us too.

▼ An industrial saw enables us to remove large amounts of excess wood.

▼ The clamping points should be remembered when trimming.

► **Camí,** *Pawn* (1989). Service wood dyed at both ends. 10" (25 cm).
Minimalist sculptures are usually considered finished after trimming or turning, as in this case.

◄ Although the chainsaw makes cutting easier, a gouge is necessary for roughing.

◄ An elm trunk with one of its sides trimmed.

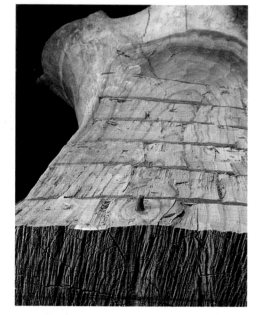

We can resort to using a chainsaw when starting to trim large blocks and trunks if hand or bow saws are insufficient or if we do not have access to a carpenter's circular saw. It would be ridiculous, however, to use a chainsaw on small sculptures, as it is not a precision instrument.

A chainsaw also allows us to make different, parallel incisions perpendicular to the drawing of the silhouette, creating a series of teeth that can then be removed with the broad chisel.

When using a chainsaw, you must follow the direction of the chain, which rotates forward. The machine is held in one hand while the other ap-

plies the correct rhythm and pressure on the wood.

A die grinder has different applications depending on whether we fit it with a chain or cutting disc.

In the first case we can fit a chain around the circumference of a normal disc. Although a die grinder with chain can replace a chainsaw, its use is very limited, as the cut can be only as deep as the radius of the disc.

It is more useful to fit a cutting disc to the die grinder. This has large alternating teeth around the perimeter and is specially designed for cutting wood. It can be used for trimming, rough-dressing, and carving in a continuous process. It is usually sold with a guard to protect the

◄▼ A cutting disc allows us to make shallow incisions.

► Using a gouge or broad chisel, we remove the wood between the parallel cuts.

user from flying shavings, although it cannot prevent them from littering the workshop.

The type of cut depends on the pressure applied and the angle of the disc with respect to the surface of the wood. Placed perpendicular to it, it saws; if oblique or parallel to it, it roughs or models. A rocking motion can also be used, which would be extremely dangerous when using the chain on the disc.

Hold the machine firmly, applying more pressure at the beginning and less as you approach the drawing.

Although a die grinder and cutting disc rough-dresses and models at the same time, it also requires the user to follow a particular method. First, the overall outline is sawed as an approximation of the form, a kind of silhouetting, and then the figure is modeled, turning the wood continuously so that the process is applied evenly.

The marks left by a die grinder may be suitable for the finish of large surfaces. But because the disc cannot be used easily in nooks, nor cut angles or sharp edges, we will need to turn to the gouge for modeling crannies and cavities.

A die grinder with cutting disc is easy to handle, although some practice sessions are advisable.

When working with a chainsaw and especially with a die grinder and disc, you should employ maximum safety measures. In addition to strictly following the manufacturer's instructions for use, also check the fit of the disc, as a vibrating one can cause an accident, especially if it flies off.

Because die grinders create a large amount of wood shavings, suitable work clothes (leather apron and gloves) should be used, and your face should be protected by a full mask rather than goggles. After this kind of tool is used, the workshop will need overall cleaning.

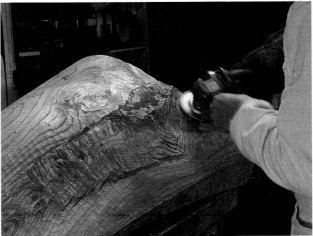

◄▲▼ The cutting disc can replace other tools for trimming, rough-dressing, and even modeling.

► **A. R. Penek,** *Der Gesist von L* (1981). 82" (208 cm). Neo-expressionists consider their work finished after roughing, meaning the saw cuts themselves are the major attraction of the work.

Beams and Trunks: A Challenge

Working with blocks is the safest method, despite the difficulties of gluing. But if we want to capture expressivity, it is more of a challenge to turn to the organic forms of trunks or to recycle construction beams.

Before doing so, it is worth considering the risks and the change in approach these entail. When gluing cuts together, we adapt the wood to the project; when working with trunks and beams, the model must adapt to the wood.

Beams were once tree trunks, and although they were squared to make them usable as beams, they sometimes retain organic anomalies that, despite their interest, can cause problems.

Beams are unlikely to undergo any important development, as they were normally felled "under a good moon" and, over the years, have dried right through to the center. The cracks they may have should be of little concern because they are unlikely to worsen. The most common defect is usually a certain sagging in the center, caused by the weight they were supporting. We can try to cover up these supposed defects, though it is preferable for our project to adapt to them and actually highlight any cracks or sagging.

Recycling beams entails certain problems such as eliminating any possible woodworms or nails, controlling splinters when working near a crack, accommodating internal cavities, and others.

The metal fittings used in building are often found in beams. If a nail is whole, it will not cause any surprises; the surprise comes when it is broken and the tip remains hidden in the wood. When trimming, therefore, the saw's teeth or chains are at risk and could even break off; later, during carving, gouges may chip.

Carving a sculpture from a trunk is even more risky, as it is difficult to know if the tree was felled at the right time. Probably it was not submitted to any insecticide treatment, and although the trunk may have been carefully dried, this drying is unlikely to be even, given the varying thickness. Before carving a tree trunk, it is preferable to practice first with a piece of the same wood and leave it for some time to see how it evolves.

◄ **Zadkine,** *Diana the Huntress* (1937). 130" (330 cm).
   Carved from a single trunk, this work retains the marks of the saw to emphasize its expressivity.

▼ **Chillida,** *Abesti Gogorra IV* (1960-64). Poplar. 37 ³/₄" (96 cm).
   By highlighting the internal tensions of several trunks, this sculpture leaves the surrounding space charged with energy.

Although this will not guarantee us a perfect result, it will help us to understand the characteristics of the trunk in question.

We begin by eliminating the bark, the sapwood, and other live areas. Then we will bore through the insect holes to locate them or their larvae.

After removing any areas that may contain microorganisms, we study the trunk's form, knots, warps, or twists. This knowledge will help us to define our project, although the maquette is not yet definitive. If the trunk conceals any surprises, we can change the model we have made.

It is best to let several days go by between roughing and carving to allow for internal drying and thus prevent cracks.

The knots in beams and trunks can be an important challenge to the sculptor because, due to their hardness, they can either flaw the gouge or fly out whole. The project should take the knots into account, either to utilize their expressivity or to prevent them from becoming too conspicuous.

When working with very large trunks, it is important to hollow them out. This reduces the weight and volume of living matter. The more pith we remove, the more evenly the trunk will dry, preventing it from splitting.

Ideally, this process should turn the carving into a kind of hollow vessel, although it is not necessary to go that far. To reach the interior of the trunk, we will have to alter some part of the sculpture's surface. We should choose the least visible part, which is usually the base on which it stands.

Usually it is sufficient to hollow out just the base, making sure the sculpture does not become unbalanced. Sculptures that are to have one side facing a wall are the easiest to hollow out, as the hidden opening can be made much wider. Then, if we want, we can cover up the hole with a board or felt so as not to scratch the furniture. This will not affect the ventilation of the piece.

Hollowing out is done at the end of the process so that the internal mass dampens the blows struck during carving. For deep hollowing, it is best to use large gouges; if just the base or the rear side, we can use the die grinder and disc or any other roughing tool.

▶ **Jorge Du Boon,** *Roc del Que* (1992). Bolondo. 29 ½'-42 ½' (9-13 m).

In this sculptural group, the pith has been replaced by an iron interior. This raises the sculpture a good distance from the ground to protect it from humidity. Properly treated wood, the absence of the pith, and the ventilation holes enable it to weather the high mountains of Andorra.

97

Pointing

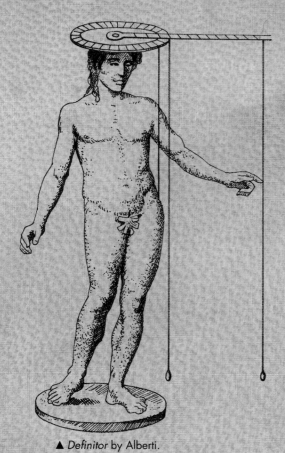

▲ *Definitor* by Alberti.

▼ Baroque framework.

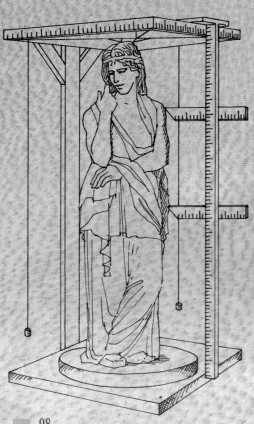

A lthough this book deals with what is properly termed direct carving, that is, sculpting unique works, we should not forget that the reproduction of sculptures has played an important role in the history of art.

Over the centuries artists have sought a method that would enable them to copy statues with the greatest accuracy and in the shortest time. The central aim of this search was applying to volume a method that was already successful for flat surfaces: copying or enlarging a drawing using a grid system.

The different techniques they invented had one idea in common: to grid a three-dimensional form, a sculpture, we need to envision it within an imaginary parallelepiped (rectangular box with parallel opposite sides), the maximum dimensions of which are determined by the most salient projections of the maquette being copied. It is as if we were to pack the sculpture inside a glass box.

The resulting parallelepiped defines the maximum dimensions of the block of wood needed for the copy. Then if we draw a grid over the imaginary faces of the block, we can compare and easily transfer the external drawing, that is, the points of contact between the sculpture and the glass.

Continuing with our example, if we were to immobilize the sculpture inside the box, we would need to adapt strips of wood of different sizes between the discontinuous surface of the sculpture and the plane of the box. The length of these strips and their position with respect to the grid allow us to copy a sculpture on different scales.

Pointing consists of determining these distances on the maquette and transferring them to the inside of the block of wood using a hand drill.

Naturally, the more points we have, the more accurate the new profile will be. To copy a life-size bust with reasonable accuracy, about 250 points are necessary.

Once these internal points have been located, the wood can be roughed. But how can we locate them in the first place? Or transfer them to the block? What method is the most reliable and time-saving? History has found different solutions.

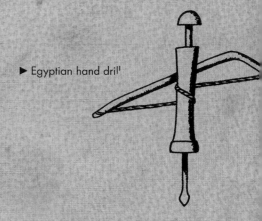

▶ Egyptian hand drill

From the Plumb Line to the Pantograph

I n classical Greece the points were located by using a plumb line. The distances from the contact points to the most salient parts of the model were measured. Then holes were bored in the wood in accordance with the measurements taken. We have not only written records of this technique since the beginning of the fifth century B.C. but also unfinished works that show the marks of the drill used for determining the distance, marks that would have been removed in the final modeling. These were, of course, marble sculptures, but the technique is also applied to wood, and records of this date back to the Renaissance.

This technique of copying sculptures came to be mastered to such a degree during the Greek and Roman periods that the artist not only could delegate his work to a craftsman but could even divide up the work. The different parts were carved separately and then assembled.

This technique was recovered during the Renaissance, and many theoretical treatises appeared. The method for determining points has been perfected and new instruments incorporated for transferring the points with greater ease.

The main theorist on methods of copying by points was Alberti (fifteenth century). In his treatise *De Statua*, he described a complex system that made it possible to copy the two aspects he considered fundamental with great accuracy: proportion and detail.

To determine dimensions, he proposed an instrument he named an *exempeda*, consisting of a straight and flexible ruler for measuring lengths and a couple of movable squares for measuring diameters.

For locating profiles he invented the ingenious *definitor*. This is a calibrated, circular instrument that is attached to the highest point of the model. A swiveling, calibrated arm extends from the center, from which hangs a plumb line that can slide along the arm. It treats the sculpture as if it were inserted in an imaginary cylinder.

The different contact points of the line and the sculpture, measured in degrees and length, provided the measurements to be transposed to the block by means of similar devices.

Leonardo da Vinci proposed a more instructive technique. We will quote his exact words, which, given their simplicity, illustrate a system that might otherwise be considered as solely for professionals.

"If you wish to make a marble figure, first make one of clay. When it is finished, let it dry and place it in a box big enough to hold the block of marble with which you want to carve the copy. With the clay figure inside the box, insert thin white rods through holes in the sides until they touch the figure, each at a different point. Then paint the part of the rods outside the box black and mark each rod and its hole so that later it will be reinserted correctly. Then take the clay figure out of the box and place the block of marble inside. Remove the material necessary so that all the rods can be inserted into the holes up the black marks." (*Manuscript A*, French Institute, Paris).

In a search for simplicity, Vasari suggested taking all the measurements from a single, front plane. When making the copy, the form will emerge from the material as if it were submerged in a tank and the water were released. This was the method used by Michelangelo, even when carving directly.

Combining the two methods of Leonardo da Vinci and Michelangelo, over the following centuries frames were built that were a type of wooden cage over which plumb lines were dropped and squares and compasses used for the measurements.

During the baroque period, another, more complex method became popular, called the *three compasses*, one of

which was always curved. These were used to take the measurements. Beginning from the base, first the main points were determined and reproduced on the copy. Then the secondary ones were transferred, and lastly the detail. This method is particularly suited to relief yet also allows a round volume to be reproduced.

In 1822 the manufacturers Durard and Girard presented before the French Academy a *pointing machine*. Invented by Gatteaux but perfected by them, it made possible quicker and more faithful copies than previous systems. It is an upside-down, T-shaped instrument that possesses the advantages of the three compasses while simplifying the procedure.

Yet the definitive solution, which is still used today for mass reproduction of sculptures, appeared at the end of the sixteenth century when Dillinger invented the pantograph, an instrument that consisted of four articulated rulers that allowed artists to copy, enlarge, or reduce a flat drawing just by going over its lines. In 1743 Langlois gave it its definitive form, although it was necessary to wait a few years until Collas adapted it for sculpting.

As we said earlier, a type of pantograph is used together with industrial machinery for mass reproduction of sculptures.

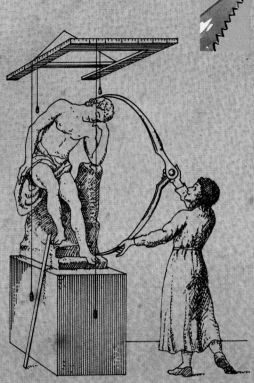

▲ The method of the three compasses.

▼ Pointing machine invented by Gatteaux.

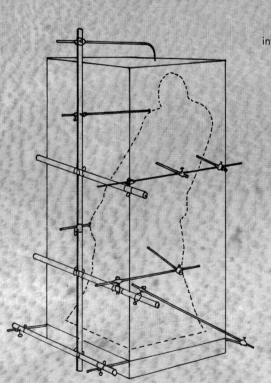

CARVING

We have now arrived at the chapter on sculpting itself. Without the knowledge provided earlier in this book, any impatient attempt to work with the gouge would have been frustrating. We now better appreciate the finest sculptures, understand how and why to choose a particular type of wood, and how to prepare a good project.

First we will discuss how to use gouges correctly, depending on the amount of wood we wish to remove and how to position it with respect to the wood fibers.

Sculpting is a continuous process of removing excess wood, but for our purposes we will divide this into three stages: roughing, modeling, and finishing.

The chapter also provides some hints on how to solve specific problems and ends with an invitation to broaden our techniques of wood sculpting beyond the limits of the gouge.

Possessed by a restrained passion,
freed from the marble block of language
the graceful form that I had seen in spirit.

Thomas Mann

With Gouge in Hand

Before carving our first sculpture, it is advisable to do several exercises with the gouge in the same way we did before beginning to write our first letter. With practice, our "writing" will become more skillful and, with time, will unconsciously reflect our personality.

First begin by gripping the gouge properly. Pick it up with your least able hand, keeping the other for the mallet. When holding the handle of the gouge, we must place our thumb on the outer part so as not to strike it with the mallet. The blows must be firm and precise. To have better control over detailed, finishing work, the hand holding the gouge should rest on the wood. We should always grip the gouge with the blade on the outside so that the chips will fly away from us. For safety reasons, do not touch the cutting edge of the gouge or gesticulate with it.

Steadying our hand, we can make several incisions in the wood, using the same gouge but

▲ Observe the position of the thumb when gripping the gouge.

varying the inclination with respect to the surface of the wood.

We will soon notice that the more perpendicular the gouge is, the deeper the cut. A large chip will then come away. Yet if the gouge is held almost parallel to the surface, the cut is more superficial and the chip finer and longer than in the previous case. For this type of cut, simply hit the handle with the fleshiest part of the palm.

We will immediately notice that each blow causes the gouge to tilt. The hand holding it should not try to resist this movement; on the contrary, we can reinforce it so that the edge digs into the wood and returns to the surface, cutting out the chips. This rocking movement means the degree of inclination is continuously changing

◀ Oak showing the bite of flat, tubed, and V-shaped gouges.

so that the gouge reappears, while the depth of the cut depends on the original angle.

We can continue to practice, trying different gouges to see the cuts they produce in the wood, depending again on the inclination of the blade.

Now we can try something new: a chisel point. This resembles the tip of a pencil. For sculpting or roughing hard wood, the edge must be resistant and therefore have a short bevel. A long bevel is required for retouching a surface. So that the bite is clean, the bevel and the point should be sharpened regularly.

After many exercises combining the above elements—grip, impact, inclination, cutting edge, and chisel point—we will acquire a certain intuition as to the solution for each problem as it arises.

Practice will show us that the gouge, apart from cutting, can ridge, canter, bevel, draw, model, and so on. For roughing we need a large mallet and a wide-bladed gouge, tubed or half-round, but with a short bevel and about 45° initial inclination. To rough, we need to bite into a lot of wood in a short time and have no need yet to concern ourselves with detail.

For modeling, we will choose a smaller mallet and a half-round, medium-bevel gouge. We should also reduce the angle of inclination.

Finally, for the details, we can even strike the gouge with the palm of the hand and use almost flat gouges with a longer bevel and narrower edge. The

▼ Bite of the gouge when roughing.

▲ To rough-dress, we use lightly beveled gouges, tubed or half-round, placing them at a high angle with respect to the carving surface.

▲ When modeling, we reduce the inclination of the gouge, which should have a smaller, flatter, sharper edge.

▼ The final blows are decisive. Greater precision is obtained by striking with the hand.

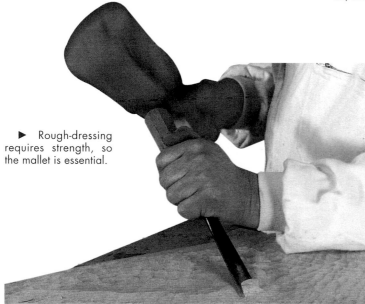

► Rough-dressing requires strength, so the mallet is essential.

angle of inclination should not be reduced too much or we risk accidentally lifting fibers.

The reduction of the wood should be gradual. Until we have dressed the entire surface with wide-mouthed gouges, we cannot start carving the underlying surface.

When sculpting, the gouge should cover only a short distance and always emerge from the wood. It should never remain stuck or cover a long distance that would scratch the wood or lift up splinters. Both these things would hap-

pen if we started to carve in the center of the surface. We should always begin at one end and work backward so that we can determine the length of each shaving.

The cleanness of the cut is the test that determines the quality of the technique we are using. The wood of the hollow is usually shinier than that of the surface, so if it appears scratched, this is an obvious symptom that the gouge has nicks, in which case it needs grinding, sharpening, or simply honing.

This type of cut depends not only on the characteristics of the gouge itself but also on another fundamental element: the hardness and fibrousness of the wood.

◄ Marks left by a cutting disc.

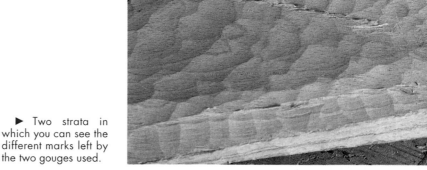

► Two strata in which you can see the different marks left by the two gouges used.

Learning to Handle Wood

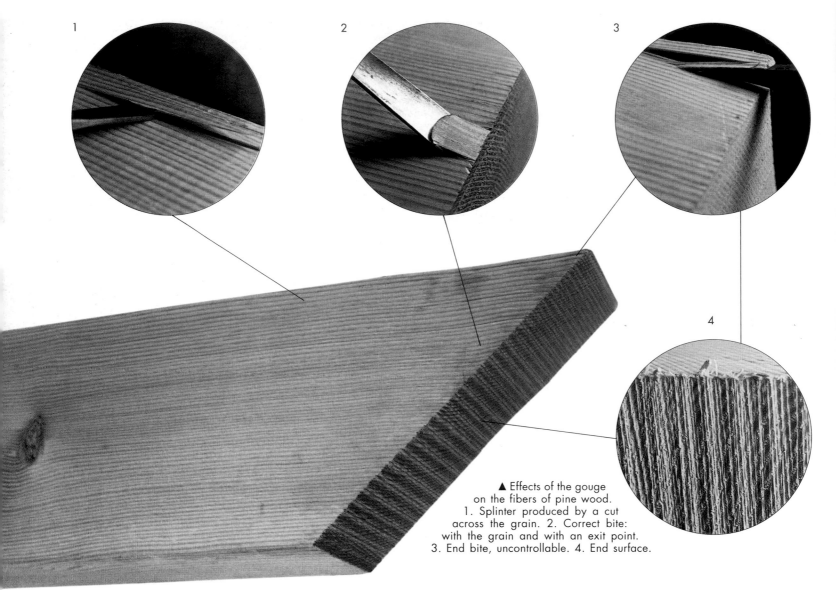

▲ Effects of the gouge
on the fibers of pine wood.
1. Splinter produced by a cut
across the grain. 2. Correct bite:
with the grain and with an exit point.
3. End bite, uncontrollable. 4. End surface.

Carving, then, depends not only on the gouge but also on the hardness and fibrousness of the wood. Even using the same piece of wood, the results will be different if we carve in one direction versus another.

Before carving, it is important to understand the behavior of the *fibers*. We suggest you try scraping a piece of poplar wood in several directions with a coarse rasp. You will see that if we do so across the grain, we tear out large pieces of grain. If we do so with the grain, we notice two things: if we go against the order of growth, we raise rough ends, while if we scrape in the right direction, we will notice that the rasp slides along more smoothly and leaves a much smoother surface.

This happens because the grain is the external face of the wood's structure: the fibers, which grew in the direction of the treetop. If we analyzed the shavings, we would see that they twist as a result of the tension released on being separated from the other fibers.

When gouging, we can see that the wood responds in a similar way as it does to the rasp, although the resistance is less and the effect is not so apparent.

If we wish to carve across the fibers, they will resist, and if we force them, they will tend to break off. The cut cannot be controlled and results in splinters.

When we wish to make a lengthwise cut, against the order of growth of the fibers, that is, *against the grain*, the resistance will be less than if we cut across the grain, although the cut will still be rough.

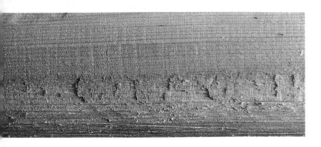

◄ Beech planed with the grain (top) and against the grain (bottom).

We will obtain a clean texture, with little effort and controllable results, only when we carve following the ascending direction of the growth of the fibers, that is, *with the grain*. When we look at a piece of wood, we can calculate the position of the fibers by the grain, but it is more difficult to detect which way is ascending. Here our sense of touch can help us: when running the tips of the fingers over a rough surface, we are more likely to get splinters if we do so against the grain than with it. So we situate the gouge pointing in the direction in which we would not get splinters and begin to carve. This way the cut will be clean.

It is not always easy to follow the grain, as there are woods whose fibers often change direction. In the two step-by-step demonstrations on pages 156 and 162, we chose elm and bolondo because they possess this characteristic. It is not always such an important factor, as there are also woods that can be worked in different directions without any difficulty.

When a tree is felled, its fibers are cut, the same as when we cut across a plank. The resulting surface is called an *endpiece*. We should try to avoid carving endpieces, as the gouge will either get stuck or create splinters. We can flatten one endpiece of a plank or trunk to act as the base and carve on the other indirectly, working it down until it will present no problem. If we do need to carve an endpiece directly, the gouge should be well sharpened and held oblique to the wood. Also, if possible, we should carve from the inside outward, concentrically.

Because endpieces have a tendency to split, it is advisable to wait a certain time between trimming and carving. If they do split, it is best cut them off and reduce the dimensions of the sculpture.

Another basic factor in the behavior of the gouge is the hardness of the wood. Naturally, to get the same bite in a hard wood as in a soft wood, the blow with the mallet will have to be more forceful, even though we are using the same gouge. Because hard wood offers more resistance, to keep the gouge from becoming nicked, we

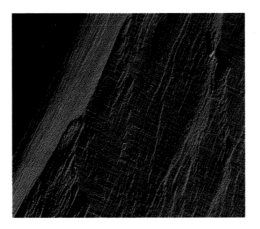

▲ Ordered structure of cherrywood fibers.

▲ Twisted elm fibers.

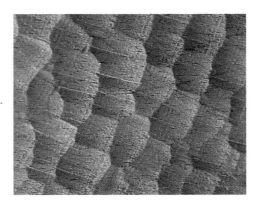

▲ Beech carved with the grain.

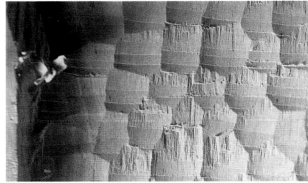

▲ Effects of carving against the grain: the cut is not clean.

can use one with a short, tough edge. Soft wood can be carved with a gouge with a deeper edge. This way we will obtain a finer cut to compensate for its greater porosity.

If we watch how a master carver works, we will see that he often changes gouges without hesitating. This is due to

his experience with the wood, changing the treatment according to each circumstance. This understanding of the wood is what should guide our work with the gouge. Since each wood has its own temperament, generalizations are unreliable; it is better, after a certain amount of practice, to follow your intuition.

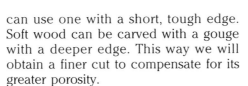

▼ When planed with the grain, vermilion produces fine sawdust.

▼ Applying the plane across the fibers tears them out in the form of shavings.

Like Shelling an Almond

To carve, it is important to control the technical aspects, but carving wood sculptures also requires mastery of volume. Remember that there are two basic processes for creating sculptural volume: addition and subtraction. Addition consists of adding material, usually malleable material, to a central nucleus. As the sculpture grows, the forms begin to take shape. In this process the sculptor imagines the volume from inside to out. Starting with a nucleus, material can be added or removed.

Technically speaking, addition does not entail any risks: if we are unhappy with a certain detail, it can be rectified until we consider it satisfactory. After any changes, we can always modify the proportions of the whole. This is what we do when modeling with clay, Plasticine, or plaster, even when joining wood.

This, then, is useful for building our models but not for carving, which this is based on subtraction or removal. This consists of creating a form from a block by cutting material away. On removing this material, the volume is achieved from the outside in. The sculptor's job, as Michelangelo would say, consists of freeing the shape contained in the block from the excess material.

We can distinguish three important stages in this process: roughing, modeling, and finishing.

Roughing is eliminating the greatest amount of wood during the carving process. This determines the distribution, the proportion, and the balance of the main volumes, what in figurative terms we call proportioning.

This stage is so important that the image makers would assume full responsibility for it and would never entrust it to their

▶ The process of carving is similar to shelling an almond. After removing the green pod, the silhouette appears. Breaking the shell is the equivalent to rough-dressing, and peeling away the fine skin can be compared to modeling.

▼ Trimmed sculpture, or *pod removed*.

▼ Rough-dressed, or *shelled*.

▼ Modeled, or *skin removed*.

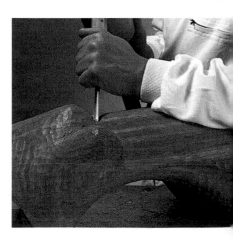

assistants. If they made a mistake, they preferred to abandon the sculpture and start with a new block.

Modeling is profiling the outline of the sculpture and then all the details of the figure until the correct shape is achieved.

Finally, during the finish, the texture becomes the most important aspect of the sculpture. We may choose to leave the marks of the gouge visible or use techniques such as smoothing, polishing, or burnishing.

Because the process of subtraction is irreversible, a deeper cut than intended can alter the entire sculpture. When faced with a mistake, it is advisable to reduce all the dimensions of the sculpture or reject it.

As a last resort, new wood can be glued on, but it is better not to do this, as the added wood will probably develop differ-ently to the block and, over time, this "repair work" will be-come apparent.

The sculpture should always be horizontal when we are sculpting, even when we have imagined it vertically; this is to make it easier to clamp.

We can rough and model the main face and then the secondary ones, or turn the sculpture so that the process is more even. Al-though Michelangelo and other masters risked finishing one face before starting on another, we recommend turning the wood so as to control the volume better, as if working on a potter's wheel.

Later we will offer further details about this process. Here we just wish to remind you that when sculpting wood, you should never lose sight of the work as a whole; that each step is irre-versible; and that you must remove the wood in increasingly finer layers, as if shelling a nut.

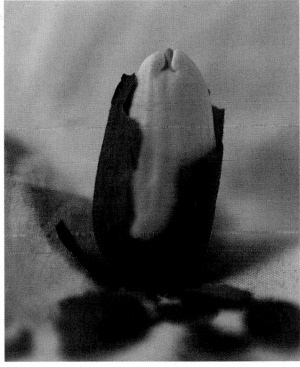

▼ We recommend turning the wood as you work. This will help you to maintain the right proportions.

▼ Cleaning away the rest of the *skin*, or finishing.

Rough-Dressing

▼ Traditional system of rough-dressing large surfaces.

► A cutting disc allows us to rough-dress or model depending on the angle it is held against the surface.

In the previous chapter we discussed trimming. This is really a way of speeding up the first stages of rough-dressing. After trimming, we continue to remove wood until the main volumes are proportioned.

If we do not know how a wood behaves, we can start by experimenting with the pieces cut away during the trimming. Thus we can calculate the necessary force when striking it and the direction of the fibers so as to carve with the grain.

We should study the wood closely, the pattern of the grain, and any possible knots or twists in order to anticipate any difficulties. We can even modify the model to avoid any unsolvable problems or to incorporate new elements depending on the characteristics of the chosen block or trunk.

Using our imagination, we should try to see the model inside the wood on the right scale. Then we draw the axes on the six faces of the block to situate accurately the points that define the form. We will also mark out the maximum silhou-

◄ Trimmed bolondo.

▲► Bolondo during and after rough-dressing.

ette and, above all, the most salient angles. Since rough-dressing is not intended to reach the definitive shape, to make sure, we can draw the perimeter some 2 to 5 mm larger than the actual size of the sculpture.

When marking these areas, do not forget the clamping points. It is precisely during the rough-dressing when the wood has to be totally immobilized, as this is when we are using the most force.

We recommend placing the wood horizontally and turning it often. It is therefore best to save the wood cut away from the silhouette and use it to make the baseboard and adjust it as needed.

Following Michelangelo's advice, we will begin rough-dressing the most salient points. Then we shall sculpt in a series of layers. We reduce the wood layer by layer, paying equal attention to the different faces of the sculpture and resisting the temptation to get carried away with detailed work; for the moment, all we are concerned with is the proportioning, that is, the distribution of planes, edges, and volumes.

Since we are working horizontally, we should occasionally place the sculpture in its intended position: vertical, horizontal, inclined, or hung. Having removed the clamp, we can see how the form is evolving. This will help us to maintain a view of the work as a whole because, we must insist, this should be our only concern during the rough-dressing phase. On changing the sculpture's position, we create a new play of light and shadows on the wood, which can help us to spot areas that need modifying.

To detect disproportions, we recommend projecting shadows of the different profiles on the wall. When enlarged, the defects stand out more.

You must be very demanding with the proportions when rough-dressing and have no qualms about rethinking the sculpture or even stopping work on it if the basic structure is faulty. It is in this hierarchy of criteria that the difference between sculptors and craftsmen lies: the sculptor tends to form an overall appreciation of the work, whereas the craftsman tends to be more concerned with detail.

The tool most often used for rough-dressing large sculptures is the die grinder with cutting disc or a straight-bladed, short-edged gouge. The sizes of the blade and the mallet depend on the dimensions of the block and the hardness of the wood.

As we remove wood, it is preferable to redraw the axes and rectify the marks that indicate the maximum profile, a profile that will get nearer and nearer to the thin safety margin that we will later model with more care.

The stage of rough-dressing can be considered finished when the wood resembles a cubist sculpture; when a series of planes, with or without edges, suggests the form still hidden within.

Controlling the proportions is fundamental, as they cannot be changed after the wood has been rough-dressed, even if the sculpture in question is abstract.

▲ The Egyptian priests determined the divine proportions of Osiris and expressed them in this roughly hewn limestone, which, with its cubist forms, served as a model for sculptors. Musée du Louvre, Paris.

▼ **Pablo Picasso,** *Figure* (1907). Painted pine. 32″ (81 cm).
The Cubists finished their sculpting at this stage. This gave it greater impact by turning the volume into the main feature of the sculpture.

◄▲ Comparison between trimming and rough-dressing a wengue plank.

Modeling

◄ When we model, we remove layers of wood, in this case elm.

After rough-dressing a large amount of wood, when the volumes are distributed, we then have a new aim: to make the surface even and continuous, somewhat cubist, in order to shape the desired figure.

First we should check that we have not gone too far when trimming or rough-dressing, because if any wood is missing, we will have to reduce the size of the entire sculpture to avoid altering the planned proportions.

Modeling gradually brings us closer to the final volume. The closer we are, the more meticulously we must work.

So we recommend continuing with the gradual reduction we started when rough-dressing. Working around the figure, we will be able to concentrate on the sculpture as a whole. It is a good idea to redraw the marks of the axes and the important points as they disappear. Since we will continue working with the sculpture horizontal, we should remember to stop occasionally to contemplate it in its intended position.

It is best to start each new stage with the most difficult or critical areas. In a realist figure, for instance, it would be absurd to devote time to the details of the clothes or to the rear side of the statue and then have to abandon the project after making a mistake with the face or hands.

We start to model using straight-bladed gouges, but narrower and more open than the previous ones. If the sculpture is of considerable size and we decide to continue using the die grinder, it should be used almost parallel to the wood so that the reduction is shallow and more gradual.

As we approach the desired form, we should use narrower and flatter gouges. To achieve greater precision, we can rest the forearm of the hand holding the gouge on the sculpture, strike the gouge weakly, and use small mallets. It is preferable to sharpen the gouges occasionally and hone them constantly to ensure a clean cut. So we need to keep the sharpening stones and a good range of gouges close at hand.

When removing the last layer, no amount of precaution is too much. The cut must be scrupulously clean. For this we use narrow, almost flat, deep-edged gouges that we should hone constantly. The gouge should slide smoothly, barely touching the wood. Use a very low inclination and strike it with the palm of the hand. As the impact is less intense, we can even hold the gouge between thumb and index finger to free the other fingers to steady the hand.

The deepest parts should be the last to be carved. To get into recesses, we can use curved gouges, either elbow or counter-elbow; although the mouth is no different, the blade makes them more suitable for cutting into wavy or

▼ The V-shaped gouge is suitable for carving internal angles and for opening up ridges.

▼ The elbow gouge and flexible shaft are useful for modeling concave surfaces.

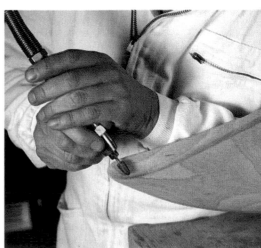

◄▼► Different moments when modeling olive wood, maintaining the axis of symmetry and the proportions.

concave surfaces. As an alternative to these special gouges, we can use a flexible shaft, fitting the most suitable grinding bur for each need.

As we finish the modeling process, we recommend you try to detect any possible anomalies by stroking the surface with the palm of the hand or by placing a strong light behind it and turning the sculpture around. Any protuberances, waviness, discontinuous planes, or alterations in the rhythm of the marks left by the gouge will stand out clearly.

It is best to conserve the clamping points as long as possible, although we can reduce them in height if they interfere with the modeling. But at some point we will be forced to remove them. Then, using foam or other materials, we will need to fashion a baseboard to grip the sculpture and prevent any abrasions.

When the modeling is finished, we can choose between giving the sculpture a meticulous finish or considering the work complete as is, with the expressive marks left by the gouge. In the latter case we need only protect the wood with suitable materials.

We ought to point out that, although such texture lends the work the beauty of an impressionist style, it is sometimes used to conceal defects and has been exploited to excess by the wood industry itself.

If, on the other hand, we want to present a surface free of any marks, we will start the finishing process, which is described further on. If not,

we can sign the sculpture as proof that we are satisfied with the result. A V-shaped gouge or a flexible shaft drill with a very fine grinding bur will serve as a writing implement.

► **Kirchner**, *Woman Dancing* (1908-12). Painted wood.
The Expressionists would stop their work at this stage to manifest their rebellion, expressed by the forceful use of the gouge.

◄ Each surface requires suitable treatment.

The Finish Crowns the Work

We have now reached the final stage of carving. We can put away our gouges and, before starting on the finishing process, ponder the Latin saying *finus coronat opus*, a good end crowns the work. Finishing consists of three phases: first the edges left by the gouge are smoothed, then any rough ends are removed, and finally the piece is sanded.

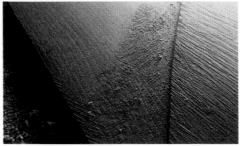

▲ The scraper removes the marks of the rasp.

▲ Effect of incorrect smoothing against the grain.

▲ Smoothing with a rasp and polishing with a riffle file near an angle.

Smoothing. Because the marks left by the gouge create an endless number of planes, we will scrape the wood with rasps to obtain a continuous surface. We should choose the right one for the dimensions of the sculpture and the hardness of the wood.

First, we begin with a coarse rasp. We recommend a curved one with replaceable blades because it adapts better to the different types of surface. Only after scraping the entire sculpture will we replace it with another, semi-fine rasp, finishing with the extra-fine. If we want an even more perfect smoothing, we can repeat the process using files in the same way as the rasps.

The teeth of a rasp will scrape according to the pressure applied, so it is best to slide it across the wood applying an even pressure, although we can increase this pressure to remove any protuberances.

The rasp should be drawn over the wood using the longest strokes possible so as to produce a level surface. We should draw the tool toward us, following the wavy areas of the surface and the direction of the fibers.

We should avoid smoothing against the grain so as not to raise rough ends. If ridges begin to form, we must apply less pressure. To spot any faults, the same as when we were modeling, we can stroke the surface or study it against the light. Riffle files should be used for concave or convex surfaces, changes of direction, and above all, for corners. There is such a wide variety of them—double-headed, curved, knife-bladed—that we can find one suited to each task. Hold it by the center and apply pressure with the fingers.

When we finish the sculpture, it should be firmly gripped, but since the clamping points will have been removed by this stage, we need to place sponges between the clamp and the wood, as mentioned earlier.

Removing rough ends. During filing, the ends of the surface fibers are raised. This phenomenon, easily identified by touch, is called *rough ends*. To remove them, we can use a simple piece of glass or carpenters' scrapers. These are not actually designed for cutting, as what appears to be the cutting

▼ The difference between the texture created by the gouge and the rasp.

▼ Smoothing with a traditional rasp.

▼ The size of the riffle files enables the artist to smooth even in difficult areas.

▲ Using a scraper for removing rough ends.

edge is rectangular. There is a wide range of these scrapers that adapt to any surface: rectangular, convex, concave, and so on.

The scrapers are used oblique to the wood. It is best to hold them with both hands at an inclination of some 45° to the surface of the wood, so that the edge removes the ends. Slide one of the scraper edges from the farthest part of the wood toward you, pressing down with the grain, that is, following the direction the fibers are growing in.

In addition to removing the ends, this process can produce a special shine on hard woods, similar to burnished metal. This burnishing can be emphasized by rubbing the wood with a hard mineral such as agate or simply with a harder wood, such as ebony.

Sanding. The grain becomes the most important aspect after the piece has been sanded. It is another component of the wood that determines the texture. Grain is formed by tiny particles that vary in thickness depending on the type of wood, and when they are removed they become sawdust.

Fine-grained woods are excellent for perfect finishes.

Although the rasp has removed the marks left by the gouge, the surface of the wood is still not smooth. There are still some tiny hairs that harbor sawdust, block the pores, and detract from the wood pattern. These fiber ends accumulate loose grain and spoil the beauty of the grain that still forms part of the wood.

To remove these tiny ends that resist the scraper, we can use different types of sandpaper. We can also fit a sanding disc to a drill or, for large flat surfaces, use an orbital sander or belt sander.

Since the long fibers have already been removed and only the round grain is left, we can rub the paper in circles, so that the grain of the paper comes into contact with that of the wood.

If we want a more highly polished effect for the entire sculpture or a part of it, we can make the rough ends stand up so they can be removed more easily. This is done by wetting the wood we want to treat. The moisture will swell the porous areas, which, on drying, will contract again and free the ends of the fibers.

A few minutes after wetting it, we will notice that the surface is rough to the touch again. We then let it dry completely and sand it with finer-grit sandpaper. We can repeat this operation as many times as necessary until we are satisfied. Because certain soft woods have many rough ends, it is advisable to wet them several times.

Now all we have to do is remove the dust that blocks the pores and prevents the grain from becoming shiny. We can

do this by rubbing it with an esparto brush or a powerful blast of air from a compressor.

If we want a perfect result that highlights the texture of the wood pattern, we can subject the sculpture to an industrial sand-blasting process.

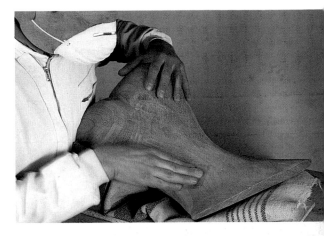

▲ Traditional finishing with sandpaper.

▼ The surface of elm wood, smoothed and sanded several times after dampening it.

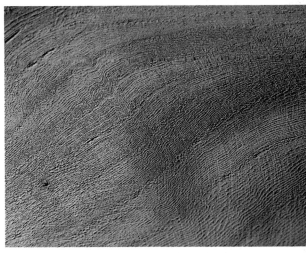

▶ Using a drill and sanding disc for finishing.

◀ Belt sander for flat surfaces.

Foreseeing the Unexpected

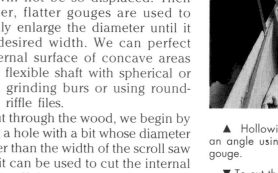

◄ Having controled the length of the fibers, we can continue to carve without producing splinters.

▲ When forming a ridge, we cut the fiber to give the gouge an exit point.

▼ Carved at the head, from the outside toward the center.

▲ Cutting with a drill.

As a general rule, we should always sculpt with the grain and from one end of the wood to the other. Sometimes, however, the form of the sculpture forces us to carve against the grain, across the end, or across the width from inside to out.

In any of these atypical cases, we should work with well-sharpened and honed gouges. When we are forced to go against the fibers, we must make incisions using flat or V-shaped gouges to cut the grain where we want. We can then carve the rest without fearing that the fibers will come away, as the gouge will emerge when it reaches the incision we made earlier.

This is a general rule, so now we will describe the solutions to some specific and frequent problems. To hollow out an internal angle, we can use a flat gouge or a broad chisel. We can use it to work down the vertical and horizontal planes alternately, until we get the desired angle.

If we want a rounded cavity, we can open up the angle in the same way but finish it off with a narrow half-round gouge; we begin at the end indicated by the grain and work progressively backward.

Concave areas are a rather more complicated subject. For these, we begin by opening up a middle point with a drill bit or gouge. Four bites with a half-round gouge are preferable to two with a tube gouge, as the fibers will not be so displaced. Then narrower, flatter gouges are used to gradually enlarge the diameter until it is the desired width. We can perfect the internal surface of concave areas using a flexible shaft with spherical or conical grinding burs or using round-pointed riffle files.

To cut through the wood, we begin by forming a hole with a bit whose diameter is greater than the width of the scroll saw so that it can be used to cut the internal silhouette. If the saw cannot be turned, make holes with the bit in the angles to make the cut easier.

If the cut is small or has a difficult shape, the bit is used again to make as many incisions as necessary around the perimeter until the interior comes away. The work is then finished with the gouge, rasp, or flexible shaft. Before carving a cylindrical form or turning sharp edges into half-rounds, it is wise to remember that all curved surfaces are many-faceted. So to obtain a half-round, for example, first we carve the sharp edge, then we reduce it on both sides, and finally we join the surfaces using a rasp until we have the desired rounded form.

However many precautions we take, wood can always hold surprises. If these occur during the rough-dressing stage, we

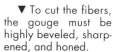

▲ Hollowing out an angle using a flat gouge.

▼ To cut the fibers, the gouge must be highly beveled, sharpened, and honed.

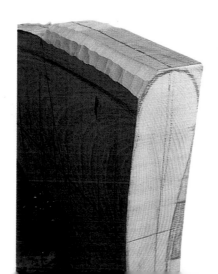

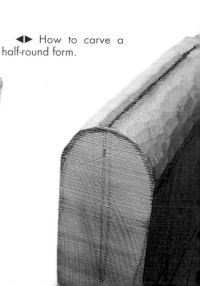

◄► How to carve a half-round form.

will still have enough material to rectify the project. The problem is worse if it appears when we are on the verge of completing the work.

We are not in favor of "repair work," but we should accept the challenge posed by a knot, crack, or colt, for example. We believe it is better to find an ingenious and creative solution that transforms an imperfection into expressivity. Despite this, we give here a few solutions to these problems. Only when we are familiar with them can we choose to use them or not.

If we encounter a knot or even the pith and want to give it similar treatment to the rest of the wood, we recommend using a medium-edged gouge that is suitable for the wood's degree of hardness. It should also be very sharp so as to carve at the first blow. This will prevent the knot from moving.

We reduce the knot using oblique, shallow cuts, following a concentric shape, working from the outside inward. After a time the knot may bleed and form a circular crack.

To disguise a crack, either a natural one or one caused by a lack of glue, we can use fillers. If the crack is small, we can fill it with glue, apply pressure with the clamps, and when it is dry, file down the area. If the surface to be covered is large, we can make a paste with glue and dry, fine sawdust from the same piece of wood. We can also add pigments to the glue to match the color of the wood.

There are polyester resin pastes that imitate the most common wood colors, although the problem with many of them is that they turn hard and shiny when dry.

Using our imagination, we can find many creative solutions, such as accentuating the cracks, encrusting them with different kinds of wood or other materials, or simply leaving them as they are. Why not?

When we encounter holes made by woodworm, or colts or internal damage, we can use similar solutions to those described above. Another cause of problems is the fissures caused by the blows of the gouge. Soft woods are more prone to these but also offer the best solution. It is usually the porous part and not the fiber that gives way. The solution is simple: apply a wet

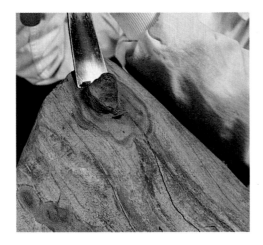

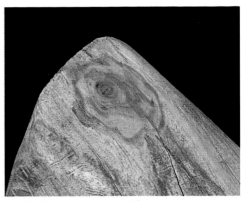

◄▲ Extracting a knot with concentric incisions until it is weakened.

cloth, wait for it to swell the wood, then file down. If this does not work, we can dampen the cloth a couple of times, but if the wood still does not swell, we will have to reduce the entire area.

If the sculpture receives a blow when it is already covered in wax or varnish, we will have to file it to open up the pores again to allow the humidity to enter.

Light can highlight the difference of tones between two adjacent surfaces. If we want to unify the color, we will have to use anilines; but if the sculpture is finished, we will have to remove the layers of wax before dyeing it, as we will describe in the following chapter.

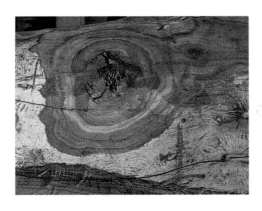

▼▶ Preparing and applying a filler to conceal defects in the wood.

▲ Why hide the expressivity of a colt?

Unorthodox Carving

H ere we will enlarge upon the concepts of gouges, carving, and wood. If the gouge modifies the form of the wood, let us consider other instruments that serve the same purpose. We shall enlarge our definition of wood to include wicker and even chipboard.

Bladeless gouges. What better way to prepare a trunk or a branch that to *direct its growth* while still a tree? It requires years, but the results are impressive. This suggestion is not new, nor related to bonsai. The Egyptians used tensors to make the wood grow according to the requirements of the part of the ship they were building.

In West Africa we also find live trees, of the ficus family, whose trunks and roots are rough-hewn and polished regularly to turn them into seats and backrests used in the meetings of the elders.

The props and walking sticks used by our grandparents were also formed before being carved from hackberry wood.

A similar approach is that which inspires David Nash to direct the growth of trees to transform them over time into a sculptural whole (p. 27).

Controlled *fire* has also been used as a sculpting instrument. In West Africa canoes are built of iroko, and after the exterior is shaped, the interior is scorched and hollowed out with an adz. Drums in the Pacific are also hollowed out using similar techniques.

Heat is also used for making casks. To make the staves (the strips of wood) flexible, a small fire is built inside the half-finished cask. The chestnut wood or oak gains in flexibility on being heated, which allows the staves to be bent. Like the iron rings, they expand with the heat and produce a better fit when cool.

It was also a contrast in temperature that was used to fit the wheel rims of traditional wagons, whose oak or ash axles were strong because of the length of the fibers.

Steam makes wood flexible and causes it to dilate. Industry uses this method to bend planks and model all kinds of objects made from laminated wood.

The same effect—bending wood—was achieved by Chinese boat builders using a simpler approach: they would place heavy sandbags on the damp beams to give them the shape necessary for the hull of their junks.

Joining woods. The ingenuity of the Surrealists showed how true sculptures could be created by combining different objects instead of using the gouge. The sea and the weather are professional carvers, modeling trunks, branches, furniture, making them appear alive. Artificial woods were also used, their decorative paneling removed, leaving a skeleton formed by badly joined wooden blocks. It was Gauguin who first brought such works into the museums.

We too can perfect these sculptures, using different combinations, though we do run the risk of turning nature's work into something more baroque.

In Arabian countries, where wood is scarce and brusque changes in temperature alter it, sculptors have developed the art of fitting together small boards. Motivated by the desire to create an intimate atmosphere, designed more for enjoyment than for exhibition, skillful artisans have constructed regal coffered ceilings, checkered platforms, lattice work, or highly detailed jewelry boxes.

Recapturing our childhood enjoyment of architecture in wood and learning the techniques of marquetry and intarsia or inlay—embedding different woods in the piece—we can create highly subtle sculptures.

Yet the powerful structures of a building and the solidity of the mounted beams have also served as inspiration for sculptors such as Chillida, who pursue the expression of vigor and strength.

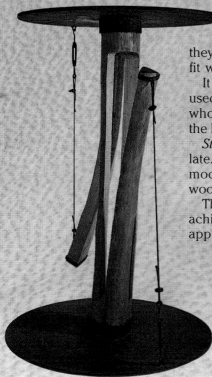

▲ **Guinovart**, *"Crui-lla de mirades"* (1995). Flanders pine. 51" (130 cm).

Using fire on pieces of holm oak, the artist has created different textures. (Photo: J. Pijoan.)

◀ **Pladevall**, *Titan XI*. Ash and iron. 40 ½" (103 cm).

By incorporating tensors, an illusion of potential dynamism is created and the weakness of the wood is transformed into strength.

▲ **Miquel Planas**, *Amfn II* (1988). Bolondo with inlaid hubinga and pine. 42" (107 cm).

The artist uses the inlay technique to combine strength and subtlety.

More wood

Wicker is also wood and very flexible too. It can be a fine complement to our sculpture, and if we know the art of basketmaking, we can also use it as the raw material for light and spacious sculptures, highly appropriate for hanging. The nomadic tribes of Mongolia even used wicker to make their huts.

The cultures of the Pacific, as we have seen, are masters of sculpting; they are by no means purists and do not hesitate to use raffia, esparto, straw, palm fibers, or anything else that nature has provided them with.

Canes, especially bamboo canes, can also lend body to a sculpture. We can learn from the technique of Chinese masons, who still use bamboo to build the framework of buildings having several stories. Chinese carpenters bend bamboo by cutting notches in it and joining the canes without using nails; they simply thin the ends so that they will fit into each other.

Most of Villelia's sculptural work is based on bamboo. His colorful, detailed mobiles can be a source of inspiration for us concerning the potential of cane.

Panels and plywood and other forms of "disguising vulgar woods" are also worthy of being mentioned here. We should remember that, although they are not found everywhere, they are an ancient invention and have never been used for sculpture. The phrase quoted is from the Roman Plinius.

Of the artificial woods, made by grinding, gluing, and pressing poor-quality woods, plywood can easily be handled without any problems with the grain. We can use it for exercises before transfering the volume from the maquette to the wood for making sculptures that will later be covered.

And what of the first material we ever used for sculpting? Using a simple pocketknife we would model cork, make canoes from pine bark, or assemble airplanes using balsa wood. Why not have some of these materials in our workshop and let our imagination, our childlike fantasies, run loose?

◄ Mask made by the **Malanggan,** New Zealand. Polychromed wood, vegetable fibers, cloth, and shells. 17 ¾" (45 cm).
The sculptors of the Pacific are not purists and mix both materials and techniques.

▼ **Mendiburu,** *Zugar.* (1970). Acacia and walnut. 45" (115 cm).
Purism taken to its ultimate consequences can also produce an unorthodox result. In this case, no material has been used other than the wood itself, even for the fastenings.

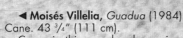

◄ **Moisés Villelia,** *Guadua* (1984). Cane. 43 ¾" (111 cm).
Cane, in this case bamboo, given its light weight and flexibility, allows the artist to experiment with space, tension, and color.

FINISHES

In this chapter we will deal with textures, complements, and especially patinas that are used to protect the wood, emphasize its characteristics, or transform it.

To be consistent with our criteria so far in favor of the nobleness of wood, we should in theory renounce such practices and defend wood sculptures left in their natural state.

But who can define what the most natural state of a living being like wood actually is? In effect, while it retains its resins, it has some flexibility, light, and coloring, but as it dries, the color fades and the surface becomes rough.

So we can choose between maintaining the smoothness of young wood by adding waxes, oils, or varnishes or showing it in its natural process of aging without any form of protection.

We also present details on different techniques to obtain a satisfactory finish.

In one thing Apeles could not be imitated. When the work was finished, he would coat it in varnish which shone and protected it from dust and other damage; but in such a way that this shine did not hurt the eyes but left the paint like a glossy stone and lent hidden weight to the colors.

Plinio

◄ **Gerardo Rueda**, *Still Life of a Pear* (1992). Several dyed woods. 16 ¾" (42.5 cm).

► Mask from the Mmwo society, Igbo, Nigeria. Polychromed wood and cloth. 17 ¼" (44 cm). Musée National des Arts Africains et Océaniens, Paris.

119

Imitating Nature

Wood exposed to the weather undergoes many transformations. Its texture is visibly changed, and the main alteration we notice is the appearance of ridges that lend relief to the grain. This happens because the softest part, the young wood, is the first to be eroded, while the part of the annual ring that grew in dry periods is more resistant.

When considering the final texture for our sculpture, we may have decided to leave the marks of the gouge visible or to give it a smooth surface. Another possibility is to emphasize the ridges, cracks, or knots, imitating the natural aging process.

Premature Aging

The techniques for speeding up this process are varied. The first ones were applied to Japanese furniture. In the West they became fashionable during the 1960s when artificially aged wood invaded bars, churches, and homes.

The ideal wood for a process that emphasizes the surface is that with a pronounced grain, the result of growing in a climate with rainy springs and dry summers.

Ancient sculptors used bones as the first instrument to achieve this artificial aging. Today, however, we can obtain a texture that resembles aging by using a metal brush on the wood, burning it with a blowtorch, or subjecting it to sand-blasting. To imitate the color of old wood, we need caustic products, anilines, dyes, and oils, which we will deal with over the following pages.

When any of these agents is used, the rough-ending process described in the past chapter can be omitted.

A metal brush is used on soft woods following the grain. With patience we can reduce the young wood until ridges appear that resemble the desired aging.

If we wish to illuminate the sculpture with anilines, it is best to cause the rough ends of the wood to stand up by dampening them as we explained earli-

▲ **Camí,** *Nomenclature* (1989). 17″ (43 cm). In this work the artist has not only respected the cracks and roughness of the banana wood but also imitated the color of the bark using oil glazes.

◄ The dead trunk of an almond tree; in this state it has lost its natural resins.

► Angkor Buddhas (10th-15th centuries). Cambodia.

The gouge of time has enriched the expressivity of these sculptures, while the patina of years has softened their colors.

er. This time we remove them with a scourer, as this adapts better to the new texture. We should avoid rubbing with a material that contains iron particles because, if they adhere to the wood, they could rust and cause black stains.

Metal brushing enlivens the tone and does not alter the color of the wood, unlike what occurs when a blowtorch is used. We advise the latter method if the wood is very hard. The aging is achieved by scorching the surface; to make this task easier, the wood can be softened with hydrochloric acid or ammonia applied with a brush.

The whole surface of the wood should be treated evenly and gradually, taking great care when working with fire.

Then we roughen with the grain using the metal brush until the charcoal powder has been removed and then scrub with an aluminum scourer to lighten the most scorched areas. Because this process darkens the wood, if we want to color our sculpture we will have to resort to decolorants or choose from semi-dark tonalities.

Another aging system is sand-blasting. In certain industries that work with metal or glass, a closed cabin is used where sand is blasted under pressure and originates a texture similar to the erosion of the desert.

The duration of this process needs careful calculating so as not to attack the hard part of the veins and damage the most sensitive parts of the work. We can also limit the area we subject to this process by covering up the rest with a resistant material.

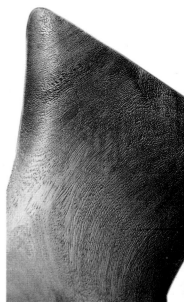

▼▶ Use and effect of the metal brush on damp bolondo.

▶ Sand-blasted Douglas fir.

▼ Old elm beams. The weather has eroded the young rings, leaving a ridged texture.

The Alchemy of Color

Having resolved the volume and texture of the work, we can either respect its natural color, alter it chemically, or modify it using dyes.

Here we shall deal with how to use certain caustic products and, later, anilines. Before starting, we should remember that it is always wise to experiment with wood left over from the trimming process, as the results could be different if we tried them on wood with a different degree of humidity.

There are many caustic products, such as soda, ammonia, bleach, or peroxide, which, properly prepared, can be used to alter the color of our sculpture.

The formulas that accompany the photos are just some among many other possible ones. We can get further information from a hardware store. Here we only want to offer some advice on entering the surprising world of the alchemy of color.

Certain precautions need to be taken when applying these products: wear a mask and rubber gloves and avoid any splashes that could stain the surrounding area, clothes, or the skin. If we are using a brush, it should be an acrylic one, as these products cause natural bristles to shrink.

Due to the odor and gases they can give off, it is advisable to work in the open air and, if possible, in the sun, which intensifies the effect by opening up the wood's pores.

COLORINGS:
1. By applying a solution of 1½ ounces (50 g) of soda to 1 quart (1 l) of water, we can obtain tones that range from yellow to grayish brown. 2. When 1½ ounces (50 g) of nitric acid is diluted in 1 quart (1 l) of water and applied to the wood, it turns brown initially before being dyed a greenish gray. 3. Brown tones can be obtained by using 1½ ounces (50 g) of ammonia diluted in 1 quart (1 l) of water. 4. Iron filings, left to soak in vinegar for half an hour, can be used to obtain a variety of tones ranging from brown to gray.

Before applying a new layer it is best to wait for the previous one to dry.

These products should be applied following the grain, with uniform brushstrokes if we want a homogeneous effect.

Any products left over can be stored in glass jars, not in certain plastic jars, which are liable to be attacked by these substances.

The definitive color is usually unforeseeable, because during the application process, the tonality, even the color, may change. It is preferable to be patient and hope that the results of the test we carried out can be obtained with the sculpture.

Even so, the results cannot be guaranteed, as small changes in temperature or the humidity of the wood can affect the process.

Remember that not all woods are sensitive to these products. Some, such as beech or walnut, hardly change and only parts of them, such as the knots, roots, or twists may undergo any change in color.

After applying the product and waiting, we will see that the sculpture appears to be covered in saltpeter. This can be removed by applying plenty of water with a sponge; this will also stop the corroding process. If a good squirt of vinegar is added to the water, the results will be optimum. Sunlight will accelerate the drying.

▼ Beech decolored using 40 drops of peroxide at 40% plus 20 drops of ammonia, dissolved in 1 quart (1 liter) of water.

▼ Beech steamed without any chemical ingredients.

▼ The same beech treated with peroxide as before but without ammonia.

▼ Pine colored with two coats of 2 ounces (50 g) of caustic soda dissolved in 1 quart (1 liter) of cold water.

▼ Flanders pine darkened by light.

▼ The same pine treated with a solution of 3 tablespoons (50 ml) of nitric acid and 1 quart (1 liter) of water, applied hot but not boiling.

► **Camí,** *Nimfosi* (1989). 22 ½" (57 cm). Mongoy treated with caustic products.

The resulting colors can change over time, but this deterioration can be delayed by the use of wax or varnish. We can also decolor the intensity of the natural color of wood using certain products, either to lighten it or to prepare it for the application of anilines. The precautions to be taken here are the same as those described for colorings.

As we mentioned earlier, the wood industry during the steaming process not only eliminates microorganisms but also alters the tone or color of the wood. This treatment is applied when the plank is still fresh, that is, recently cut. It is subjected to a high temperature that opens the pores so that the chemical that will modify the color can penetrate deeply. The best results with this process are obtained with birch, walnut, and beech. This is the most

DECOLORANTS:
1. Wash the wood with salted water, ½ cup (100 g) of salt per quart (liter) of water, and apply oxalic acid with a brush while the wood is still damp. 2. Wash the wood with 6 tablespoons (100 ml) of bleach dissolved in 1 quart (1 liter) of hot water and then rub with peroxide at 40%.

long-lasting form of coloring, yet its technology is beyond the possibilities of a sculptor, who will need to resort to the caustic products mentioned above or dyeing with anilines, oils, or enamels.

Atmospheric Conditions

Natural light also plays a role in coloring our sculpture. It makes any added colors paler; it darkens pine, oak, or beech; and it alters the color of teak, vermilion, or iroko. This process is almost unno-

ticeable inside houses, but is much more abrupt and pronounced outdoors.

The climate also changes the form of the wood, which, upon losing its resins, acquires ridges between the veins.

For this reason a sculpture intended for outdoors cannot be improvised: we need to select oily woods, which are much more resistant to climatic changes, such as bolondo, Burma teak, iroko, or kwila, and we should avoid nails or other materials that may rust.

The oily woods mentioned above do not require any protection. Yet most of them split when their resin dries. To prevent this, linseed oil was traditionally applied, which gave them a honey-colored patina, or tars, which darkened them. Creosote is a by-product of oil that does not alter the color, protects the wood from insects and humidity, and can be effective for more than two decades. We can also use varnishes designed for exteriors, although they are usually too shiny.

If our sculpture is intended for a park, we should try to think of it as a collective work, because its finish will be decided not only by the weather but also by insects, birds, and children.

▼ **Michael Warren.** *Arter image* (1984-86). Spanish chestnut. 17'9" × 17'9" × 17'9" (540 × 540 × 540 cm).

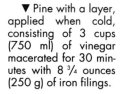

▼ Pine with a layer, applied when cold, consisting of 3 cups (750 ml) of vinegar macerated for 30 minutes with 8 ¾ ounces (250 g) of iron filings.

▼ Flanders pine darkened by the action of light.

▼ Pine dyed with a second layer of the previous solution after the first was dry.

In Color!

There are numerous ways of enriching the color of the wood, but only one fundamental difference between them: some are opaque and others, being transparent, enhance the properties of the wood.

Transparencies

Anilines are colorants in powdered form, of different origins, that are available in hardware stores. Their true color appears only when they are dissolved in liquid, so when we buy them, we must trust the indications on the packets and forget about their apparent color, which resembles that of the others. They are also available ready-dissolved, although the variety is more limited.

Anilines are the most transparent colorants that exist. Thanks to them we can enliven the colors of a chosen wood, change it, or simply unify or diversify the tones.

Because anilines are transparent, the resulting color depends on how they combine with the natural color of the wood. Light woods such as maple or mulberry provide a white background, the ideal base for any color, even luminous ones. But dark woods such as elm or walnut make anilines appear cool.

When dissolved in liquid, they are easily applied, especially to porous woods, which absorb them easily, so that the color penetrates beneath the surface. Yet thanks to their transparency, they not only don't conceal the streaked pattern of the wood but enhance it. Depending on the liquid used, they are classed into two main groups: alcohol- and water-based.

Alcohol-based anilines have the advantage that they are quick drying, although they do evaporate within a few years and the pigmentation is therefore short-lived. Furthermore, the range of these anilines is confined to half a dozen colors.

We recommend water-based anilines because, apart from the fact that they last longer and are more economical, there are over twelve colors to choose from, plus combinations that widen the range.

The ideal proportion of aniline to water is indicated on the packets. Generally speaking, 1/2 ounce (15 g) of aniline is mixed with 1 quart (1 liter) of alcohol or 1 ounce (30 g) per quart (liter) of hot water. We can obtain different tonalities of the same color by altering this proportion.

Bear in mind that all anilines fade after a certain time, and reds and blues are the first to lose their intensity.

Before applying any aniline, you need to remove entirely any rough ends, following the procedure described earlier of wetting the wood and then using the scraper. Otherwise, the liquid aniline will lift the fiber ends. The wood must also be brushed to remove all remains of sawdust, which might block the pores.

If the sculpture is small, it can be dyed by immersion,

◀ Anilines in powder form all look similar; it is when they are diluted in water that their true colors emerge, as can be seen on this steamed beech.

◄ Finished using a bordeaux-colored aniline glaze.

After dyeing with walnut pigment or any type of aniline or acrylic paint, it is best to apply waxes or varnishes to seal the pores, intensify the light, and soften the wood to the touch.

Glazes

In art-supply stores we can also find a range of oil colors; these are liquid and are derived from oil. They dissolve well in benzene or turpentine. They can be combined and diluted using these solvents.

After being applied to the wood they are semi-transparent and create a shiny patina, ideal for imitating aged wood.

Like anilines, they are applied in different layers, but have the disadvantage that, being oil-based, they do not penetrate the pores quite so much and take longer to dry, so it is necessary to wait about 24 hours between one glaze and the next.

These substances do not dampen the wood, do not lift up rough ends, and the work with the scraper need not be as perfect as with the previous method.

They are applied with a stiff brush that, to obtain a good penetration, should be drawn along and also across the grain.

They do not require subsequent varnishing. It is enough simply to polish them with a chamois cloth or coat them with a fine layer of neutral wax if we want a satiny shine.

We can also make these dyes ourselves if we use the following proportions:

8 ¾ ounces (250 g) oil-based paint of the desired color, 2 cups (500 ml) of turpentine, 6 ounces (175 g) of linseed oil, and 1/2 ounce (15 g) of dryer.

but the most common method is to extend the aniline with a brush. Aniline behaves in a similar way to watercolor: it spreads over wet areas, can create glazes, and becomes more intense as more layers are added.

So if we want to color the sculpture, the wood must be very dry; otherwise the aniline will spread uncontrollably. Every brushstroke creates a glaze. Overlapping brushstrokes create a new tonality. For this to be a success, the previous layer must be left to dry completely.

Liquid aniline should be applied with long brushstrokes following the direction of the grain, on dry wood unless we want a gouache effect.

Water-based anilines usually dry after half an hour; alcohol-based dry much more quickly. Although the intensity of the color fades on drying, it is advisable to dye using successive glazes in order to control the entire process.

As the wood becomes impregnated with the aniline, care must be taken in applying it, as stains and splashes cannot be removed.

Well-dissolved acrylic paints can replace anilines, as they behave similarly and are easier to find in the stores.

Walnut pigment behaves in a similar way. This is the coloring most commonly used in cabinetmaking and is sold in granular form to be dissolved in water. It is obtained from nut shells and can be used to darken any light wood until it takes on the dark brown that is characteristic of walnut.

▲ **Rodríguez Guy**, *Window* (1990). 28″ (71 cm).
A shutter colored with pigments.

► Dyeing the exposed endpiece of elm using walnut pigment.

▼ Walnut pigment in powdered form and the resulting dye after being diluted in water and applied to the beech.

▲ Injecting insecticide into a hole found in a wengue sculpture.

Before considering a sculpture finished, it is wise to protect it from those internal and external agents that can damage it.

Insects and fungi produced by humidity are its main enemies. While xylophagous insects feed on it and consume it from inside, fungi produce discoloration, mold, and rotting.

Anti-Woodworm Products

If we have used native woods or recycled beams, they may contain the larvae of xylophagous insects such as borers, lyctus, hornets, termites, or woodworm.

Because they are highly resistant, the only infallible method of eliminating these pests is to bore each hole with a

▼ Different sprays for xylophagous insects.

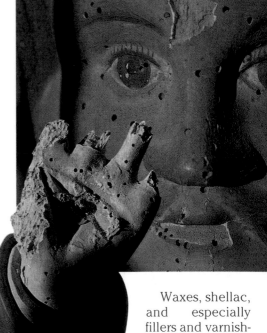

punch and extract them. This is impossible in most cases, as the holes would form a maze of galleries.

So we need to use gases to exterminate them. This was traditionally done using smoke, but today there are many anti-woodworm sprays designed to be injected accurately into each hole.

Some insects are very resistant, and so it is best to repeat the operation or even block the hole with Plasticine. In extreme cases we will have to spray the entire sculpture and leave it wrapped for several hours in a plastic bag to prolong the effects.

These products are generally highly toxic, so it is wise to use them in well-ventilated spaces and to wear a mask.

They usually contain fatty elements as well, so we have to choose the right moment to apply them because these oils will prevent dyes from impregnating the pores. If we wish to dye the wood, it is better to use the insecticides after the dyeing process. In this case it is a good idea to spray the entire surface so that the resulting color will be even.

The Subtlety of Wax

After eliminating any possible corrosive elements from the sculpture, we can turn to the job of protecting the surface. If we look closely, we will see that after sanding and brushing, the pores become more visible. These can trap humidity, dust, smoke, and any kind of dirt. They should therefore be blocked up.

Unfortunately, our enjoyment of the sight and touch of real wood is only temporary. If we wish to conserve it without it altering it significantly, we are forced to sacrifice its own texture for another, more plasticlike texture by applying sealers. In return, the wood will be easier to clean and less likely to lose or absorb humidity, which reduces the possibilities of it splitting in the future. In some cases it will even prevent mold from forming. Despite the protection a sealer offers, it is difficult to foresee the effects of the dryness produced by heating and air-conditioning.

Waxes, shellac, and especially fillers and varnishes provide the necessary protection. Before applying these, however, it is best to reflect on the aesthetic rejection caused by certain works of art on which the restorer has made excessive use of these products.

Wax is the substance that least alters the texture of the wood and, if properly applied, produces a satiny shine similar to that of young, taut wood. However, it does not block the pores well, evaporates over the years, and protects sculptures more from dust than humidity, making it best suited to interiors.

We can prepare the wax ourselves, enjoying its pleasant smell and altering the color to suit our purposes. We include a recipe for this, although it is easier to buy it in hardware stores.

▼ Pieces of virgin wax.

◄ The effects of woodworm.

▼ Larvae of xylophagous insects, life size.

We can choose between neutral wax (white or yellow) and dyed waxes that imitate the color of certain woods; there is a wide range of these tones: toasted, walnut, cherry, mahogany, and even black. A good wax-type shoe polish can be used instead.

If we applied anilines previously, we cover them with neutral wax so as not to alter the pigmentation. Otherwise, we can use dyed waxes that will intensify the natural color of the wood.

They should be kept vertically sealed so that the solvent cannot evaporate. If they do dry out, they can be rescued by warming them in a bain-marie and adding turpentine, taking care because it is flammable.

Wax is applied over smooth surfaces using a leather chamois. But if the surface is irregular, it is preferable to use a brush that can get into all the recesses to reach the pores.

The first layer is usually absorbed by the wood. We should wait a few hours until it dries and then apply additional coats until satisfied with the result.

Some people apply wax hot so that in this liquid state it penetrates better; we do not recommend this method because, if you have not mastered this technique, you can cause stains if it is not evenly applied. It is also easy for the wax to spread too much. Nor do we recommend working with wax

glazes of a different color to that of the wood because when they evaporate they will eventually stain the surface of the wood.

We will see if we have applied too much wax if it sticks to our fingernails when we scratch it. To reduce the wax, we can clean the sculpture with a cloth dampened in turpentine. If, finally, we want a delicate shine, we can brush the surface or rub it with a chamois until it has the desired patina.

Shellac, together with wax, is one of the oldest finishing materials known. It is sold ready prepared or in fine, dark, honey-colored scales exuded by a worm. These should be dissolved in the proportion of 1 pound (500 g) of scales per quart (liter) of denatured alcohol. It gives a satiny shine, but does alter the color. For best results, apply three or four coats with a brush and wait for the each coat to dry before applying the next, usually about three or four hours. Being such a slow process, shellac is hardly used in the West.

▲ Applying wax to holm oak with a brush.

MAKING WAX AT HOME:
Mix the ingredients by warming them in a bain-marie, taking great care because they are flammable. The amount of turpentine can be altered until the mixture becomes creamy. It is applied when cold.

1. Most usual formula:
   2 ounces (50 g) of carnauba wax
   3 ½ ounces (100 g) of virgin wax
   2 ½ cups (600 ml) of turpentine

2. Higher-quality formula:
   7 ounces (200 g) of mineral wax
   2 ½ cups (600 ml) of turpentine

▼ Range of colored waxes available commercially.

Sealing the Pores

◄ Spraying on varnish.

Although we prefer waxes, we must admit that varnishes and fillers are more effective. The latter are sold in paste or liquid form. Liquid form is preferable because it penetrates better and does not alter the texture as much.

Being very transparent, semi-shiny, and totally colorless, we can also use it as a first coat before applying waxes or varnishes, al-though this is not usually done because its chemical ingredients may react in an unforeseeable way with certain varnishes.

Varnishes are the most popular wood protectors, some of which are even designed for exteriors. Obtaining good aesthetic results with them, however, is a professional's job.

The Egyptians used them for protecting their sarcophagi, and the Greeks for their ships. Baroque

▼ Commercial varnishes and enamels.

writers compiled authentic recipes. We reproduce one quoted by Pacheco as a curiosity:

"Place half a pound of linseed oil in a vitrified pan and put it to cook over some good charcoal embers. When hot, add three heads of garlic, and when golden brown, remove and dip in a hen feather to see if it is cooked, and if it comes out burned, add three ounces of powdered fat, which is juniper gum (which the Arabs call sandarac) and cook until it seems to have the right consistency, and if it could be improved, use lavender oil and no garlic."

Nowadays there is a vast range of varnishes, colored or colorless, shiny, satiny, matte, transparent, or opaque, for exteriors and interiors, applied with sprays or brushes.

Each brand uses different components, so it is most unwise to mix them or even to superimpose them.

Varnishing properly is more complicated than it looks and should preferably be done by a professional, but if we do decide to do it ourselves, we recommend using an aerosol and taking care that it does not run. When it is dry, the surface should be smoothed with a tuft of cotton wool before new layers are applied.

If we are using liquid varnish, the process is similar: brush it on evenly and smooth the first layers with fine sandpaper.

Three or four coats are generally sufficient. If, after the last coat, the effect is too shiny or if we want to rectify the tonality, we can apply wax, which will only adhere if the surface is clean and dry.

Each coat should be applied with the grain, in long strokes from one end to the other to avoid overlapping sections. Take care with the edges and do not apply too much to the corners.

When varnish is wrongly used or has too much dryer, it will crack easily. It can also lose its shine if it comes into contact with solvents such as turpentine or alcohol. In these cases, the only way of restoring the sculpture is to remove the varnish and start again.

▶ **Camí**, *Llavor* (1990). 49″ (125 cm). An antique restored using traditional polychromy, from which hangs a wooden egg coated with Japanese lacquer and eggshell.

Opaque Coatings

If we want to coat the sculpture totally or in part and conceal the joints of the different pieces of wood, we can use enamels, false polychromy, or, if we have mastered such a difficult technique, Japanese lacquer.

Enamels, industrial paints diluted in turpentine, are the simple coloring method. They come in all colors and can be shiny, satiny, or matte. They seal the pores and provide long-lasting protection, so it is unnecessary to apply varnish or wax. For correct application, simply follow the manufacturer's recommendations. The first layer can be replaced by a primer. Enamels can be applied with a brush or aerosol. Two layers are usually sufficient. If the color seems excessive when we have finished, we can alter it rubbing with an aluminum scourer.

Nowadays, we can also use metal paints to impart a metallic appearance to our sculpture. If we buy them in powder form, we then use glue as a binder. There are also temperas and enamels for applying directly with a paintbrush. The easiest method, however, is to spray on fine layers and then perfect them by rubbing gently with a scourer or applying oil glazes of a toasted color, dark wax, or wax shoe polish.

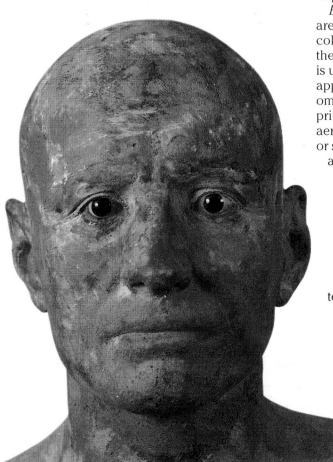

◀ **Antonio López**, *The Man* (1966-96) (detail). This hyper-realist effect has been achieved by hiding the wood under different opaque materials.

The application of traditional polychromy is so complex it cannot be fully dealt with here. The information we provide in this chapter is merely a synopsis of the knowledge of this art and cannot be considered an introduction to it.

There are various types of polychromy, but they are always applied over a coating such as tar—in the past—or plaster or other materials in more recent times.

Simple polychromy is one consisting of plain colors using egg tempera or, since the Renaissance, oil.

There are also flesh tones, obtained with tempera, designed to imitate the color of human skin.

Wood can be covered with gold leaf or, less frequently, silver. The gold can be partially covered or not.

Brocading tries to imitate true brocade, fabric woven with gold thread. This is achieved by covering the gilt surface of the sculpture with plain colors that are then scratched—simple brocade—or stippled—perforated for luster—to reveal the gold underneath.

Under the Polychromy

When the rough-dressed, modeled, and smoothed sculpture arrived at the painter's studio, it was subjected to a laborious process. We summarize here the main stages of brocading as an example of polychromy. The process for obtaining flesh colors or matte gilt was relatively simpler. The following were the main stages in applying polychromy:

Priming: A general inspection of the sculpture, extracting or sealing knots with garlic to prevent them from eventually bleeding.

Binding: Reinforcing the cracks or joints of the surfaces that did not require polychromy with bent nails.

Patching: Applying cloth or strong glue to the holes of the areas that were to be polychromed.

Gluing: Coating the entire surface with glue prepared with parchment and sheep or goat ears. Garlic was sometimes added to the second coat. This paste was known as garlic paste.

Thick plaster: Five layers were dabbed on with a brush and sanded after each drying.

Different samples of polychromy found in the museum and churches of Atienza (Castile), Spain:

1. *Christ of the Four Nails* (13th century) (detail). Majesty. Simple polychromy with subsequent retouching.

2. *San Joaquín* (18th century). Oil polychromy.

3. *Grutesco* (16th century).

▼ Brocading: detail of a chasuble, the motif inspiring brocades.

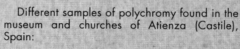

▼ Mystical lamb polychromed in gold.

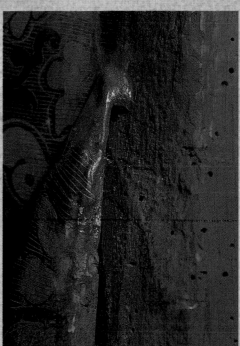

Thin plaster: Five layers were stroked on with a brush and sanded after each layer.

Reshaping: The master sculptor would restore the original forms with gouge and file. At this stage, occasionally before, the head was cut open vertically, the interior hollowed out, and glass eyes inserted.

Washing: With clean water and a few drops of weak glue.

Boling: Coating with five layers of bole, unctuous clay well fired and carefully prepared by the master using water. Special distemper and occasionally lead tapestry.

Polishing: Using a bristle polisher, taking care not to leave grease on the sculpture.

Gilding: After dampening the layer of bole, the gold leaf was applied and would adhere to the sculpture without use of any other products. These extremely fine pieces of gold foil were pre-

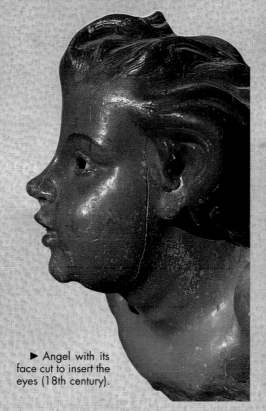

► Angel with its face cut to insert the eyes (18th century).

▲ Area adjacent to the brocade (reverse side of an image).

▼ **Berruguete,** *Apóstol* (1530). Prototype of a well-brocaded sculpture.

pared by the gold beater, who would beat coins of the highest quality between layers of leather.

Buffing: When the previous stage was totally dry and therefore hard, it was buffed until it shone.

Brocading: Applying the colors obtained from mixing natural pigments, water, and beaten egg. The drying and hardening could be accelerated by applying walnut oil.

Finally a wooden punch was used to draw the adornments, lifting up the paint or piercing the surface, trying not to damage the gold; a round-tipped punch was used to make perforations of luster.

Experts now polychrome following a simplified process when working in oil, and a somewhat more complicated one if working with water. Gold, bronze, or silver leaf is sold in foil two thousandths of a millimeter thick. More detailed manuals explain how to apply it correctly, or we can content ourselves with false gilding, as described on the previous page.

► *Dormition of the Virgin* (15th century). From Espluga Calba. Diocesan museum of Tarragona. A processional Gothic image, one of the first examples of brocading.

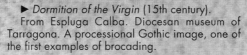

Other Finishing Materials

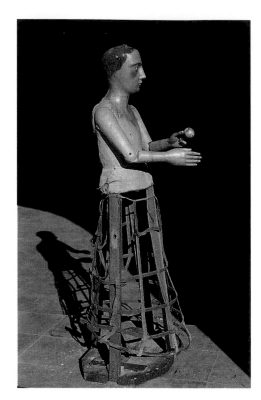

▲ An image ready to be dressed.

▼ The tailor rounds off the sculptor's work.

Although we defend the idea that sculptures should not hide the wood they are made of, we must admit that throughout history, wood has been treated not only with polychromy but also with other materials, especially metal and cloth.

Both in Eastern and Western religious imagery, it has been common to enhance the religious figure with halos, crowns, hearts, and moons, usually made of silver. These adornments may have been designed with the artist's consent or added later.

Baroque realism, and in particular the school of Gregorio Fernández, added to polychromy any element that would lend it more realism: wigs, glass eyes, mother-of-pearl, resin tears, lumps of earth, and other materials.

There are a great many popular images that are designed to be *dressed*, for which the skill of the dressmaker can be more important than that of the sculptor. The latter's role in these cases is confined to carving face and hands. The structure that imitates the body is a mere framework that may well be the work of a carpenter.

Animist carvings also incorporate elements other than wood for the purpose of decoration and especially symbolism: feathers, esparto resembling hair, magical substances in the navel, nails for spells, and so on.

We mention these here to stimulate your imagination, as they enlarge our creative field. When imagining our sculpture, we can add other materials, perhaps utilizing iron, marble, glass, or found objects.

Wood is not necessarily the most important aspect of a sculpture; we can use it as the support for a marble, or imagine a large metal stele that enhances a woodcarving, or combine them in equal proportions.

Another possibility is to take advantage of the great expressive force of wood that appears defective, by adding other elements. Instead of trying to disguise an unexpected split in the wood, for example, we can reinforce it with large staples, cover it with leather or cork, make it look like a scar, or have lead flow out of it; a colt or a simple hole made by larvae can be filled with tin, glass, flint, or other materials.

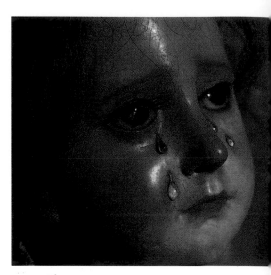

▲ Detail of a baroque baby Jesus with glass eyes and tears and natural hair.

▼ *Vili-Yombé.* Sculpture in wood, iron, and nails. 42 ½" (108 cm). Musée National des Arts Africains et Océaniens, Paris.
Although this work is a sculpture, the image is designed mainly for ritual and magical reasons.

A sculpture can be enhanced by incorporating fragments of objects that are obsolete but worth recycling.

We can also invent other forms to act as the base of the sculpture other than the typical pedestal, such as tensors, ropes, or rods. This will give us the opportunity to widen the expressive potential of our sculpture, provided we know how to assemble the different elements.

It is wise to be highly critical when using this method so as not to take it to excess. If the additions adapt to the main idea of your sculpture, they can open up new, aesthetic fields; if not, they will appear artificial. We recommend moderation.

Shall we consider the title of our work as a literary complement or an integral part of it?

Names have the basic function of defining, limiting, while art tries to express the indefinable. For this reason certain artists who defend abstract art refuse to give their works a name so as not to circumscribe their interpretation. We are not in favor of nameless art, but neither are we in favor of assigning names that state the obvious. We prefer to employ poetic language as an ally of our work to lend our creation new readings.

▲ The serenity of this mask takes on a new dimension when topped with feathers.

▶ **Katsura Funakoshi**, *Playing with Water* (1994). Camphor wood and tin plate. Although this sculptor is one of the main realists of the twentieth century, he incorporates metals that, paradoxically, emphasize the intimate nature of his work.

◀ **Camí**, *Estro* (1993). 57" (145 cm). This elm grew while trapped in a wire, which has been left. To emphasize the internal tension, a bayonet has been added.

Displaying Your Work

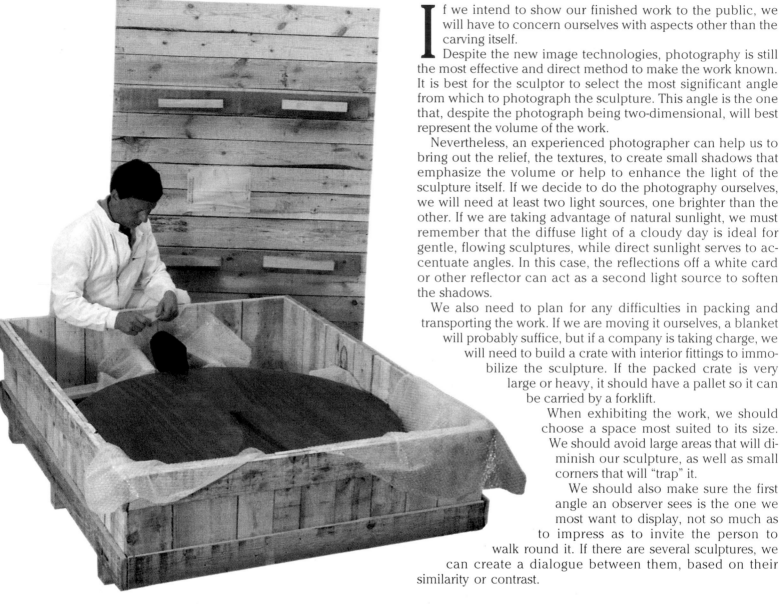

I f we intend to show our finished work to the public, we will have to concern ourselves with aspects other than the carving itself.

Despite the new image technologies, photography is still the most effective and direct method to make the work known. It is best for the sculptor to select the most significant angle from which to photograph the sculpture. This angle is the one that, despite the photograph being two-dimensional, will best represent the volume of the work.

Nevertheless, an experienced photographer can help us to bring out the relief, the textures, to create small shadows that emphasize the volume or help to enhance the light of the sculpture itself. If we decide to do the photography ourselves, we will need at least two light sources, one brighter than the other. If we are taking advantage of natural sunlight, we must remember that the diffuse light of a cloudy day is ideal for gentle, flowing sculptures, while direct sunlight serves to accentuate angles. In this case, the reflections off a white card or other reflector can act as a second light source to soften the shadows.

We also need to plan for any difficulties in packing and transporting the work. If we are moving it ourselves, a blanket will probably suffice, but if a company is taking charge, we will need to build a crate with interior fittings to immobilize the sculpture. If the packed crate is very large or heavy, it should have a pallet so it can be carried by a forklift.

When exhibiting the work, we should choose a space most suited to its size. We should avoid large areas that will diminish our sculpture, as well as small corners that will "trap" it.

We should also make sure the first angle an observer sees is the one we most want to display, not so much as to impress as to invite the person to walk round it. If there are several sculptures, we can create a dialogue between them, based on their similarity or contrast.

▲ Packing the most delicate part of *Émul,* a sculpture carved in vermilion and wengue.

▶ **Camí**, 1986. Three sculptures of sapele and iron plate exhibited in Fontana d'Or, Gerona, in a dialogue with the architecture.

Suitable lighting can accentuate or diminish the expressive features of the work or establish areas that evoke intimacy or distance.

Finally, we should listen to any praise with a certain amount of skepticism, as the person who best knows the work is its creator. We should reflect on negative criticism to be able to distance ourselves from the work, yet still remember the pleasure it gave us while we were carving.

If we take part in a competition, we may still take consolation from the wise advice of Don Quixote: *"Aspire to the second prize, as the first is due to favor."* And to the theorist who judges our work lightly, we may remind him of the Chinese proverb: *"Knowing how to is not the same as doing."*

The Style of Wood

Before proceeding to the step-by-step descriptions of the evolution of a series of works, we should remember that the beauty of wood has created its own style: its veins have been copied on other materials.

In the same way that basketmaking influenced the decoration of early ceramics, the beauty of wood has prevailed even when longer-lasting materials have been chosen.

This is the case of the early, pre-Hellenic columns that imitated an inverted tree trunk—the palaces at Crete—or the fences and doors that surround Buddhist figures such as the one in Sanci during the first century B.C.

We can also find numerous terra-cotta sculptures in Africa—Ife (eleventh century)—or bronze with a woodlike finish—Benin (fifteenth century).

In the present century, surrealists such as Miró sanctified trunks in bronze, while architecture does not conceal the mark of the woods used for framing concrete.

► **Miró.** *Stools.*
These objects in everyday use are trapped in dream time, as the original wood is transmuted into painted bronze.

► *Terra-cotta Ife* (11th-12th century). Nigeria.
Among the many different interpretations of this ridged human face is the possibility that the artist wished to imitate veins of wood.

STEP-BY-STEP DEMONSTRATIONS

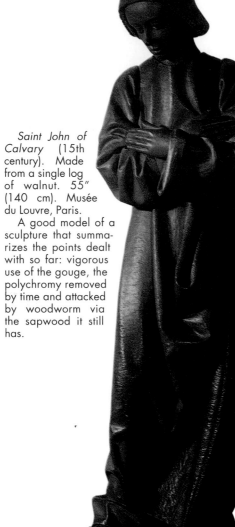

Saint John of Calvary (15th century). Made from a single log of walnut. 55" (140 cm). Musée du Louvre, Paris.
A good model of a sculpture that summarizes the points dealt with so far: vigorous use of the gouge, the polychromy removed by time and attacked by woodworm via the sapwood it still has.

H aving analyzed the entire process of carving, we now present a practical summary, illustrated with photographs, of how several sculptures, in increasing order of technical difficulty, were produced.

More than models to be copied by the beginner, they are reference points. For this reason we include the image of a classical sculpture as a prototype to stimulate the imagination.

We have attempted to include the full range of processes, tools, and materials described earlier, and for easy reference we have arranged them in the following chart.

PROPOSAL	RECYCLING	A BRANCH
PROTOTYPE	**Cristòfol**	**Marededéu de Montserrat**
MATERIALS	oars, butcher block, lead plate, and accessories	olive
TOOLS	· clamps · keyhole or scroll saw · plane · replaceable rasp · scraper drill and bits · metal shears · rubber mallet	· bench vise and clamps · hand saw · gouges and metal mallet
PROJECT	· composition on sand · experimentation	· *in mind* · experience · axis of symmetry
PREPARATION AND TRIMMING	· cleaning and cutting oars · joining an extension · perforating the base	· direct rough-dressing · clamping
ROUGH-DRESSING AND MODELING	· not carving but assemblage · sanding extension of oar · roughing the base	wide range of gouges
SMOOTHING ENDING POLISHING	· clamping the oars · fitting the lead sheet · including metals · anchor piece on base	sandpaper
FINISH	· bluing the disc and metal elements · acrylic paint · anti-wormwood · matte aerosol varnish · waxing the base · lead: no protection	· varnish with brush · toned with fine steel wool · wax
TEXTURE	· material's own texture	· smooth and with bark
COLOR	· partially colored blue	· that of olive wood
NAME	*Remol*	*Francesco*

ONE CUT	THREE CUTS	ONE TRUNK	SEVEN CUTS AND A BEAM
ancusi	**Kuan Yin**	**Sergei Konionkov**	**Cálao**
eamed beech	bolondo and iron	elm	vermilion, wengue, yellow pine, nails and rods
ench vise and clamps and saw ouge and cylindrical malle eplaceable rasp ffle files traight scraper	· plane and clamp · circular saw · gouges and conical mallet · traditional rasp · riffle files · curved scraper · metal brush · drill and bit	· clamps and strips · chainsaw · die grinder with cutting disc · mask and gloves · gouges and bell-shaped mallet · replaceable rasps · drill with sander	· very large clamps · bandsaw · die grinder with cutting disc · gouge and mallets · electric plane · belt sander · drill with sander · orbital sander · drill and bit

aper stencil
arbon transfer
ain axes
	· life-sized maquette
	  in gray clay
	· grid for transposing to block
		· sketch, clay model,
		  evolving during the process
		· marking axes
			· Plasticine maquette
			  on galvanized wire netting
			· concentric circles and axes

aditional rough-dressing
vo clamping points
	· gluing the three cuts
	· pressed with clamps
	· industrial trimming
	· two clamping points
	· baseboard
		· chainsaw and half-round
		  gouge
		· no clamping points;
		  strips used as buffer
			· double gluing of cuts
			· two clamping points
			· industrial trimming
			· support area

ouges: half-round,
-shaped, and flat
	· half-round gouges
	  with different mouths
	· traditional rasp
	  and riffle files
		· cutting disc
		· gouges, tubed and
		  wide-mouthed half-round
			· cutting disc
			· smoothed with
			  electric plane
			· retouches with
			  wide-mouthed gouge

asp, riffle files, nd flexible shaft tool traight scraper	· sandpaper and mask · curved scraper	· rasp with removable blade · sanding disc and flexible shaft	· concave areas: sanding disc · flat: belt sander · drill and bit

ash with cloth
andpaper
ater-based aniline
axed by hand
on plates on base
	· washed and scraped
	  with metal brush
	· building of base and rod
	· hand-waxed wood and iron
	· anchoring
		· cleaning and filling cracks
		· anti-woodworm
		· wash with sponge
		· industrial sand-blasting
		· hand-painted
		  with walnut pigment
		· hand-waxed
			· washed with sponge
			· orbital sander
			· gluing vermilion, wengue,
			  and yellow pine: stained
			  with walnut pigment plus
			  lights with sandpaper
			· hand-waxed

ompletely smooth	· aging and ridged veins	· relief of grain and
		  smooth areas
			· vermilion: open pores
			· wengue: stratification
			· yellow pine: roughness
			  with nails

atural and dyed wine color	· olive brown with light areas	· natural and dark walnut areas	· vermilion and wengue: natural · yellow pine: walnut with lights
ngue	*Thetis*	*Meteora*	*Èmul*

Mixed Materials: Recycling

For those starting to carve, we suggest beginning by recycling material, working without any grand preconceptions.

As a first step, we can search in the attic, gather unusual sticks in the country, or attend an auction of old items until we find a wooden object that attracts our attention; we can then contemplate it from different angles, at leisure, until ideas occur to us.

With the gathered objects we can experiment with different compositions until we are satisfied; we should be careful of baroque style forms that eventually become tiring.

Then we can assemble the different elements. A basic knowledge of woodworking is sufficient for this.

As our prototype we have chosen *Moonlit Night* by Leandre Cristófol. A cabinetmaker and, in his old age, sculptor, he was surprised to be awarded the title of artist by the critics. Today he occupies a place of privilege in the history of sculptural surrealism, together with Miró.

◀ **Leandre Cristòfol**, *Moonlit Night* (1995). Natural and dyed woods. 28″ (71 cm).

◀ Strolling along the beach, we found two fragments of oars and in a junkyard a steel disc from a sawmill.

To form a composition, we needed a base and were given an old butcher's block.

So these were the basic elements of our future sculpture: two oars with the remains of blue paint, a rusty steel disc, and a beech log.

▲▶ After experimenting with different combinations on the beach, we decided that a vertical composition would be the most evocative.

▶ 1. To accentuate the verticality, we saw the top ends of the oars into a nose-cone shape.

◀ 2. We could also have used an electric saw. In either case, before sawing, we draw the outline and clamp the oar firmly to the workbench. Later we will file down the edges.

◀ 3. Having discarded the idea of creating a tabletop sculpture, we need to extend the larger oar so that it stands up from the floor. We fit on a square strip of pine, slightly larger than the diameter of the oar. The overlapping cut will reinforce the gluing.

▲ 4. The next day the glue has dried and, with the oar firmly gripped in the clamp, we plane with the grain the four sides of the square strip until it has many facets: this brings us closer to the cylindrical shape of the oar.

▲ 5. Using a replaceable blade rasp, we smooth with the grain the different edges formed by the plane.

◀ 6. We finish assembling the two woods by smoothing the surface with sandpaper, rubbing it in all directions.

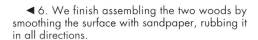

◀ 7. To obtain a uniform color, we dye the wood with a highly diluted coat of aniline. We tested this tone earlier on pieces of the same pine.

139

▲ 8 and 9. To emphasize the marine origin of the oars, we enlarge the colored areas of each oar with highly diluted acrylics to lend transparency to the veins. Before this we cleaned the wood with a brush.

◄ 10. We use the long oar as a support for the smaller one and join them with two old screws after drilling the holes.

◄ 11. The smaller oar snaps and the pith resists more than the heartwood. Using a gouge, we emphasize this feature, forming a reed shape.

▼ 12. We finish off the tip of the oar, sealing it with lead. The difficulty of imbedding metal in a thin wooden edge is overcome by drilling it and threading it with a metal rod.

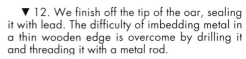

► 13. Now we turn our attention to the base. The patina of grease and dust that covers this block reminds us of its origins. We scrape it with a rectangular scraper and then the true face of the wood appears and we deduce that it is beech wood. We now feel the log "is looking at us" and decide to respect the holes and incorporate them into the sculpture itself.

► 14 and 15. We need to imbed the larger oar in the smaller one. Because we do not have a drill bit that size, we trace the circumference we have drawn with a normal-sized bit. Then we can finish the job with a half-round gouge.

▼ 16. Although the post is still in good condition, despite its age, we take the precaution of spraying the entire surface with an anti-termite solution, especially in holes and cracks.

▼ 17. To seal the pores, we choose a dark wax that emphasizes its primitive texture. We apply it with a flat brush, following the fibers so that it penetrates between them.

18. We experiment with how to place the metal disc and realize that the composition needs balancing by adding another metal to the base.

19. The butcher's block has been confused in our imagination with a banquet, a drum, and even with the throne of a tribal patriarch. So we cover it with lead plate, a ductile substance that dignifies our throne and is reminiscent of a drum skin. We use a mallet to adapt the lead to the surface of the block. Any excess lead is cut off with the shears.

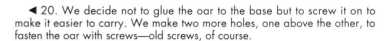

20. We decide not to glue the oar to the base but to screw it on to make it easier to carry. We make two more holes, one above the other, to fasten the oar with screws—old screws, of course.

21. The small metal elements we have incorporated—screws, lead, and a ring to frame the reed—help us to decide the color of the disc. We blue it with an industrial product that protects it from rusting and produces a uniform color with the other metals.

◄ 22. Having prepared each element separately, now is the time to assemble them.

▼► 24. Having finished the work, we now start searching for a name that captures its marine origin and exalts its verticality. In the diary of a recent trip to India, we find the name of a tree that catches our eye: remol.

▼ 23. We adjust the disc onto the long oar. The head of the bolt will be visible, while the nut, hidden between the disc and the oar, lets the disc rotate. The lower bolt does not grip anything. . . but let's play critic: *"The binary rhythm of the whole—two oars, two circular and metallic surfaces, two objects, an abstraction of masculine and feminine—requires double sets of screws."* And what if we were just trying to disguise a mistake when we fitted the disc?

Camí, *Remol.* Dyed wood and metal. 93 ³/₄" × 15 ¹/₄" × 13 ³/₄" (238 × 39 × 35 cm).

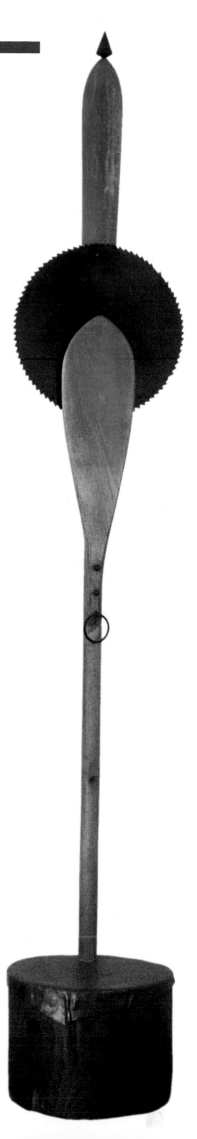

Olive Wood: The Experience of a Professional

Before you fit the handle to a gouge, we recommend you visit the workshop of an experienced sculptor. We do. By appointment we go to a shop-workshop located in the Pueblo Español in Montjuich, Barcelona. It belongs to Josep Pons. His enthusiasm for carving is contagious. His serene look is reflected in the many images he has carved, or is it the expression of the saints that has marked him? We remember Camoes: *"May the lover be transformed into the object of desire through imagination."*

Another Josep, the photographer of this exercise, cannot believe what he sees: the agility of the sculptor, which seems inherited from many generations, prevents him from capturing decisive moments. Even his photojournalist's speed seems slow when pressing the shutter.

The shop is full of olive trunks, a couple of saws, and dozens of gouges. There is no place here for electric tools.

There are many replicas, each with its own character, of the *Moreneta,* another soulful image, which is sung to so that it will illuminate Catalonia from the mountain of Montserrat.

▶ *Marededéu de Montserrat.* (end of 12th century). Polychromed wood. 37 ¹/₂″ (95 cm).

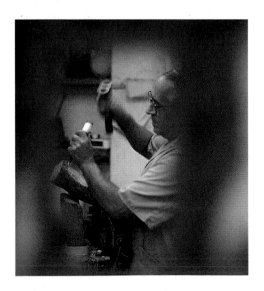

▲ Invading his privacy, we find Josep "talking" with the wood.

▲ We are surprised by the number of gouges, some of which have been ground so often they have almost no blade left. They are inherited, he explains proudly.

◀ In a few hours, this olive branch—*cut under a good moon on this land*—will take on another life.

▶ 1. He removes the bark from one side, leaving the other. He surprises us by saying that the bark he leaves will not change. He trusts the moon and we trust his experience.

▼ 2. With decided blows, he begins to dress the wood, which, as we have already seen, must remain firmly gripped by the table vise and rest on a piece of wood.

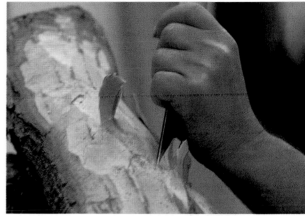

▶ 3. He begins to model with the flat gouge so that he can control the length of the fibers. The image he aspires to is so far only in his mind.

▶ 4. The outline has been determined. He constantly redraws the symmetrical axis.

▼ 5. Josep strikes with a small metal mallet; both gouge and matter seem an extension of his arm.

▼ 6. A figure begins to emerge from the wood. This reminds us of the "bathtub" method described by Michelangelo.

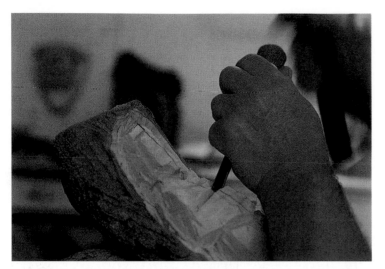

◄ 7. His firm, agile wrist directs and controls the direction of the V-shaped gouge, which cuts across the fibers.

► 8. He changes gouge so quickly it is difficult to follow, but by the marks he has left, we deduce he has mostly used a flat, wide-mouthed gouge.

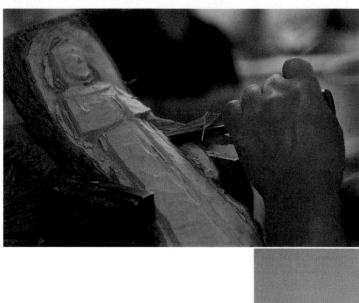

◄ 9. Using the V-shaped gouge, he carves the head and raises long fibers he knows how to handle.

▼ 10. He takes up the flat gouge again, but discards the mallet.

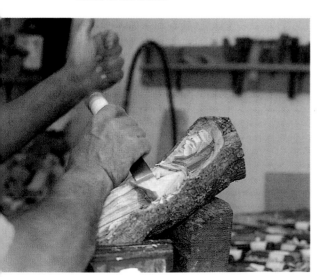

◄ 11. Not even an hour has gone by, perhaps, and the figure is already proportioned.

He stands it up to check that the proportions are correct.

◄ 12. He clamps the wood again and starts work on the detail. Using a tubed gouge, he carves a distinguishable wavy fold on the sleeve of the figure.

▲ 13. Like a musician who masters his art, he always finds the right gouge in the midst of this apparent chaos.

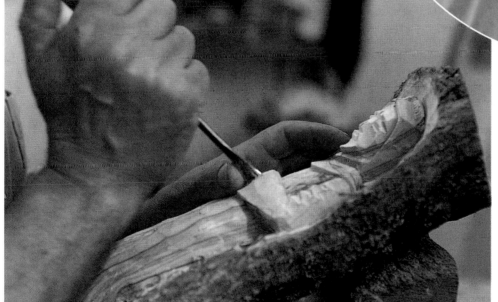

◄ 14. Now he applies a narrow-mouthed counter-elbow gouge.

◄ 15. The olive seems to be grateful for being brought back to life. We remember the initiation rites of African woodcarvers to be at peace with the wood spirit.

▲ 16. The veins of the olive are now visible, introducing a dash of color.

▲ 17. The face still has the hard cubist features left after dressing.

◀ 18. Keeping its symmetry, the gouge begins to model the face.

▲ 19. And it soon possesses the serene heartbeat of the living.

◀ 20. The image is set upright. At its feet lie the gouges that have brought it to life.

▼ 21. All that is left is to sand it to remove the grain . . .

▲ 22. . . . varnish it by hand to seal the pores . . .

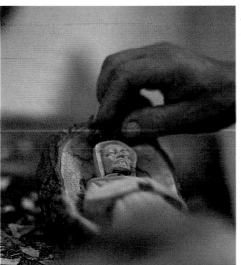

◄ 23. . . . take down the shine of the varnish with steel wool so that it shines with "hidden weight," as Plinius advised . . .

▼ 24. . . . and wax with a chamois.

► **Josep Pons**, *Francesco*. Olive. 14 ½" × 6¾" × 4" (37 × 17 × 10 cm).

Beech: Acquiring Practice

To acquire some practice with the gouge, we now propose working with a plank of malleable wood such as bosse, sapele, or cherry.

We have chosen steamed beech, which entails no risks and is easily worked.

Essential tools are a saw, a couple of straight gouges with different sized mouths, clamps, rasps, scraper, and sandpaper.

After studying the veins and patterns, inspired by how the beech is warped, we imagine a sculpture that enhances the properties of the plank without becoming too complex.

As a model we suggest Brancusi, who, in addition to sculpting large works, pursued the creation of simple, stylized, primitive forms using different materials.

▶ 1. Once the idea has been conceived, we sketch it on a life-size piece of cardboard, cut it out, and transpose it to the wood on both sides, on which we have already marked the axes and set aside the two clamping points.

▲ 2. The plank is firmly gripped by the bench vise, and we begin to silhouette it by making parallel cuts perpendicular to the fibers that create the veins.

▼ 3. With a straight, almost flat gouge, we chop our small pieces of wood from between the cuts. The gouge, rather than cutting the wood, tears it out by separating the fibers. On reaching the profile, we bite less into the wood until we are just removing shavings.

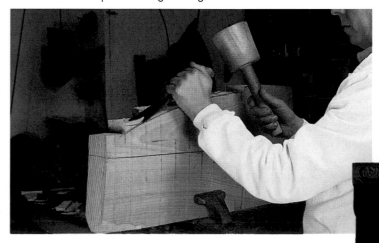

▶ **Brancusi**, *Le coq* (1924). Wild cherrywood. 36" (91.8 cm).

◄ 4. Using the same gouge, working back with the grain, we reduce the sharp edge. We repeat this process several times until we have a polygonal surface that the rasp can then transform into a half-round.

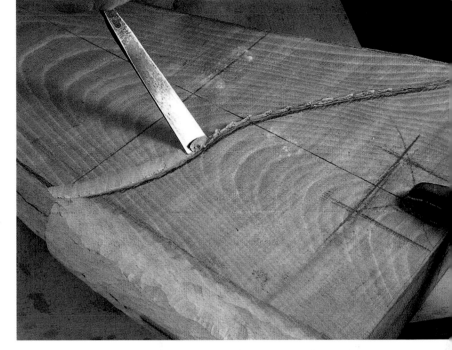

► 5. With the wood held flat and tight, we ridge the surface with oblique cuts with a beveled gouge. This way we cut the fiber and can continue rough-dressing the interior.

◄ 6. We reduce the wood in successive layers, making sure the gouge always exits from the wood.

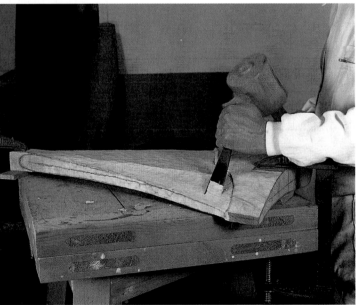

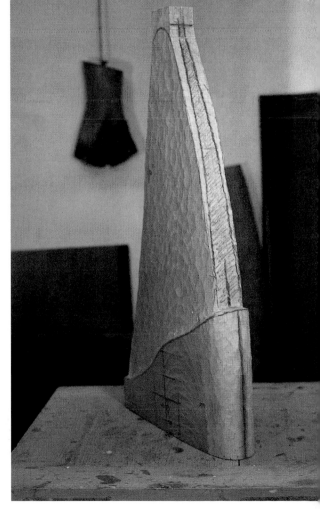

▼ 7. When rough-dressing, we must respect the clamping points.

► 8. The carving is set upright frequently so as not to lose sight of the overall appearance.

▲ 9 and 10. Having drawn the area we wish to reduce, we proceed with a well-sharpened narrow gouge, resting an arm on the wood to steady our work.

◄ 11. The layers become increasingly flatter as we approach the desired shape.

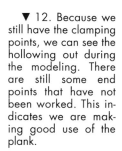

▼ 12. Because we still have the clamping points, we can see the hollowing out during the modeling. There are still some end points that have not been worked. This indicates we are making good use of the plank.

▼ 13. The base also shows the effect of the reduction. The sculpture now has its definitive volume, so from now on we will turn our attention to the surface.

◄ 14. With the wood well-clamped and protected by a cloth, we work on the edge. With a well-beveled gouge we open up a central ridge that will widen as far as the edges.

▼ 15. One of the clamping points has been removed, and we consider the modeling finished after checking, against the light, that the wavy surface is correct.

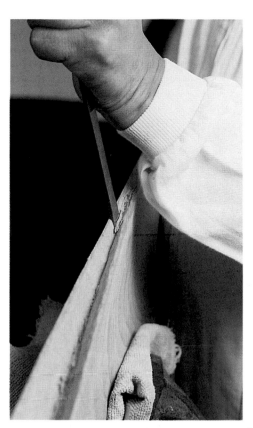

◄ 16. Using a round-bladed rasp, we remove the marks left by the gouge. The growth order of the veins indicates which direction—with the grain—we have to slide the tool.

▼ 17. Using a riffle file, we work the detail, first on the flat surface and then on the vertical head.

► 18. Also with the grain, we pull the scraper toward us to eliminate the rough edges raised by the file.

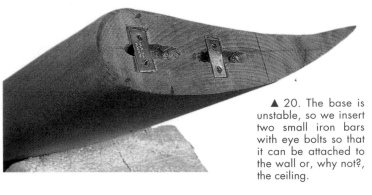

▲ 20. The base is unstable, so we insert two small iron bars with eye bolts so that it can be attached to the wall or, why not?, the ceiling.

◄ 19. Now we can eliminate the remaining clamping point using a well-refined gouge, rasp, and knife.

▼ 22. Then we dampen the entire surface to raise the rough ends and open the pores so that they will absorb the aniline we'll apply later.

◄ 21. After covering the work surface with a cloth to prevent scratching, we rub fine sandpaper in the direction of the waves. The grain comes away in the form of sawdust.

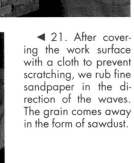

▲ 23. We sand the surface again until it is smooth.

► 24. We apply two coats of aniline dye to obtain the tone we tested earlier on another plank of beech.

► 26. We have given the work the tentative name of *Lethargy* because of its resemblance to another sculpture. This gave us the idea to hang it . . . *until the inanimate beings awake from their lethargy*. First we placed it on the wall, but then a visitor mentioned lingam. Neither lingam nor lingua, we hung it from the ceiling and gave it the name of a Chilean tree whose bark is used to tan leather: lingue.

▼ 25. We sealed the pores with dark wax, the surface with dyed wax, and the rest with neutral wax.

Camí, *Lingue*. Steamed beech. 14″ × 12½″ × 2½″ (36 × 32 × 6.5 cm).

Bolondo: Classical Forms

Now we are going to carve a classical sculpture, not so much for its appearance as for the method of work. We will build a block with three cuts and leave the wood its natural color, although traditionally on the Buddha pictured here or on Catholic images, the join of the cuts was hidden and polychromy applied by a specialist.

For this sculpture we need a greater range of tools than for the previous one. We will meet them as we go along.

We have chosen bolondo, but because it is difficult to work, we recommend practicing with walnut or teak, which are harder.

► **Kuan Yin,** *The Bodhisattva Who Hears the Cry* (12th century). The Art Institute of Chicago, Buckingham Collection. Divinely human.

◄ 1. We start with a life-sized maquette modeled in clay. Taking the drawing of the base as a reference, we grid the surface of the maquette to define the distances with precision.

▲ 2. We flatten the sides of the cuts to be joined with a plane, leaving the surface slightly rough so the glue will penetrate properly.

◀ 3. After applying the glue evenly, we press the three cuts with clamps and leave them overnight to set.

▼ 4. After marking the axes of the maximum outline and the two clamping points, the carpenter takes charge of the trimming. The bandsaw replaces the traditional saw. The most salient points reach the very edges of the block, which indicates we have made good use of the material.

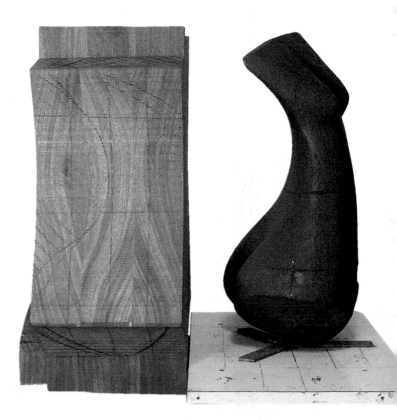

▲ 5. We compare the maquette with the industrial silhouette to see how accurate it is.

▶ 6. We then draw the profile of the sides of the block, using the symmetrical axes and grid as a guide. We mark off the area to be removed from the silhouette, but because it is asymmetric, we trim it with a straight, half-round gouge instead of sawing it off.

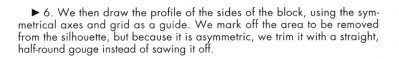

7. The sculpture is now proportioned and our eyes are irritated by some substance the bolondo has given off. The clamping points show how much material has been removed, while the ends and the base define the initial block.

8. We lend volume to the breasts without concerning ourselves with details for the moment. We leave the modeling of the two planes from the original surface of the plank for later.

9. We redraw the lower area and notice that the edges need to be reduced.

10. We round off the forms using a straight gouge, until the Cubist-like planes created by the rough-dressing disappear. We also reduce the clamping point, which is beginning to interfere with our work, and replace it with small pieces of wood.

11. The modeling progresses, and we are now some 2 or 3 mm away from the desired form, so we will need to be extra careful from now on.

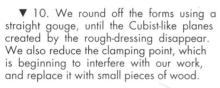

▲ 12. With a steady hand, accurate blow and a small gouge, sharpened and filed down, we carve the internal areas, making sure the gouge always re-emerges from the wood.

▶ 13. We see the harmony of the carved surface and compare it with the maquette. There is still a plane that has not been carved.

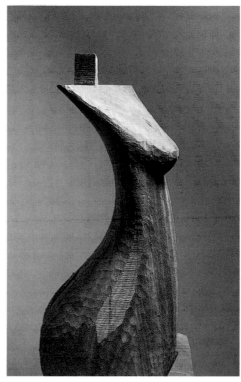

▲ 14. We continue to lift off the last layers. The bite of the gouge becomes increasingly smaller, and the wood is removed in shavings.

▼ 16. The modeling is now finished, and to unify the many planes created by the gouge, we use a traditional rasp along the grain, first a coarse one and then the fine one. We can control the tool more easily by drawing it toward us; we increase or lessen the pressure as necessary.

◀ 15. To reduce certain internal areas, we have to make an exception to the rule of always carving outward. So we groove the limits to prevent the wood coming away unexpectedly.

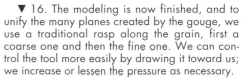

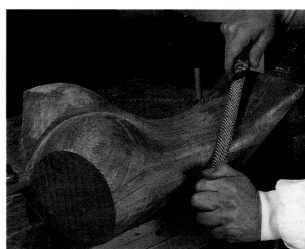

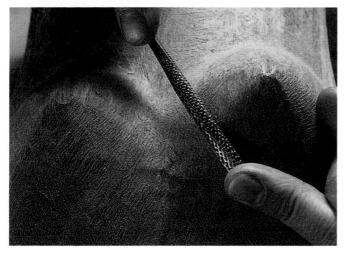

◀ 17. The most hidden areas or those that require the most precision are smoothed using increasingly smaller rasps.

▶ 18. We use a curved scraper to remove the small ridges left by the rasps and to cut off the rough ends.

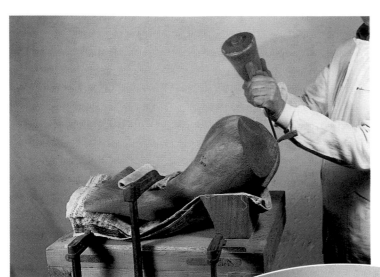

▲ 19. Because our sculpture lacks a base, we build one to keep it steady and safe. We can now remove the clamping points. On the bottom, because we need to leave a curved surface after removing the point, we use a highly beveled gouge to cut the fibers concentrically.

▶ 20. Since the upper side of the sculpture is flat, we can saw off the other clamping point and then smooth with a rasp.

◀ 21. We want to elevate our sculpture on a metal rod, so we drill the base first with a small bit, then, when we are sure the hole coincides with the center of gravity, a larger one.

◀ 22. At the same time we have designed the base and commissioned a metalworker to build it.

▶ 23. Using the flexible shaft, we sign the work. The artist is happy to do so, although this style of sculpture belongs to his aesthetic concerns of earlier years. The wax maquette was made in 1981.

► 24. After polishing the piece, we realize that this wood, with its interwoven fibers, irregular grain, and alterations in color, requires a treatment that highlights its characteristics. We dampen it and scrape it with a metal brush to accentuate the pattern and relief of the veins.

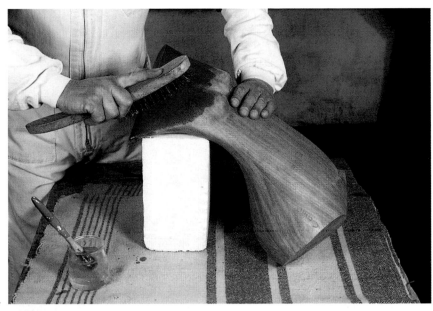

◄ 25. To conclude, we seal the pores with neutral-colored wax.

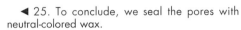

► 26. While we were carving, someone joked about giving the name Thetis to the work. Then the idea of this goddess and the name of the sea from which the mountain ranges emerged inspired the idea for the support, replacing the original idea of hanging it from a string.

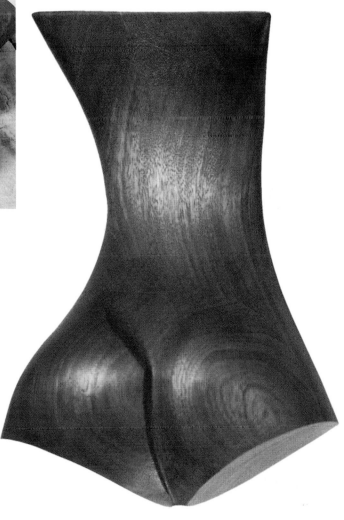

► **Camí**, *Thetis*. Iron and bolondo. 71 3/4" × 10" × 11" (182 × 25 × 28 cm).

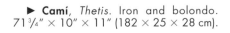

Elm: Carving a Trunk

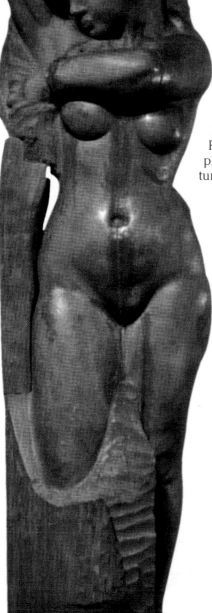

To increase the level of difficulty, we now propose carving a trunk. The results will depend on our inventiveness and skill, as the factor of surprise is a constant feature of this type of direct carving: we encounter knots, colts, fibers that change direction, insect galleries. . .

Although African carvers and Henry Moore carved green trunks, we do not recommend it because they crack if not treated with polyethylene glycol.

We will use traditional and electric tools to show how they are used, although they are not always necessary.

Here we are going to carve an abstract figure, but as a prototype we have included a female figure that emerges from the trunk and on which the marks of the gouge are still visible in places. We recommend you visit the Zadkine Museum in Paris or scan bibliographies for images of sculptures by this artist.

◄ **Sergei Konionkov,** *Caryatid* (1918). Carved from a single trunk of elm.

▶ 1. We start with a trunk found beside a river, the remains of one of the many elms cut down because of Dutch elm disease, which has virtually wiped out the species in Europe.

◄ 2. With fear, we make a lengthwise cut that reveals the beauty and direction of the veins and that shows, apart from being completely dry, the disease has not affected the heartwood.

▶ 3. We model a maquette, keeping it damp throughout the entire process in order to adapt it to any surprises the wood may give us.

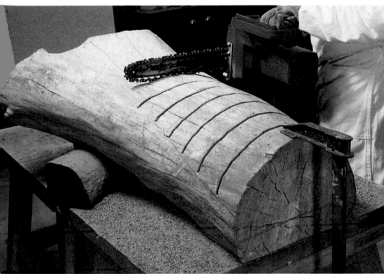

▲ 4. We clamp the trunk firmly to a low workbench and trim the other main side, making parallel cuts with a chainsaw up to the limit we have drawn.

▼ 5. Using a wide-mouthed, straight, almost flat gouge, we remove the excess wood.

◄ 6. We mark off the main axes in red and the silhouette in blue, using the maquette as a guide.

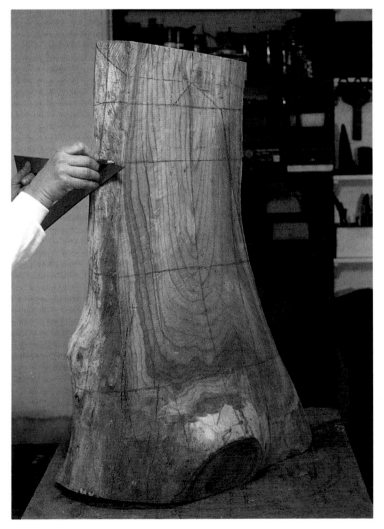

► 7. We discover that the base is not flat and smooth it with an electric plane, although this could also be done using a gouge.

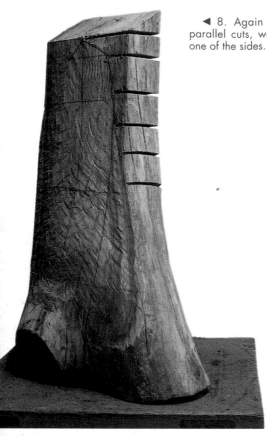

◄ 8. Again using parallel cuts, we trim one of the sides.

◄ 9. In the same way we saw and carve the upper end, up to the limit set by the drawing of the desired profile.

▼ 10. We finish the trimming of this profile using the means at our disposal to immobilize the trunk in such an unstable position: clamps, two stands, and an iron weight.

▼ 11. On the remaining side the only part we wish to remove is the sapwood, and because the cuts are therefore shallow, we use the die grinder with the cutting disc.

▼ 12. We remove the sapwood with a gouge. Although the trunk is immobilized by its own weight, we use three strips of wood gripped by clamps stop it from moving.

▼ 13. A knot has suddenly appeared. Using a sharp gouge, we cut out the hard pith in concentric circles. A hard blow with a slightly beveled gouge would rip it straight out.

▶ 16. We continue to redraw the axes as they disappear and compare the piece with the maquette, as our main concern is the proportions of the work.

▲ 14 and 15. We rough-dress the piece and model at the same time, using the cutting disc. We bring the disc down in short, diagonal movements, varying the inclination depending on the amount of wood we want to remove. A bitter-acid smell fills the air.

◀ 17. We pay special attention to how we model the upper part of the sculpture because the wavy forms and the pattern of the veins will attract the spectator's attention upward.

▶ 18. Elm being such a strong wood, we can thin out the edge even more.

▶ 19. We have reached the pith and work as carefully on it as on the knots.

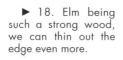

20. The red axis lines indicate how much wood has been removed with the disc. The knot will be reduced later using a gouge.

21. We hollow out the pith with a sharp gouge held almost parallel to the wood so that it exits quickly.

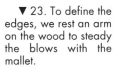

22. It is easier to control the work with the piece laid flat, because in a somewhat unorthodox way, we are forced to carve inward to define the last layer.

24. The volume has been outlined. Now we can turn to the details.

23. To define the edges, we rest an arm on the wood to steady the blows with the mallet.

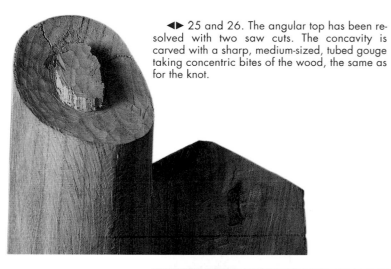

◄► 25 and 26. The angular top has been re-solved with two saw cuts. The concavity is carved with a sharp, medium-sized, tubed gouge taking concentric bites of the wood, the same as for the knot.

► 27. The elm is now fully modeled. We could leave the marks of the gouge visible, but will contin-ue with the finishing process.

► 28. We smooth the piece using a curved blade rasp. If we push it downward, we will work more quickly but will also raise rough ends at the same time by working against the growth of the veins.

► 29. Elm fibers grow in an anarchic fashion, so we have to adapt the direction of the rasp to each particular area; we will smooth the knot with a circular motion.

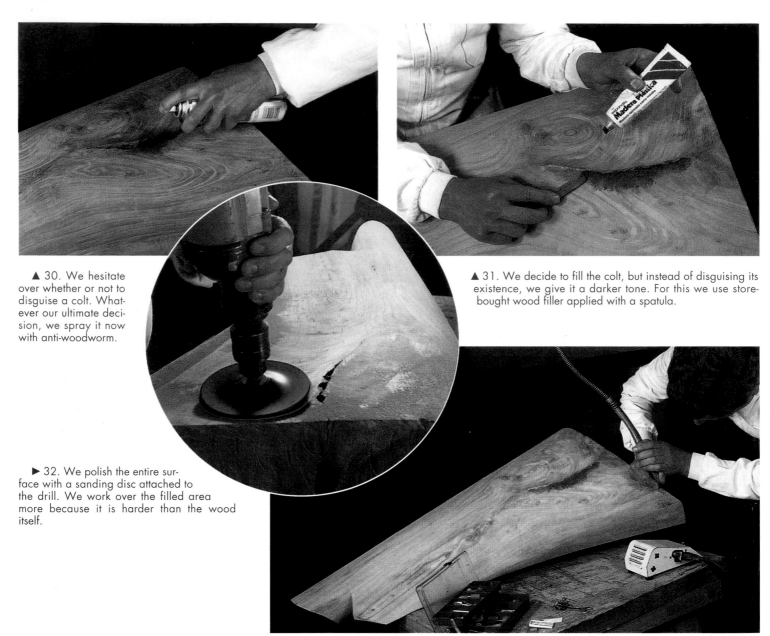

▲ 30. We hesitate over whether or not to disguise a colt. Whatever our ultimate decision, we spray it now with anti-woodworm.

▲ 31. We decide to fill the colt, but instead of disguising its existence, we give it a darker tone. For this we use store-bought wood filler applied with a spatula.

► 32. We polish the entire surface with a sanding disc attached to the drill. We work over the filled area more because it is harder than the wood itself.

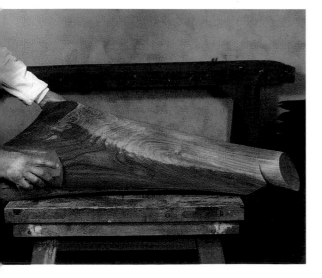

▲ 33. And the signature, in proportion to the size of the sculpture.

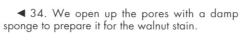

◄ 34. We open up the pores with a damp sponge to prepare it for the walnut stain.

► 35. We have applied a coat of walnut stain to the lower part to give it a solid appearance, and apply dark wax, using light wax for the rest of the sculpture.

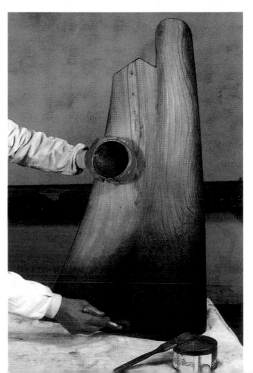

▼ 36. Erosion, the silhouette of a church, a landscape of Capadocia, Meteora in Greece? Meteora—beyond the wind—will be its name.

TO A DRY ELM

On the old elm, wounded by the lightning . . .
some green leaves have appeared . . .
Before he fells you, elm of the Duero,
the woodcutter with his ax, and the carpenter
makes you into a wagon or yolk,
before becoming embers in the fireplace, tomorrou
may you burn in a hut,
next to the roadside . . .
elm, I must describe
the gracefulness of your newly green branch.
My heart hopes also,
toward light, toward life,
another miracle of spring.

Antonio Machad(

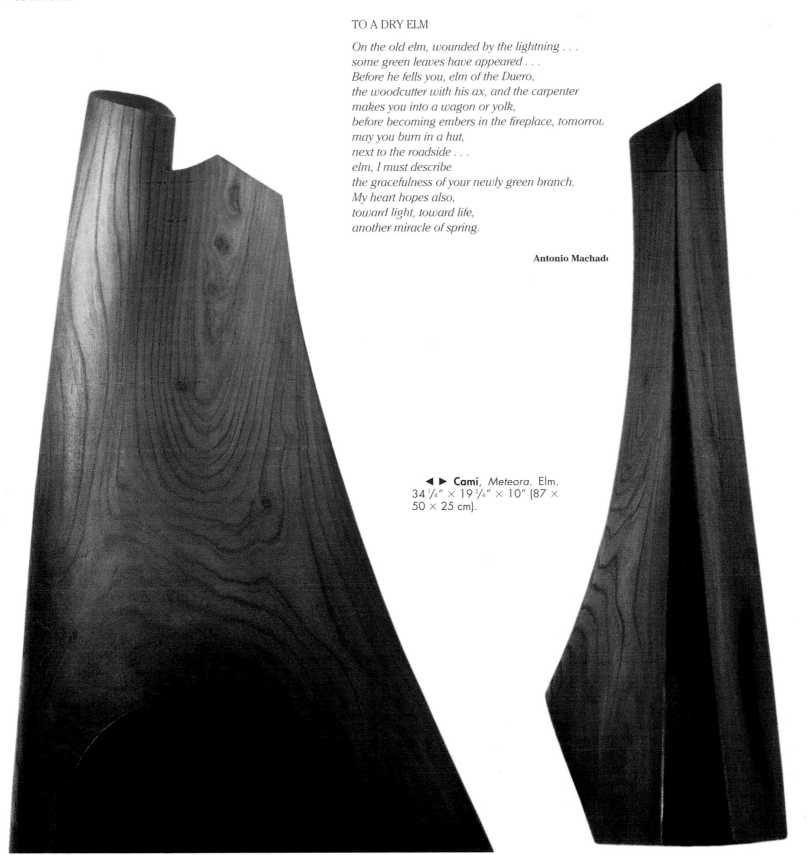

◄ ► **Camí**, *Meteora*. Elm. 34 ¼″ × 19 ¾″ × 10″ (87 × 50 × 25 cm).

Vermilion, Wengue, and Yellow Pine: The Challenge

Once we can control volume and have acquired the necessary skill, we can undertake more complex sculptures. We have imagined a sculpture that forces us to overcome new problems, such as gluing cuts by their narrow side, using several electric tools, and combining different woods.

While we were carving, we proudly believed that our sculpture was original, yet on a recent visit to the Musée de l'Homme in Paris, we rediscovered one of the many representations that the Senufo people of the Ivory Coast make of the calao, a black bird of the savanna. Also represented with wings outspread, it symbolizes fertility but presides over funerals as well. Why not admit that these sculptures could penetrate our subconscious and influence us?

▲ This is our maquette: black Plasticine over galvanized wire netting. We have deliberately sought a certain solemnity of the lines.

▼ And here is the chosen wood: vermilion and dark wengue with light-colored sapwood. Yellow pine will be used for the base.

◄ *Cálao.* 49" (126 cm).
Musée de l'Homme, Paris.

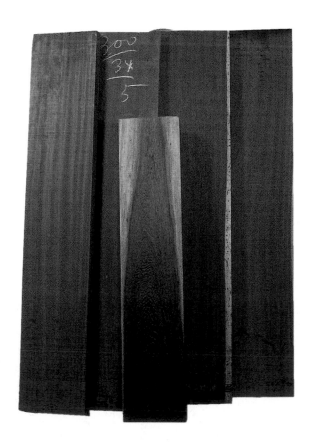

▲ 1. We have had to borrow some very large clamps to press the four planks horizontally. Our clamps grip a wood strip to prevent warping.

▲ 2. The bed of the saw is rather small, but Tomás, an expert carpenter, can handle any circular trimming.

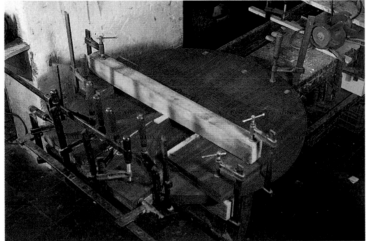

◄ 3. He also sets up this device so we can thicken the lower section with two pieces left over from the trimming.

◄ 4. We will discuss the base later. Now we mark the axes and several concentric circumferences that guide us in creating a thicker area in the middle of the vermilion.

►5. This is when we start to carve.

▲ 6. The vermilion is held firm, leaning on the wall and immobilized by its own weight. It only requires anchoring at the base, as we have seen.

▲ 7. The circles remind us that the rough-dressing should be deeper toward the perimeter. We like the marks left by the disc . . . we may even leave some visible.

▲ 8. We start on the rear side of the vermilion. The disc is applied with the grain, against, across . . . our only concern now is effectiveness and safety. Crimson shavings rain down on us as the workshop is flooded in red.

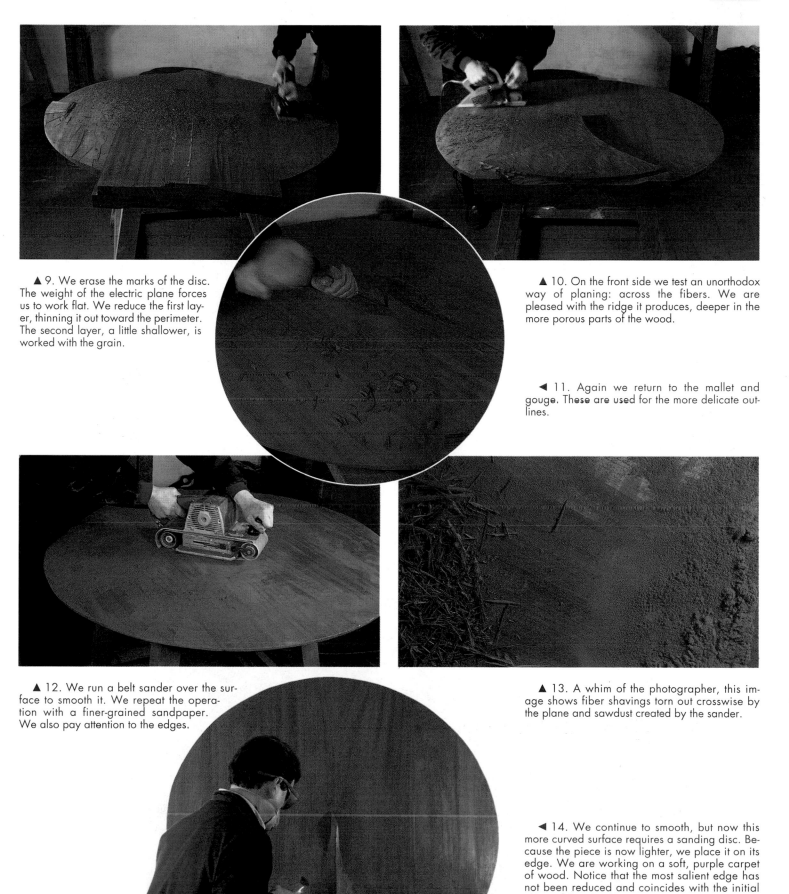

▲ 9. We erase the marks of the disc. The weight of the electric plane forces us to work flat. We reduce the first layer, thinning it out toward the perimeter. The second layer, a little shallower, is worked with the grain.

▲ 10. On the front side we test an unorthodox way of planing: across the fibers. We are pleased with the ridge it produces, deeper in the more porous parts of the wood.

◄ 11. Again we return to the mallet and gouge. These are used for the more delicate outlines.

▲ 12. We run a belt sander over the surface to smooth it. We repeat the operation with a finer-grained sandpaper. We also pay attention to the edges.

▲ 13. A whim of the photographer, this image shows fiber shavings torn out crosswise by the plane and sawdust created by the sander.

◄ 14. We continue to smooth, but now this more curved surface requires a sanding disc. Because the piece is now lighter, we place it on its edge. We are working on a soft, purple carpet of wood. Notice that the most salient edge has not been reduced and coincides with the initial plane of the glued cuts.

◄ 15. The supporting area is no longer necessary. We prepare the way for the bow saw with the mallet and a broad chisel, as with traditional trimming.

► 16. Two steel rods will attach the vermilion to the base. We calculate the distances and the spacing before drilling with a 20 mm bit.

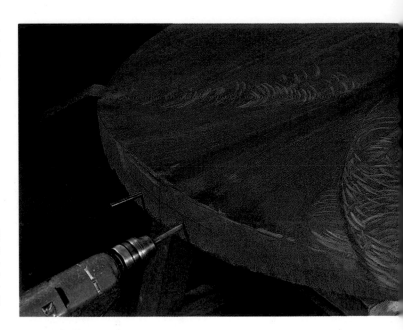

► 17. A damp sponge intensifies the red color of the vermilion, opens its pores, and raises it fibers.

▼ 18.Vermilion: This showy semi-hard wood reveals a fine grain and regular fibers when dry. To balance the composition, we have included chaotic areas with the disc.

▼ 19. We remove the rough ends and finish with the orbital sander to smooth the wood entirely. It is a pleasure to feel the vibrations! We keep a handful of scarlet sawdust as a souvenir.

► 20. Now we turn to the head and tail. A complex silhouette; beautiful, almost metallic wengue.

▼ 21. Rough-dressing is done with a gouge and cutting disc. Modeling: a well-sharpened gouge for the layers, edges . . . plus a very narrow, half-round gouge.

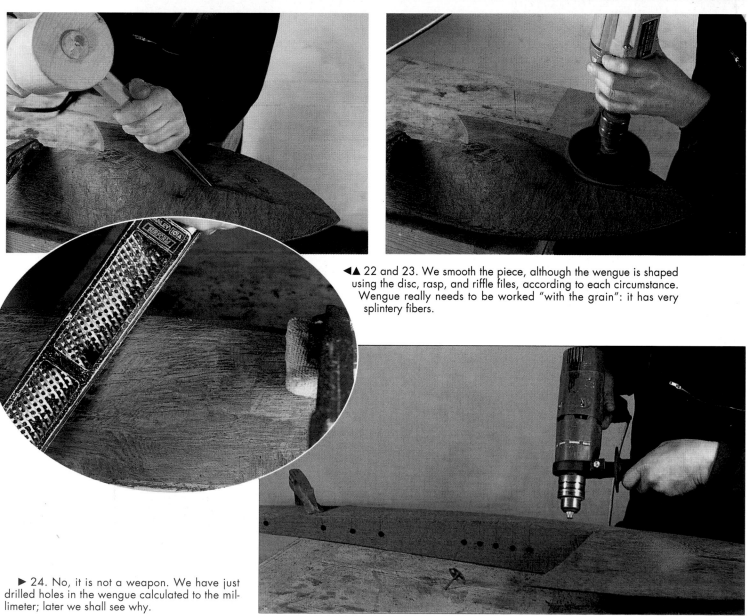

◄▲ 22 and 23. We smooth the piece, although the wengue is shaped using the disc, rasp, and riffle files, according to each circumstance. Wengue really needs to be worked "with the grain": it has very splintery fibers.

► 24. No, it is not a weapon. We have just drilled holes in the wengue calculated to the millimeter; later we shall see why.

◄ 25. We plant metal "mushrooms" next to the crest. Decorative? Expressive? Earlier on we used anti-woodworm.

► 26. A last look before gluing. Something is wrong with the symmetry! Back to the gouges.

▼ 27. We attach the wengue and the vermilion. Dowels are inserted in the holes made in each wood to join them. Carpenter's glue is used to guarantee the result.

◄ 29. There is no need to carve it. We scrape the paint with a rasp; it has aged well. Its resin dulls the rasp by filling the teeth; its sweet smell overwhelms us.

▼ 30. We again use the 20 mm drill bit and a steady hand so as not to stray from the perpendicular. Two steel rods are to be inserted between the pine and the vermilion. Each rod will be able to move independently of the other.

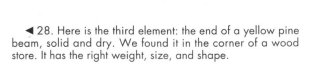

◄ 28. Here is the third element: the end of a yellow pine beam, solid and dry. We found it in the corner of a wood store. It has the right weight, size, and shape.

◀ 31. One, two, or more layers of walnut stain, until the pine matches the wengue.

▼ 32. The walnut stain is now dry and we sand the pine, bringing out the shinier veins. This is not a true brocade but produces a satisfactory result.

▼ 33. Fighting the woodworm again! We will respect this crack: it lends the work a taste of old age.

▶ 34. Danger! Our bird is being attacked by a colony of nails. Some have even reached the head. Others are weak and we have pried them out with a drill bit.

◀ 35. This test was done after trimming the wengue, but looks better on this page.

◀ 36. Protected by wax: red for the vermilion and dark for the rest.

▶ 37. We have emulated the representations of a bird from the savannas of Africa. Emu, an Australian bird almost 6 feet (2 m) tall . . . ÈMUL!

◄► **Camí**, *Èmul*. Vermilion, wengue, and yellow pine. 7'2" × 3'8" × 13 ½" (218 × 112 × 34 cm).

179

Mass Production: Replicas on Demand

Perhaps, after reading though this book, we are still incapable of carving a toy boat from pine bark. Not to worry: there are factories that can reproduce wood sculptures in much the same way the hardware store can make copies of a lost key. If we take them a prototype, we can get copies for all our friends.

We visited one of these factories in Breda, near Gerona, Spain, although when we see a report from a colleague we feel a certain nostalgia: it was to disappear in a fire some months later.

We were surprised to see that along with the sculptures, they also reproduced chairs. And we thought *we* were original introducing the idea of plebeian wood in the first chapter! Of course, in this case they were Gaudí chairs . . . destined for Japan.

▼ **Gaudí,** *Chair.* Designed for the Calvet House. Gaudi Museum. Barcelona.

▲ 1. A general view of one of the factory bays.

◀ 2. A collection of prototypes already reproduced. Despite the dust, we can see they are made of metal. Remember: to place an order for reproductions, we need to provide sculptures made of materials harder than common wood.

▼ 3. Preparing the cuts. German clients, they tell us, prefer maple.

◄ 4. A prototype in action. The copy at the end turns around.

► 5. The arm of the mechanical sculptor supports one of the dozens of milling cutters used.

▲ 6. Here we can see the trimming process . . .

▲ 7. . . . the rough-dressing, using smaller cutters . . .

▲ 8. . . . and the modeling, always based on the prototype.

▼► 9 and 10. In the foreground is the machine that reads the form of the bronze image and multiples it. To perfect the detail, it seems they use pins instead of cutters.

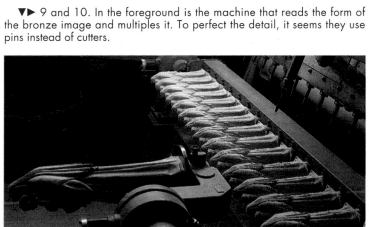

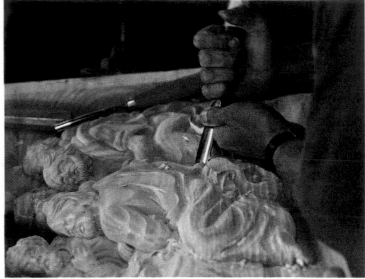

▲ 12 and 13. Certain customers prefer traditional carving. An expert surrounded by gouges gives a piece that handmade touch.

► 14. The hands can be so expressive! It is best to model them separately, according to tradition.

▼ 15 and 16. The arms and sleeves can also be reproduced separately. But before gluing, they need smoothing to adjust the fit. This is a simple task done with a plane.

▶ 20. Colors to choose from.

17, 18, and 19. The sculptures await their turn to enter the "beauty salon."

▶ 21. These figures have been treated with walnut stain.

►22. A makeup session in the dressing room.

◄▼ 23 and 24. Shipwrecked in a sea of varnish.

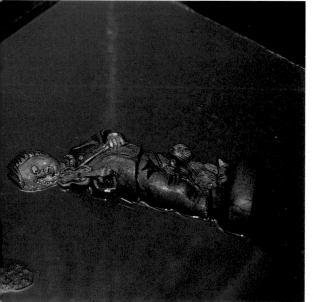

▲ 25. Bronzed under fluorescent light until the varnish dries.

► 26. A touch of distinction: the excessively shIny areas are softened with a chamois disc.

► 28. And in the shop: perhaps the label reads *handmade*.

▼ 27. On the train of merchandise.

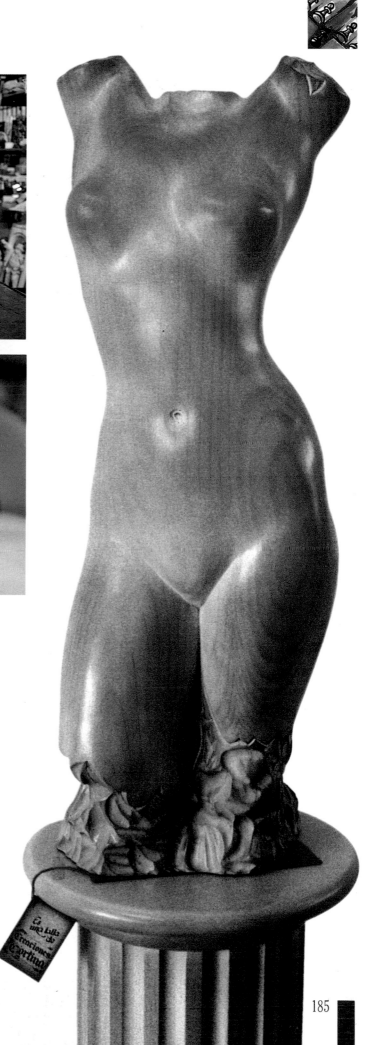

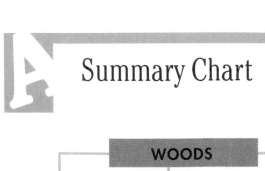

Summary Chart

CARVING

PROCESS

WOODS

they are sold

soft
semi-soft
hard

they contain

they develop

cracks
shrinkage
warping
twisting

without bark
whole
quartered

TRUNKS

bark
sapwood
heartwood
pith
roots

STRUCTURE

sides
heart

PLANKS

CUTS

protuberances
wounds
colts
knots
flakes
crystallization

external | **internal**

veins | fibers

texture | grain

· on endpiece
· with the grain
· against the grain
· across

TRIMMING

ROUGH-DRESSING

MODELING

SMOOTHING

ROUGH-ENDING

HISTORY

Time as sculptor

natural

gouged

smooth

aged

texture

PROVOKED
chemical
metal brush
sand-blasting

NATURAL
wax
varnish

Plebeian wood
Musical instruments
Certain *animists*

Noble wood
Choirs and organs
Certain altarpieces

DYES
anilines
walnut pigment
dyes

color

animists | unction
rites

Japan
China | lacquer

Buddhism-Amida
Romanic | temple...

Baroque | oil | polychromy

Renaissance
Baroque | brocade

ALTERED

modify
the relief

cover
the vein

aerosol
paints

SANDING

FINISHING

TOOLS

CUTTING

Handsaw
· Keyhole saw
· Chainsaw
· Bandsaw

· hand clamps
· bench vise
· tabletop clamp

CLAMPING

· baseboards, strips
· buffers
· protectors

CARVING

CUTTING DISC

GOUGES

blade
· straight
· curved
· elbow
· counter-elbow

mouth
· flat
· half-round
· tubed
· V-shaped

RUBBING

· sanding disc
· belt sander

RASPS

· traditional
· replaceable blade
· riffle files
· files

· straight
· curved

SCRAPERS
· straight
· curved

· orbital sander
· sanding disc
· sandpaper
· steel wool

▼ **Tilman Riemenschneiden,** *The Last Supper* (16th century). This sculptor is one of the first who deliberately ignored polychromy.

SCULPTORS

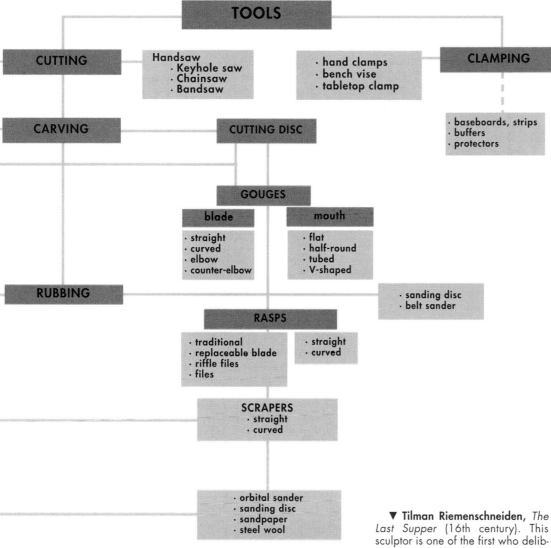

A LIST OF THE ARTISTS
WHOSE WORK
APPEARS IN THIS VOLUME:

▲ Photo on page...
☆ Commentary on page...

GLOSSARY

◄ *A School* (beginning of 16th century). Polychromed wood. Musée National du Moyen Age, Thermes de Cluny, Paris.

A

Addition. Sculptural process that creates volume by adding material.

Against the grain. Rough cut against the direction in which the fibers grow.

Altarpiece. Wooden decoration for an altar.

Aniline. Water-based pigment.

Baseboard. Wood and cloth device for immobilizing and protecting the sculpture.

B

Bench vise. Metal or wood clamping device, forming part of the workbench.

Bevel. Oblique surface along the edge of a gouge.

Bite. The effect of the gouge cutting into the wood.

Blade. Metal part of a gouge.

Bleed. Release resin.

Block. Set of glued cuts for sculpting.

Brocade. Polychromy resulting from applying paint to gold leaf and then partially removing it to let the gold show through.

C

Cambium. Part of the trunk that generates the growth of new rings.

Chisel. A heavier, thicker carpenter's tool than the gouge.

Clamp. Metal instrument for gripping wood.

Clamping point. Wooden section used for gripping the piece.

Coat. Layer of paint, dye, stain, or varnish.

Colts. Internal cavities in wood.

Crack. Splitting of the wood caused by the drying out of the ducts that transport the sap.

Creosote. By-product of tar used to preserve wood.

Cuts. Fragments of a plank used to form a block.

D

Decked. Adorned with precious jewels.

Decorum. Suitable treatment of a theme.

Descent. Sculpture that represents Christ being taken down from the cross.

Direct sculpture. Sculpting without using any copying method.

Dye. To color wood without altering the pattern of the veins.

E

Edge. Cutting end of a gouge.

Endpiece. Surface of wood after sawing perpendicular to the fibers.

F

Fell. To cut down trees.

Fiber. Dry sap ducts in the form of threads that rise from the roots up to the leaves.

File. Metalworkers' tool with a grooved surface used for smoothing.

Finish. In carving: smoothing, roughending, and sanding. In general: additions to the sculpture to protect, modify, or decorate it.

Finishing. Removing the grain to buff the wood.

Flakes. Shiny dry sap trapped in the wood.

Flexible shaft. Flexible arm fitted to a drill to hold grinding burs.

G

Gilt. Coating a sculpture with gold leaf or similar paint.

Gold leaf. Extremely fine foil made from this metal and used for gilding or brocading an image.

Gouge. Chisel suitable for carving curved surfaces.

Grain. Direction that wood fibers grow.

Grind. Create a new beveled edge on a gouge, chisel, or knife.

Grinding bur. Small toothed metal bit used to reduce wood.

Grotesque. Capricious relief, sometimes mocking or surreal.

H

Heart. A plank the diameter of the trunk.

Heartwood. Part of the trunk that is ideal for carving because it is dry and compact.

Hone. To perfect the edge of a gouge, chisel, or knife.

I

Image. Statue of a religious nature.

J

Join. Uniting two pieces of wood.

K

Knot. Part of the trunk from which a branch emerges.

M

Majesty. A crucifix representing Christ reigning on the cross.

Mallet. Curved hammer, made of wood or soft metal, for striking the gouge.

Maquette. Provisional model of a sculpture.

Mask. Not only to cover the face; may cover the entire head or be kept in the temple.

Misericord. Carved prop on the choir seats to allow the person to rest without actually sitting down.

Modeling. Shaping the forms and the details of a sculpture.

Moiré. Wavy pattern of grain.

Moon. Time of the year when wood is cut. Good moon: when the tree grows more slowly, the date changing according to species and climates. Bad moon: time when the tree is developing most: wood felled in spring cracks and rots easily.

Mortise. Hollow in the handle for fitting the shank of the gouge.

Mouth. Cutting edge of the gouge.

N

Nicks. The broken edge of a gouge.

► *Figure in Ritual Pose* (6th century). Mayan. Mexico. 14" (35.6 cm). Rockefeller Collection, Metropolitan Museum of Art, New York. One of the oldest examples of the few pre-Columbian carvings still existing.

P

Patina. Soft tone that the surface of a sculpture acquires over time. Can be created artificially.

Phloem. Sap duct.

Pith. Innermost part of the trunk, harder than the rest and prone to splitting.

Plank. A board ready-cut to be sold.

Pointing. Traditional system for copying a sculpture as faithfully as possible.

Polychromy. Multi-color coating of a sculpture. Here we use the term only when between the wood and the paint there is another material used as a neutral base color.

Pores. Hollow points in young wood that absorb the humidity.

Priming. Covering the carving with glue, gesso, or other bases for polychromy.

Proportioning. Dressing the piece to obtain the correct proportions.

Prototype. A maquette that acts as the original for making copies of a carving.

R

Rasp. Tool with metal teeth used to remove the marks of the gouge.

Riffle files. Smaller than normal files and used for smoothing difficult-to-reach surfaces.

Ring. Annual growth indicator of a tree.

Rough-dress or -hew. Eliminating a lot of wood to obtain the volume of the sculpture.

Rough ends. Ends of wood fibers.

S

Sand-blasting. Wood polishing using a jet of sand.

Sanding. Removing loose grain by rubbing with abrasive paper.

Sawdust. Grain that comes away from the wood when sawing or sanding.

Scraper. Unbeveled, flat steel used for removing rough ends.

Sharpening. Putting a cutting edge on the bevel of a gouge, chisel, or knife.

Side. Side plank of a trunk, thinner than the heart plank.

Sketch. Drawing done before modeling the maquette.

Smoothing. Removing the edges of gouge bites.

Stand. Sculptor's bench with a turntable.

Strata. Each of the layers removed when carving.

T

Texture. Distribution of the elements that form a surface and are noticeable to the touch.

Totem. Mythical ancestor, the protector of a clan. Sculptural post.

Trimming. First stage in carving, using a saw to remove a large amount of wood to obtain an approximate profile of the sculpture.

Turpentine. Juice obtained from pines and other conifers and used in varnishes.

Twist. Contortion of fibers and wood itself.

W

Walnut pigment. Coloring obtained from walnut shells and dissolved in water.

Warping. Bending of planks.

Whole. A beam as large as the trunk will permit.

With the grain. Cutting or rubbing in the direction of the fibers.

X

Xylophagous insects. Insects that destroy wood.

Y

Young wood. More porous rings that have grown in spring.

▼ Detail of two large figures outside a Hawaiian temple.

Much of the technical data presented in this book has been provided by professional sculptors or by cabinetmaking manuals. Historical information has been obtained from different books, which we consider unnecessary to list here. Any general history of art, especially those dealing with the Romanic, Baroque, and non-European cultures, will provide more information on the subjects presented in this volume. Another good source for information on tribal wood sculpture is the monographic studies published by ethnological museums, which usually contain images and contents of great quality.

This is a selection of some particularly useful volumes.

HISTORICAL:

· Coldstream, Nicola. *Masons and Sculptors (Medieval Craftsmen).* University of Toronto Press, 1991. Covers a critical period in the history of sculpture.

· Kraus, Dorothy. *The Hidden World of Misericords.* George Braziller, New York, 1975. One of several books by this author on woodcarvings in medieval and gothic churches.

· Maskell, Alfred. *Wood Sculpture.* Metlven and Co. Ltd, London, 1912. A Eurocentric relic.

· Meilach, Dona Z. *Contemporary Art with Wood.* Crown, New York, 1968. Creative techniques and appreciation of 20th-century woodcarvings.

· Moore, Henry. *Wood Sculpture.* Universe Publishing, New York, 1983. Woodcarvings of sculptor Henry Spencer Moore, 1898-1986.

· Palomino, Antonio. *Lives of the Eminent Spanish Painters and Sculptors.* Cambridge University Press, Cambridge, England, 1997. A useful and informative account of 16th- and 17th-century Spanish artists and sculptors.

· Read, Herbert. *A Concise History of Modern Sculpture.* Frederick A. Praeger, New York, 1964. A discussion of the works of the masters of modern sculpture.

· Roukes, Nicholas. *Masters of Wood Sculpture.* Watson-Guptill Publishers, New York, 1980. A survey of contemporary wood sculptors.

· Willet, Frank. *Ife in the History of West African Sculpture.* McGraw-Hill, New York, 1967. Primitive sculpture from the Nigerian region of Ife.

WOOD AND TOOLS:

· Better Homes and Gardens. *Classic Woodworking Woods and How to Use Them.* Des Moines, 1993. Forty different wood species are discussed.

· Blackburn, Graham. *The Illustrated Encyclopedia of Woodworking: Handtools, Instruments & Devices.* Simon and Shuster, New York, 1974. Use, history, and development of every hand tool from the 18th century to the present.

· Edlin, Herbert L. *What Wood Is That? A Manual of Wood Identification.* Viking Press, New York, 1977. Includes 40 actual wood specimens.

· Jackson, Albert, and David Day. *Good Wood Handbook.* Betterway Publications, Cincinnati, 1992. Excellent color photos of 74 woods, plus text on their characteristics, uses, and workability.

· Jackson, Albert, David Day, and Simon Jennings. *The Complete Manual of Woodworking.* Knopf, New York, 1989. Updated information on endangered species of wood. Also deals with carving.

· Lincoln, William Alexander. *World Woods in Color.* Reprint edition. Linden Publishing, 1997. A classic illustrated guide to exotic woods.

· Pye, Chris. *Woodcarving Tools, Materials and Equipment.* Sterling Publications, 1995. An introduction to the workshop.

· Vesey, William. *Power Tools.* Schiffer, Atglen, Penn., 1985. The care and use of power tools, many of them used for wood sculpture.

TECHNIQUES:

· Bouché, Brieuc. *A Master Carver's Legacy: Essentials of Wood Carving Techniques.* TAB Books Inc., Blue Ridge Summit, Penn., 1986. Expert guidance on the techniques of woodcarving from a master craftsman.

· Carstenson, Cecil C. *The Craft and Creation of Wood Sculpture.* Dover Publications, New York, 1981. A well-illustrated survey.

· Gross, Chaim. *The Technique of Wood Sculpture.* Arco Publishing Co., New York, 1977. A master craftsman and teacher goes through all phases of wood sculpture and recognizing grain, color, and attributes of wood.

· Lindquist, Mark. *Sculpting Wood: Contemporary Tools and Techniques.* Davis Publications, Worcester, Mass., 1990. A solid introduction to techniques and tools.

· Orchard, David. *The Techniques of Wood Sculpture.* North Light, Cincinnati, 1984. A detailed guide to tools, materials, and skills involved.

· Rich, Jack C. *Sculpture in Wood.* Reprint edition. Dover Publications, New York, 1992. A clear and concise practical guide, originally published by Oxford University Press, 1970.

· Wilbert Verhelst, *Sculpture: Tools, Materials, and Techniques.* Prentice Hall, Englewood Cliffs, N.J., 1988. Introduction to woodcarving techniques and wood fabrication.

· Wills, Ferelyth and Bill. *Sculpture in Wood.* Arco Publishing Co., New York, 1975. Heavily illustrated with over 300 black-and-white photographs.

► *War Mace.* Marquesas Islands. 29" (75 cm) (upper part). Similar examples can be found in different collections.

Index

▶ Ritual spoon. Dan, Liberia. 20″ (51 cm). Rockefeller Collection, Metropolitan Museum of Art. New York.